A HISTORY OF
BRITISH TRADE UNIONISM

Henry Pelling was born at Birkenhead in 1920 and was educated at Birkenhead School and at St John's College, Cambridge, where he read classics and, later, modern history. His undergraduate career was interrupted by war service in the army. From 1949 to 1965 he was a Fellow of The Queen's College, Oxford. His first book, *The Origins of the Labour Party*, was published in 1954. He has paid several visits to the United States, and has written a history of the American labour movement. He is now a Fellow of St John's College, Cambridge, where he continues research in modern British history. Among his most recent books are *The Labour Governments 1945–51* (1984), *Britain and the Marshall Plan* (1988) and *Winston Churchill* (2nd edn, 1989).

A HISTORY OF
BRITISH
TRADE UNIONISM

HENRY PELLING

FIFTH EDITION

PENGUIN BOOKS

PENGUIN BOOKS

Published by the Penguin Group
Penguin Books Ltd, 27 Wrights Lane, London W8 5TZ, England
Penguin Books USA Inc., 375 Hudson Street, New York, New York 10014, USA
Penguin Books Australia Ltd, Ringwood, Victoria, Australia
Penguin Books Canada Ltd, 10 Alcorn Avenue, Toronto, Ontario, Canada M4V 3B2
Penguin Books (NZ) Ltd, 182–190 Wairau Road, Auckland 10, New Zealand

Penguin Books Ltd, Registered Offices: Harmondsworth, Middlesex, England

First published 1963
Reprinted with minor revisions 1970
Second edition 1971
Third edition 1976
Fourth edition 1987
Fifth edition 1992
1 3 5 7 9 10 8 6 4 2

Printed in England by Clays Ltd, St Ives plc
Filmset in Monophoto Imprint

CONTENTS

Contents

PREFACE TO THE FIFTH EDITION

FOR this edition, as for previous revisions I have extended the narrative, revised the bibliography and altered the text in the light of fresh research.

ST JOHN'S COLLEGE   H. M. P.
CAMBRIDGE

INTRODUCTION

NOWADAYS when one in every three or four adults is a member of a trade union, and when all of us are likely to be affected by the decisions of a union's leaders, there is no need to emphasize the importance of the study of trade unionism. But why should we examine its past, when what we are really concerned with is its present and future?

For better or for worse, the structure of present-day British trade unionism can be understood only in terms of its historical development. An acute foreign observer described it at the end of the Second World War as 'an ancient city full of architecture of different periods and styles'. This is no less true today: it is a characteristic due in part to the early development of British industry, in part to the absence from our national history in the last two centuries of any social upheavals such as have been caused elsewhere by revolution or military conquest.

But there are other reasons, too, to study British trade-union history. It is concerned with the aspirations and the fears of ordinary people, with their endeavours and their struggles, with their modest successes and their setbacks. In following their slow and often painful progress, we may obtain some understanding of human problems in general, and in particular of those likely to exist in an emerging industrial society. Of course, no other country has developed or will develop quite as Britain has done; but as the greatest of the classical historians pointed out, so long as human nature remains as it is, similar situations will recur, and we can learn from history in the same way as from personal experience.

PART ONE

THE EMERGENCE OF TRADE UNIONISM

THE SETTING

THIS book is divided into three parts, each consisting of four or more chapters. In the first part we shall be considering the evolution of local clubs and societies and eventually unions (the term was not used until the early nineteenth century) up to the point when a national organization embracing all forms of union was formed to win legal recognition from Parliament. The period covered is a long one, for the first clubs can be traced in the later seventeenth century, and the Parliamentary struggle to secure legal status for trade unionism did not take place until the late 1860s and early 1870s.

One obvious reason for the length of the period was that until the later nineteenth century working men could hardly ever vote in Parliamentary elections, still less stand for Parliament themselves. Enfranchisement came mainly in the Second and Third Reform Acts of 1867 and 1884 respectively, and the union leaders played a part in the public agitation for their passing; the first trickle of M.P.s drawn from the ranks of labour appeared in 1874. At any time before then, the claims of labour could be put before Parliament and the Government only by petitioning or lobbying, by public demonstrations and pamphleteering, or, more crudely, by disturbance of the peace. Ministers of the Crown in most cases knew very little about the lives or feelings of the manual workers; and any signs of organization among them were frequently regarded with alarm, as being potentially criminal and even seditious. This was in fact the main reason for the passing of the Combination Acts of 1799 and 1800, during the crisis of the war with revolutionary France.

It would be a mistake, however, to speak of a homogeneous 'working class' in Britain at any time before the later nineteenth century. Contemporaries did not use the expression, at any rate in its singular form. They referred sometimes to 'the working classes' in the plural, and perhaps more frequently to the different economic 'interests' which cut across class lines. The 'agricultural interest', comprising all those who worked in agriculture or who benefited from it economically, remained the most important 'interest' in the country for almost the entire period that we are considering; but agricultural labourers and smallholders were naturally the least able to combine or to express themselves politically. Many other industries were at least partly rural, owing to the prevalence of outwork; but of those which were concentrated in the towns, the majority were on a very small scale. Master and man customarily worked side by side, and there was often less social difference between them than there was between the craftsman, with his 'capital' in the form of his skill and the tools of his trade, and the unskilled labourer, who could rarely be sure of regular employment.

It is true that this picture began to be altered in the eighteenth century, and was much transformed in the early nineteenth, by the processes which we associate with the Industrial Revolution – the application of steam power, the growth of factories, and the increase of the scale of industry owing to transport improvements. But the new processes spread only gradually from one industry to another, leaving many virtually untouched for a long time, and others by no means deeply affected. Even in the textile trades, many small businesses rose and fell in the latter part of the period, and sub-contracting was common both there and in the mining industry. The engineering industry, too, which was at once the product of the new processes and their agent, consisted largely of small firms employing both highly skilled and unskilled workers, rather than any undifferentiated mass of semi-skilled.

Until the beginning of the Victorian age communications were so indifferent that the market for both goods and labour tended to be local or regional rather than national. Internal migration was usually limited to quite short-distance travel.

The freer movement of men and materials had to wait for the coming of the railways in the 1830s and 1840s, and it was not until thereafter that national unions of particular industries or trades became practicable. Even so, local loyalties and rivalries remained strong and hindered wider developments of unionism after they became desirable.

But on the whole the greatest obstacle to the development of trade unionism arose from the hostility of the employers of labour. They were usually well aware that their interests, in the short term at least, were bound to suffer as a result of collective instead of individual wage bargaining; and they were encouraged in this view by the theories of the economists, and especially the doctrines of *laissez faire* which became prevalent in the late eighteenth century. It is true that combination among employers, even for the purpose of fighting unions, was often weak and temporary, and that there were trades in which small masters found themselves more or less at the mercy of their skilled workers. But as a general rule, it was a good deal easier for employers to combine than for their workers; and early in the nineteenth century it was not uncommon for employers to try to force all their workers to abjure unionism altogether.

Under these circumstances, unionism up to the middle of the nineteenth century was largely confined to artisans. The scarcity value of their skill enabled them to extract concessions from their employers; their regular earnings allowed something to spare for union contributions; and their ranks included a sufficient proportion of persons able to read and write and thus to see to the union accounts and organizing. The factory workers in general, and the miners, were slower to develop unionism, because of the disruptive effects of technical change, the strength of their employers, and the less indispensable character of their skill; but their turn was clearly coming in the later part of the nineteenth century. The comparatively unskilled workers, among whom we may classify agricultural labourers and many of those engaged at the gas works and in transport, had no means of pressing their claims, and were in any case gravely weakened by illiteracy and the casual nature of their employment. In the 1860s and 1870s it was still largely the members of the 'trades'

– carpenters and bricklayers, printers and bookbinders, engineers and shoemakers – who took the lead in the establishment of a national congress of the unions, which met annually from 1868; and it need not surprise us that this was not called a labour congress but rather a trades' congress – in fact, the Trades Union Congress (T.U.C.), under which name it has ever since been known.

But let us now examine the beginning of unionism in more detail.

CHAPTER TWO

THE ORIGINS TO 1825

THE concept of a separate organization of employed workers, to determine wages and conditions by negotiation with their employers, had no place in the medieval system of industry. The recognized crafts were catered for by the gilds, which were combinations of both masters and journeymen. The journeymen were skilled workers who had served an apprenticeship to their trade. The gilds had the responsibility of protecting the standards of their respective crafts by defining the terms of service for apprentices, which usually ran for a period of seven years. Furthermore they could also fix the prices for the manufactured product and determine the piecerate to be paid to the journeyman. The journeymen were, of course, vitally interested not only in the level of the piecerate but also in the conditions of their work and in the protection of their status *vis-à-vis* the unskilled. They were anxious to restrict the number of those who could enter their craft and share their privileges; and to this end they favoured the limitation of the proportion of apprentices to journeymen. But if they combined and went on strike to enforce their views on any of these matters, they risked punishment under the common law of 'conspiracy in restraint of trade'. The incentive to combine, however, was not present to any great extent in a society where it was quite normal for journeymen to become masters in due course, and where, with skilled workers at a premium, there was a sufficient community of interest between master and journeyman to satisfy both.

In Tudor and Stuart times an increasing part was played by the State in the direct regulation of wages. As early as the fourteenth century there had been some statutory intervention, but it was probably confined at first to determining the wages of unskilled workers, who could not belong to gilds. Later, the practice spread to the skilled trades. At first it took the form of fixing wages by Act of Parliament; but this proved to be unsatisfactory owing to changes in the price-level, and the justices of the peace were given powers to make assessments from time to time. The Statute of Artificers (1563) gave the justices power to fix the wages of both artisans and labourers, and it also enacted penalties on both masters and men for any breach of contract. Wage regulation by these means continued throughout the seventeenth century, but went into decline after about 1700.

The decline of official regulation of wages in the eighteenth century was accompanied by a decay of the gilds. The reasons for both changes may be found in the increasing scale of industrial organization and the quickening pace of industrial change. The gild system operated reasonably satisfactorily while master and journeyman worked side by side, and while the journeyman could provide his own tools and raw material. But in the eighteenth century the rapid growth of commerce, the improvement of communications, the development of specialization, and in some industries the introduction of machinery, led in many cases to an increasing separation of the interests of master and man. The journeyman might now need a good deal of capital to rise into the ranks of the masters; but, on the other hand, he had less chance of saving a portion of his income if, as sometimes happened, his status as a craftsman was undermined by the new methods of working. In any case, change was so rapid that the formal system of regulation became simply an embarrassment to the masters. So far as they could, they neglected it; and this attitude was reflected in the attitude both of the magistracy and of Parliament itself. The journeymen, for their part, deprived of the protection to which they had been accustomed, began to combine separately from their employers, often with the overt and presumably legal object of petitioning Parliament for the redress of their grievances, but not infrequently also with the purpose of enforcing wage demands against their employers by the direct sanction of bad work, 'go-slows', or 'turn-outs' (later known as strikes).* Naturally, if Parliament failed to respond to the petitions the direct sanction became the only practicable one.

It will be seen that these combinations of workmen did not grow out of the gilds; but as the gilds declined, so the need for combination grew, in order to enable the workers to maintain rights and privileges formerly guaranteed to them either by the gilds or directly by Act of Parliament. Generally speaking, up to the middle of the eighteenth century Parliament endeavoured to satisfy journeymen who petitioned it for the restoration of gild practices or the regulation of wages; after that time virtually nothing was done except in the case of the Spitalfields weavers – a strong pressure group rather close to Westminster – who obtained an Act regulating wages in 1773. It became accepted by Parliament that new industrial conditions had made both gilds and wage regulation out of date; instead, a policy of *laissez faire* was adopted. At the same time Parliament endeavoured to prevent the emergence of combinations, whether formed by the masters or by the men. This was done by the enactment of legislation to make combinations in particular industries definitely illegal.

We must not exaggerate the misfortune suffered by employed workers as a whole as a result of the decline of the gilds and of wage regulation by the State. The growth of industry in the eighteenth century meant greater opportunities for many of them as well as for many employers. While some skills, formerly regulated, were undermined by industrial change, others were strengthened or came into existence for the first time. Unregulated wages were often far higher than they would have been if regulated, in some cases purely as a result of the scarcity of labour. But in the nature of things, while some prospered, others suffered; and of those who prospered in one season, by no means all maintained their prosperity in another season. From the late eighteenth century onwards it was clear that if there was to be any defence for the artisan against the vicissitudes of economic

* The use of the word 'strike' in the sense of 'a stoppage of work' is apparently an innovation of the early nineteenth century. But the phrase 'to strike work' was used in the eighteenth century, presumably on the analogy of a ship striking sail.

change, it would come neither from the gild system nor from the legislature.

Let us now go back a little in order to examine the first traces of organization among workers of particular trades. As we might expect, clubs of journeymen existed at a very early date for what were ostensibly purely social purposes. For much of the seventeenth century, for example, the practice had existed of the journeymen in each London printing establishment forming a body known as a 'chapel'. The term 'chapel' apparently had no religious significance when used for this purpose: it may be derived from a similar usage in France, which can be traced back to the sixteenth century. Joseph Moxon's *Mechanick Exercises* (1683) quotes a list of rules drawn up by a chapel in London, together with penalties for non-observance. Benjamin Franklin encountered rules of this sort when he took a job in a London printing-house in 1724: he tried to ignore them, being used to the more indivi-dualistic environment of American printing establishments, but soon found that his workmates could enforce them by 'little pieces of private mischief', such as transposing his pages, mixing his type, and so on, 'and all ascribed to the chapel ghost'. Although most of the rules listed by Moxon are concerned simply with maintaining social behaviour and work arrangements of mutual advantage to all those in the printing shop, it is noteworthy that they also included such remarks as: 'It is now customary that Journeymen are paid for all Church Holy days that fall not on a Sunday, Whether they work or no . . .' This suggests that, although the main purpose of the chapel was social, it could be expected to act as a focus for resistance to the infringement of the journey-men's conditions of work by the masters.

It was also not uncommon for workmen to combine as early as the late seventeenth century for the purposes of mutual insurance against sickness, old age, or death. Thus in 1699 the Newcastle keelmen (lightermen in the coal indus-try)

unanimously agreed among themselves to sequester and set apart some small portion of their dues or wages to be a public fund or bank for the relief of themselves, their widows and children, and also aged skippers.

At first they relied on their employers to look after the funds, but this proved unsatisfactory, and after a few years they made the collections 'at their societies or box meetings'. 'Box meetings' were meetings at which the box containing the funds was opened and its contents checked. In the course of the eighteenth century these 'friendly societies', as they were called, spread widely throughout the country. Eden, the author of *The State of the Poor*, wrote in 1797 that 'since the commencement of the present century friendly societies have gradually extended to most parts of Great Britain'. In 1793, indeed, Parliament specifically recognized them by the Friendly Societies Act, which provided them with a legal status and protection for their funds. Even so, the dividing line between friendly societies and combinations for wage bargaining remained in doubt, especially as workers combining for wage-bargaining purposes, which were of doubtful legality, could use the organization of a friendly society as a legal mask for their activities. Thus, when Francis Place in the 1790s joined a Breech-Makers Benefit Society he found, as he later explained, that it was 'intended for the purpose of supporting the members in a strike for wages'.

The first well-documented example that we have of an organized and at least semi-permanent combination to raise wages is that of the Journeymen Feltmakers. In 1696 we hear of a delegation of twelve journeymen in this trade negotiating with their masters in an effort to prevent a cut in wages, and two years later they were induced to give 'an ingenuous account and full discovery of their combinations and collections of money against the Company', which later provided a basis for the prosecution of several of them. Early in the eighteenth century combinations are more frequently mentioned, and sometimes appear to have been very elaborate. Thus in 1721 the Master Tailors of London petitioned Parliament against their own journeymen, saying that 'to the number of seven thousand' they had

lately entered into a combination to raise their wages and leave off working an hour sooner than they used to do; and for the better carrying on their design have subscribed their respective names in books prepared for that purpose, at the several houses of call or resort (being publick houses in and around London and Westminster) where they use; and collect several considerable sums of money to defend any prosecutions against them.

As a result, an Act was passed to fix tailors' wages and to prohibit the combination, but the fact that the masters' complaints against their journeymen were repeated at intervals later in the century suggests that some degree of combination, however informal, remained.

We are told that the initiative of the journeymen tailors encouraged combinations in other trades in the London area among 'curriers, smiths, farriers, sail-makers, coach-makers, and artificers of divers other arts and misteries'. But the evidence of activity among the trades is by no means confined to London. Even before 1721 there were reports of organization among the weavers in the woollen industry of Devon and Somerset. In 1718, as a result of a petition, a Royal Proclamation was issued against

lawless clubs and societies which had illegally presumed to use a common seal, and to act as Bodies Corporate, by making and unlawfully conspiring to execute certain By-laws or Orders, whereby they pretend to determine who had right to the Trade, what and how many Apprentices and Journeymen each man should keep at once, together with the prices of all their manufactures, and the manner and materials of which they should be wrought.

This suggests a considerable degree of development in the process of combination. We may note especially the concern of the journeymen that the permitted proportion of apprentices should not be too large, lest there should be an oversupply of journeymen and consequently an unemployment problem. It was a matter that the gilds used to be responsible for: now it became a grievance making for the voluntary combination of the journeymen. Although the Proclamation apparently had some effect in suppressing combination, complaints later in the century suggest that its effect was only temporary.

In spite of the fact that combinations were held to be illegal, they proved very difficult to suppress. Masters needed the goodwill of their workers, especially in the trades expanding rapidly or in those requiring the more recondite skills; and so they often tolerated what was virtually a system of collective bargaining. For the late eighteenth century, a time of rapidly rising prices, there is naturally a good deal of evidence of wage claims and employer–employee negotiations. The London printers again provide eloquent testimony. In 1785 the compositors presented a memorial to the master printers requesting an increase in their wages, or rather in their 'price of work', for they were paid by the piece. The masters held a meeting 'to consider of the Propositions of the Compositors', and they agreed to an advance. Seven years later, however – that is, in 1793 – the compositors, suffering as they were from the 'more than proportionate increase of prices of every article of life since the last rise in 1786', sent an address to the masters asking for a further improvement. The address was couched in very respectful terms: the compositors opened by expressing gratitude for the consideration given to their earlier application, and went on:

As we disclaim all proceedings militating against justice, or that are subversive of decent and respectful behaviour, we presume that any communication, which the present situation of the business renders necessary to be opened with our employers, will be received in a manner suitable to its importance, and with candour coinciding with its equity.

The presentation of an address of this character, and the securing of signatures – which numbered 539 – betoken effective organization; and it is not surprising to find that a body called 'The Phoenix, or Society of Compositors' was founded in March 1792 'at the Hole in the Wall, Fleet Street'. The name suggests that it was a revival of some earlier society; and it was apparently a friendly society as well as a body for bargaining with the masters, for it had a subscription of no less than 2s. 3d. monthly, which must have been largely used for providing either insurance benefits or entertainments for members. Shortly afterwards, of course, the Friendly Societies Act was passed, and the number of such bodies became legion.

Although the beginning of combinations among workmen implied, to some degree at least, a widening of the gap between master and man, the first societies were almost invariably of skilled artisans rather than of labourers, and the skilled artisans were a conservative group who were anxious to maintain their status and standard of living in a changing industrial environment. They were not factory workers; and the societies were not the product of the Industrial Revolution in its customary definition. Rather, they were a response to changes in the structure of industry which had been taking place since at least the later seventeenth century – changes which broke up the traditional mould of a system regulated by the State, by gilds, and by long centuries of custom.

It was no doubt partly the extent and efficacy of combinations in the later eighteenth century that provoked the active hostility of Government and Parliament. Many combinations were illegal under statute law; all were increasingly suspect under common law; and now, with the growing prevalence of *laissez faire* doctrine, it seemed highly inexpedient to allow the law to be so often flouted as it had been earlier in the century. To some extent, in addition, the Commons were influenced by the growth of the employers' interest among their own membership. But whatever the economic motives in the sterner attitude displayed towards combinations in the later eighteenth century, it is probable that after the 1780s the decisive element in the situation was the Government's concern for public order at a time of revolution abroad, and its feeling that combinations were often productive of unrest and even violence, and could easily become the cloak for rebellious conspiracies on the Jacobin model.

Probably there was a good deal of superficial justification for these fears. The industrial towns in the North were growing rapidly, but the arrangements for the maintenance of public order were quite inadequate. Most workers were still illiterate and could readily be swayed by rumour and prejudice. A certain amount of rioting and other disturbance had been an endemic feature of popular society, and now it was made worse by the dislocations of war and price inflation. Disaffected artisans or labourers could easily band together and terrorize their employers or their fellow-citizens in general. There is a good deal of evidence of such occurrences, and of the concern of the magistrates, in the Home Office papers for the 1790s. The concern was naturally all the greater for the fact that the men who were organizing their fellow-workers feared prosecution, however peaceful their objects, and hence were inclined to a certain furtiveness of behaviour. Thus, in 1792 the Mayor of Liverpool wrote to the Home Secretary that he suspected that a meeting of the town's journeymen carpenters would be a prelude to rioting, but he did not know whether the object of the disturbances would be to increase their wages or to protest against the proposed abolition of the slave trade.

The very last years of the eighteenth century seemed to be particularly critical. In 1797 there was the mutiny at the Nore; in 1798 there was a rising in Ireland and a landing of French troops in its support. In 1799, therefore, the Government was in a mood to tighten the laws against conspiracy and to secure the summary trial of offenders. Early in the year the master millwrights of London petitioned Parliament for action against combination among their employees; and on the initiative of one of the M.P.s for the City of London a Bill to this effect was passed through the Commons without a division, in spite of counter-petitions by the workers concerned. In the course of the debate, William Wilberforce suggested that a general measure 'to prevent unlawful combinations of workmen' would be desirable, as the existing law did not seem to be adequate. This suggestion was taken up by the Government, which was particularly worried at the time by reports of an Association of Weavers in Lancashire extending from Oldham to Stockport and from Blackburn to Wigan. As the Duke of Portland, then Home Secretary, put it in a letter to a Bolton magistrate,

If nothing injurious to the safety of the government is actually in contemplation, Associations so formed contain within themselves the means of being converted at any time into a most dangerous instrument to disturb the public tranquillity.

The result was the dropping of the master millwrights' Bill and the substitution of a general Bill against combinations, which was passed into law within a month of its introduction.

This Act of 1799 was, however, replaced by an amending measure passed the following year; and the Act of 1800 remained in force until the repeal of the Combination Laws in 1824.

There has been a good deal of misapprehension about the significance of the two Acts passed in 1799 and 1800. The combinations against which they enacted penalties were already being treated as illegal in England, both by common law and under existing statute. The novelty of the fresh legislation lay in the provisions for summary trial, and it was on this aspect that Benjamin Hobhouse, who almost alone attacked the Bill on its way through the Commons, concentrated his criticism. The penalties, however, were very mild: a maximum of three months' imprisonment or two months' hard labour. This was a remarkable contrast to the sentences of up to seven years' transportation which could be imposed under other almost contemporary legislation, such as the 1797 Act against Unlawful Oaths. Partly for this reason, and partly because the provision of opportunity to appeal to Quarter Sessions weakened the effect of the summary procedure, not very many prosecutions actually took place under the 1800 Act. Furthermore, the Act also forbade combinations among employers, and included arrangements for the arbitration of industrial disputes: and while neither of these provisions was put into operation, the Government felt increasing embarrassment in later years in using the Act against workers only. Finally, the measure did not incorporate any special clauses adapting it to Scottish legal procedure, and consequently it was a dead letter in Scotland.

It is true that the process of summary conviction was successful in the hands of determined employers. An interesting case appears in the Home Office papers for 1801, concerning some of the workers in Messrs Bulmer's shipyard at South Shields. They sent an anonymous letter to their employer saying:

You Bulmer if you do not give the carpenters a guinea a week as sure as Hell is hot O before winter is done you must be shot O . . .

Bulmer quickly identified those responsible, threatened them with the provisions of the new Act, and secured a public apology and thanks to himself and his partners 'for their withdrawing their prosecution commenced against us, on the last Act of Parliament for prosecuting unlawful combinations of workmen'. The men also made promises of good conduct for the future.

Yet at the same time, innumerable combinations remained or came into existence for the first time. In some trades the employers were willing to negotiate with the leaders of combinations, and did not desire to suppress them; not infrequently, they were positively intimidated by their workmen, and feared the consequences if they initiated any prosecutions. In 1804 the Attorney-General, Spencer Perceval, was asked to give his advice to the Home Secretary on a request for Crown prosecution of a combination. The request came from some employers in the London boot and shoe trade. Perceval replied that it was 'too notorious that similar combinations exist in almost every trade in the kingdom'; but he advised against a Crown prosecution, on the grounds that it would discourage the masters from initiating proceedings themselves, and also because

... in all these cases there are always, whether well founded or not, complaints on both sides, and the impartiality of government would be awkwardly situated, if, after undertaking a prosecution at the instance of the masters against the conspiracy of the journeymen, they were to be applied to on the part of the journeymen to prosecute the same masters for a conspiracy against their men.

After another dozen years of the operation of the Act, combinations were at least as widespread as before, and probably more so. The Home Secretary of that time was the very conservative Lord Sidmouth, and he might have been expected to respond favourably to a petition which he received in 1816 for the strengthening of the Combination Laws. But after consulting the law officers of the Crown he replied that while he recognized 'the alarming extent to which the combinations of workmen in different branches of trade and manufactures have been carried', he could not recommend any increase in the severity of the law, especially as

the great practical inconvenience which is felt arises from the difficulty of providing the necessary facts to convict offenders.

He thought that the only remedy would be to make examples of selected cases, if evidence could be systematically collected by 'persons worthy of trust'. But government agents were too busy with purely political espionage to have time for this.

This is not to say, however, that workers in all trades were able to defend themselves against the economic vicissitudes of the time. In fact, the most unfavourable feature of the existing law was that it made things especially difficult for those who for economic reasons were most completely at the mercy of their employers. In unskilled work, where there was always a reserve of men to take the place of those dismissed, or in trades where skilled artisans were threatened by the introduction of machinery, combination was difficult to maintain, and it readily degenerated into violence both against employers and against workmen unwilling to adhere to the combination. In the declining handicraft trades the violence culminated in organized machine-breaking in the years 1812–14, when in any case demand for manufactures was restricted by Napoleon's Continental System. The title of 'Luddism' has been given to these disorders, derived from the name, or pseudonym, of 'Ned Ludd', above whose signature a declaration was issued announcing the Nottingham framework knitters' intention to 'break and destroy' the new machinery in the lace trade. Various acts of machine-wrecking both preceded and followed this declaration. 'Ned Ludd' was also active in the West Riding woollen industry, destroying shearing gigs, which were displacing the labour of the shearmen. Of course, we do not know in all cases how far these acts displayed a direct hostility to machinery which was replacing labour, and how far they were simply designed to intimidate the masters who owned the machines into giving better terms to their men. At any rate, if peaceful combination was impossible, it was not unnatural in the circumstances for desperate men to resort to violence. As if to add insult to injury, Parliament chose this moment (1813–14) to repeal the obsolete clauses of the Statute of Artificers, which gave legal sanction to the fixing of wages by justices and to the seven-year apprenticeship requirement for artisans.

In 1815 the long war against Napoleon at last ended in victory, but it did not bring any immediate softening of the official attitude towards industrial combinations. On the contrary, there was fresh concern about public order as a result of the economic distress of the immediate post-war period. Luddism continued, and spread to agricultural districts; and in the towns there was agitation for political reform. In 1817 plans were made by some Manchester weavers to stage a protest march to London, in order to demand government action to ease their plight. Some hundreds set out, carrying blankets or coats, and consequently they are known to history as 'the Blanketeers'. But they were soon dispersed after the arrest of their leaders. In 1819 came the unnecessary tragedy of 'Peterloo', when eleven members of a peaceable political demonstration in Manchester were killed by a charge of the Yeomanry. This was followed by the passing of the 'Six Acts', most of them designed to restrict public meetings and demonstrations. It was not until two or three more years had passed that the general alarm in governmental circles had sufficiently subsided to permit some relaxation of restrictive laws.

Meanwhile Francis Place, the London Radical whose Breech-makers' Society we have already mentioned but who had become a master tailor, was setting about the reform of the Combination Laws. He now had no enthusiasm for combinations: he was convinced that wages tended to find their own level as a result of the operation of supply and demand, and that combinations existed only because the workers, resenting the ban on their existence, regarded them as their safeguard. In these views he was encouraged by the Benthamite economist J. R. McCulloch, who also advocated repeal. In 1822, with the liberally minded William Huskisson at the Board of Trade and Robert Peel as Home Secretary, the time seemed ripe for action; and in 1824 Joseph Hume, the Radical M.P., on prompting from Place, secured the appointment of a Select Committee of the House of Commons to inquire into matters affecting industry, including the operation of the Combination Laws.

The Committee heard a great deal of evidence from both employers and workmen of different trades, and Place saw to it that as many of them as possible were men of liberal views.

All the same, there is little doubt that they spoke no more than the truth when they said that the existing law tended to aggravate ill-feeling between masters and workmen without effectively suppressing combination. In his own evidence Place suggested that the effect of the law was to make combinations into secret authoritarian bodies. 'Apprehension of prosecution,' he said, 'causes unlimited confidence to be given. If the cause were removed, the effect would cease.' The Committee agreed with him, as may be seen from two important paragraphs of their conclusions.

That the laws have not only not been efficient to prevent Combinations, either of masters or workmen; but, on the contrary, have in the opinion of many of both parties, had a tendency to produce mutual irritation and distrust, and to give a violent character to the Combinations, and to render them highly dangerous to the peace of the community.

That it is the opinion of this Committee that masters and workmen should be freed from such restrictions, as regards the rate of wages and hours of working, and be left at perfect liberty to make such agreements as they eventually think proper.

The Committee therefore recommended that 'the statute laws that interfere in these particulars between master and workman' should be repealed, and that the common law should also be altered to allow peaceful combination; but it added a rider, that there should be effective safeguards to prevent 'threats, intimidation, or acts of violence' by either masters or workmen against the freedom of labour and capital.

The result was the Combination Law of 1824, which repealed all statutes concerning combinations from Edward I's reign onwards, and also declared that the mere act of combining should not be grounds for prosecution under the common law. At the same time it authorized summary jurisdiction, as under the 1800 Act, for persons using 'violence to the person or property' or 'threats or intimidation' in order to impose the rules of a combination. The Act was passed through both Houses of Parliament almost without discussion.

Unfortunately for the sponsors of the 1824 Act, it came into force just at the beginning of a period of good trade and rising prices. The result was a sudden crop of strikes, accompanied in some cases by far-reaching demands for the regulation of conditions of work, exclusion of non-society men, and so on; there was also a certain amount of violence. A general alarm ensued among the employers most affected, and with the aid of *The Times* they persuaded the Government, in the persons of Huskisson and Peel, to move for a fresh committee of inquiry. This body, the Select Committee on the Combination Laws, 1825, heard rather more evidence on combinations than its predecessor did, and uncovered various apparently undesirable practices, such as the restriction of output in order to prevent unemployment – 'strong young men do a vast deal too much we consider,' said a leader among the London Coopers – and also collective pressure on each non-society man, described by a witness as 'keeping ourselves separate from him, treating him as one who does not belong to us'. In some trades 'moral violence', as another witness described it, was apparently not enough: in the Scottish cotton industry at least one weaver was disfigured by a vitriol attack, and in Dublin non-members of combinations in the skilled trades ran the risk of being waylaid and maimed by unidentifiable assailants. But the most extensive intrusions by the men upon what the masters regarded as the privileges of their position took place in the shipping and shipbuilding industries, where the term 'union' was already coming into use. Members of the Shipwrights Provident Union Society, which flourished in the Thames shipyards, drew up stringent rules for the employment of their members and for the conditions of their work, and insisted on a high standard of professional knowledge on the part of foremen. The Loyal Standard Union, composed of seamen of the Tyne and Wear, actually issued a propaganda pamphlet entitled *A Dialogue Between Tom and Harry*, which advocated the principle of combination; and the members of the union refused to go to sea with non-unionists as shipmates. This provoked the masters into a counter-combination of their own, designed to encourage the employment of 'sailors not belonging to union societies'. All these things seemed to the members of the Commons Committee to be deplorable results of the laxity of the existing law.

As a result of the new Committee's report, a compromise Bill was framed and quickly passed into law in the summer of 1825. This reaffirmed the repeal of the earlier Combination Laws, but made the provisions against violence and intimidation more stringent than they had been in the 1824 Act. 'Molesting' or 'obstructing' persons at work was forbidden, and the definition of the purposes of legal combination was narrowed to questions of wages and hours of labour – thus excluding such matters as the proportion of apprentices to journeymen. All the same, it was still practicable for combinations to exist completely in the open, and so it could be said that the main principle of the 1824 Act was maintained. As Peel himself put it:

Men who ... have no property except their manual skill and strength, ought to be allowed to confer together, if they think fit, for the purpose of determining at what rate they will sell their property.

On this basis the organizations which had emerged a few months earlier from the shadows of illegality were allowed to remain in public view, to form the nucleus of the trade-union movement as we know it today.

CHAPTER THREE

HIGH HOPES AND SMALL
BEGINNINGS, 1825–60

THE evidence given to the Select Committees of 1824 and 1825 provides us with some idea of the general character of combinations early in the nineteenth century. A few of them were very elaborate in their structure. The West Riding Fancy Union, for instance, recruited textile workers in a wide area of Yorkshire, and had a hierarchy of committees leading up to a General Council, which alone could authorize a strike by any of the local branches. In London the Tailors had several thousand members, and an organization described by Francis Place as 'martial', linking together the local groups at the 'houses of call' or public-houses where masters could contact journeymen. But most combinations were of a much smaller and more localized type. There were innumerable clubs, each with usually not more than a few dozen members, yet each pursuing an existence which was either completely independent or only very loosely linked to other clubs in the same trade. Among the journeymen brushmakers, to take one example, the so-called United Society was in fact a network of autonomous clubs up and down the country, sharing no more than a mutual undertaking to provide hospitality for a day or two to any club member who might be 'on tramp'.

The artisan 'on tramp' was an interesting phenomenon of this period of comparatively restricted horizons for the working-man. At a time when railways were not yet in existence, and when the cycle of boom and slump was more regional than national or international, it was quite practical for a skilled man who was unemployed to set out, 'his kit packed on his back and walking-stick in hand', in order to seek work in his trade in some other town. In towns where the men of his trade were organized in a club, his own card or ticket of club membership with its 'emblematical engraving' would be accepted as entitling him to hospitality for a brief period while he looked for a job. If he failed to find one he set out on his travels once more. Sometimes the 'tramp' would find work in a town where no trade club as yet existed; in such cases he might well set about founding one himself.

Although many of the clubs were thus bound together by informal links within a particular trade, in other ways they were usually very independent. There was as yet virtually no machinery for cooperation between clubs existing in different trades; but the clubs were often generous in their response to exceptional appeals for assistance, and in such cases as a difficult strike or a prosecution in some other trade, they would make liberal contributions out of their own funds, or at least arrange to take up a voluntary collection from their members. In London the need to make representations to Parliament at the time of the repeal of the Combination Laws led to the establishment of a committee claiming to represent a wide range of trades; and in Lancashire, as we shall see, there were some attempts to combine the workers of that already crowded industrial area. But these were only temporary efforts, and it was apparently only in Dublin that the trades were in continuous association early in the century for industrial as well as political purposes.

The extent to which the clubs stressed the 'friendly society' aspect of their functions depended in part upon whether they had been founded before or after the repeal of the Combination Acts. After 1824 they were free to disclose at least some of their industrial aims. But in any case the reasonably prosperous artisan looked to his trade club to provide him with sickness, old age, and funeral benefits; and for the purpose of strengthening the organization, it was usually found convenient not to draw any rigid distinction between funds for providing strike pay and funds for ordinary benefit purposes. Thus, all the clubs required regular contributions from their members, often at a high rate; and the clubs were faced with the difficult problem of safeguarding their funds against embezzlement at a time when they had no legal means of redress. Since the club meetings were usually held at a public-house, it was customary for the funds to be left in a box in the custody of the landlord. This was similar to the methods of the friendly societies, whose 'box meetings' we have already encountered. The box would be secured by a number of locks, usually three, each with a different key. Only one of the keys would be held by the landlord; the others would be held by officers of the society.

Membership of artisans' clubs was normally restricted to men who had served the seven years' apprenticeship which was still required in many trades; and the indenture might have to be produced for authentication before a man could join. In trades where apprenticeship had died out, or was dying, obviously this condition did not apply; but some other condition concerning length of work at the trade might be substituted for it so that the club could maintain a degree of limitation upon membership. Thus when William Lovett, the well-known London Radical, first arrived in the metropolis and took work as a cabinet-maker, he could not become a member of the Cabinet-Makers Society until he had 'worked or served five years to the business'. But in any case there were likely to be exceptions to such regulations for the sons of members, or at least for the eldest sons, if they wished to work at the trade. Candidates for membership had to be proposed and seconded by existing members; an entrance fee was normally exacted, and in some cases it was spent at once on the entertainment of the general body of members. If this implies some laxity of behaviour it should be added that there were often penalties for misconduct at meetings, such as drunkenness or blasphemy.

So far as the election of officers was concerned, the provisions were markedly democratic in character. Probably the Friendly Society Acts, with their emphasis on committees, general meetings, and printed rules, set a pattern for the trade clubs as well. A clerk or secretary and a treasurer, together with a small committee, would be elected by a general meeting, and the committee would elect its president or chairman. If the club belonged to a larger combination it would send a delegate to join the committee of the body to which it belonged. It was still very unusual, however, for any local club to yield up any considerable proportion of its funds to an outside organization.

Generally speaking, clubs of the type described above were most common among the skilled trades of London and other large towns. The coalminers and the workers in the new textile factory industry of the North were still very largely devoid of permanent organization; and like the agricultural labourers and to some extent also the unskilled labourers of the towns, they tended readily to resort to individual acts of violence or intimidation, of the type which precipitated the 1825 Select Committee. For them, low wages, lack of education, and the hostility of employers militated against effective and continuous combination. It seemed to the more intelligent of them that the only way to get the better of the employers was to form a 'general union' of workers in all industries, and this was what the Lancashire Spinners endeavoured to do even before the repeal of the Combination Laws. In 1818 a 'union of trades' was established at a meeting of delegates, most of whom were from some part of the Lancashire textile industry. The body that they founded was called the 'Philanthropic Society', and its rules indicate that it was no more than a very loose federation of clubs, whose members were 'recommended' to support each other from their funds in time of need. It was evidently designed to serve the needs of the Lancashire area and not much more; but its sponsors got in touch with the leaders of unionism in London, and the Londoners almost at once set up a similar body of their own, which they called the 'Philanthropic Hercules'. But neither the London nor the Lancashire organization lasted any length of time, and the only real link among the trades in London at this time was provided by the weekly journal the *Gorgon*, with which Place was associated and which devoted a good deal of space to news of the clubs.

It was ten years before any noteworthy new attempt to found a 'general union' was made; but again the initiative came from Lancashire. John Doherty, a young Irishman who had been building up a cotton spinners' union in the Manchester area, found himself making little headway at a time when the introduction of new spinning machinery was weakening the operatives' bargaining position. After an unsuccessful strike in 1829, he decided that his efforts would benefit very much from the support of a 'union of all trades'. First, however, he sought to enlarge the scope of the spinners' union in order to embrace members of the trade throughout the United Kingdom; and he summoned a conference in the Isle of Man in December 1829, at which a 'Grand General Union of the Operative Spinners of Great Britain and Ireland' was set up. In the following year he went on to hold a further conference in Manchester to establish a 'general union', which was called the 'National Association for the Protection of Labour' (N.A.P.L.). This was to consist of local unions of trade clubs, affiliated to a council meeting monthly in Manchester, and with a general committee of delegates meeting every six months. Regular contributions were to be paid to the central funds, which were to be used only for strikes against cuts in wages. Although its main strength was in Lancashire, the N.A.P.L. quickly spread as far afield as Huddersfield, Birmingham, and Newtown in Montgomeryshire; and its influence was responsible for the formation of a union among the Staffordshire potters.

At the end of 1830 the strength of the main element in the N.A.P.L., the Lancashire spinners, was again put to the test. The master spinners of the Ashton-under-Lyne area imposed a reduction of wages on their employees, who at once came out on strike. Naturally the Manchester unionists tried to secure the collaboration of their fellow-workers elsewhere, by a universal strike of all those spinners who were receiving wages below a certain figure; but the Scottish and Irish spinners would not comply, and even in England the response was only partial. By March 1831 the strike had failed, and the Grand General Union of Operative Spinners had broken up. As for the N.A.P.L., it was seriously weakened, and its reputation also suffered when its secretary absconded with £160, which was the great bulk of the remaining funds. Doherty made renewed efforts to establish it in London, but there was opposition to this in Lancashire, and he was forced to give up his connexion with the organization, which in any case seems to have disappeared in 1832.

Meanwhile in Yorkshire a 'Trades Union', quite independent of the N.A.P.L., had been formed at Leeds, probably in 1831. We do not know very much about this body: there seems to have been an element of secrecy about it, no doubt owing to the bitter hostility that it encountered from the employers. In the summer of 1833, for example, one Leeds master dyer discharged all of his employees whom he knew to be unionists; and later that year a number of employers in the same area drew up a 'Bond' whereby each of them pledged himself not to employ any members of a union. It was probably for this reason that many Yorkshire workers pinned their hopes of reform on political agitation, and joined the Short Time Committees which were being organized by Richard Oastler, the 'Tory Radical', for the statutory limitation of factory hours.

The early 1830s were in general a period of ferment among intelligent working men. The movement for the reform of the franchise had set them thinking about their own rights and prospects, and those of their number who had come across the Ricardian theory of value had developed the idea that the only important element in industrial production was the work of the artisan or labourer. It followed from this that capitalists and shopkeepers were industrial parasites, and that the way to eliminate their role was to establish a new system of cooperative production. Conferences began to be held for the discussion of methods of cooperation, and an important part in their work was taken by Robert Owen, the wealthy manufacturer who had become a keen social reformer. In 1832 a National Equitable Labour Exchange was set up in London for the exchange of goods produced by cooperative production. The idea was that goods should be priced according to their 'labour value', that is, the amount of labour expended in their production. Unfortunately the exchange did not work very well, partly because the variety of goods produced on a cooperative basis was not large, partly because goods which seemed high in price relative to the open market were naturally left unsold. Although other exchanges were set up both in London and in the provinces, the experiment did not last long.

In the building trade there were developments of unionism

which showed the influence of similar ideas. Local trade clubs had long been in existence among the building crafts, and they had by this time begun to unite into national organizations. In 1827 a General Union of Carpenters and Joiners was formed, to be followed ten years later by a national society of bricklayers known as the 'Manchester Unity'. In the early 1830s the building craftsmen were especially discontented, owing to the new practice of 'contractors' intervening as middlemen between themselves and the architects. The result was the formation in 1831 or 1832 of a comprehensive body of all the building trades, known as the Operative Builders Union. This body was governed by a 'Grand Lodge' or 'Builders' Parliament', which met twice a year in different centres of industry. Within the union the individual crafts retained a good deal of autonomy, and their organization both locally and nationally received a powerful stimulus. In 1833 the 'Builders' Parliament' took up the idea of cooperative production, and established a 'Builders' Guild' to put it into practice. The construction of a 'Guildhall' at Birmingham was put in hand.

In 1834 came the climax of these attempts to use unionism as a vehicle for the transformation of society. A 'turn-out' of workers in many trades took place in Derby, the masters refusing to re-employ the men unless they promised to abandon combination. The Derby men appealed for help, and clubs and societies throughout the country rallied to their support. It was largely in order to organize a continuance of this support that a conference of delegates met in London to form a 'Grand National Consolidated Trades Union'. The more long-term intentions of the founders of the 'Grand National' (as we may call it) were to rationalize the structure of combinations, to achieve a general control of movements for an advance of wages, and to coordinate assistance for strikes, especially strikes against a reduction of wages. Such assistance could either be financial, in which case it might take the form of a general levy upon the membership, or it could be organizational, such as by making arrangements for cooperative production by those thrown out of employment. The 'Grand National' grew with great rapidity, and may have temporarily numbered as many as half a million members; but only a tiny proportion of these ever paid any fees to its headquarters, so the figures have little real significance. At least there appears to have been some widening of the boundaries of combination at this time, to include previously unorganized groups, such as agricultural labourers, and even a few women, such as those who joined the 'Lodge of Female Tailors'. Within each trade the local clubs were to be organized nationally under a 'Grand Lodge'; and the naïve enthusiasm with which many such clubs joined in the movement is well illustrated by an account which we have of the behaviour of the Nantwich shoemakers.

After paying entrance fees our society had about forty pounds to spare, and not knowing what better to do with it we engaged Mr Thomas Jones to paint for us a banner emblematical of our trade, with the motto, 'May the manufactures of the sons of St Crispin be trod upon by all the world', at a cost of twenty-five pounds. We also purchased a full set of secret order regalia, surplices, trimmed aprons, etc., and a crown and robes for King Crispin.

The 'secret order regalia' and the denomination of the local clubs as 'lodges' indicate the prevalence at this time of various mystic rites probably based on masonic practice. At a time when unionists could easily be victimized by their employers for the mere fact of membership, such ritual no doubt played its part in maintaining the privacy of the proceedings. It had the disadvantage, however, that it persuaded the Government that a conspiracy was afoot; and consequently, the police were required to take action against any persons suspected of propagating it. A couple of 'delegates' of the union were arrested by the police at Exeter and held when found to be carrying

two wooden axes, two large cutlasses, two masks, and two white garments or robes, a large figure of Death with dart and hour-glass, a Bible and Testament.

The concern of government at this time was heightened by the incidence of a good deal of rural unrest, including rick-burning and machine-breaking, which could easily be attributed to the growth of unionism among the agricultural labourers. In 1834 Lord Melbourne, who was Home Secretary in the Whig government, chose to make an example of six labourers of the village of Tolpuddle in Dorset, who had been found to be using a form of ritual, though it was not one derived directly from the 'Grand National'. The six men were tried at Dorchester and were found guilty under an Act of 1797 which forbade the 'administering or taking of unlawful oaths' for seditious purposes. This was straining the statute, for there was no evidence that the labourers had a seditious purpose in mind; nevertheless, they were given the maximum sentence permitted under the Act – transportation for seven years, and they were all duly shipped off to Australia. The harsh treatment of the Dorchester labourers, or the 'Tolpuddle martyrs' as they have often been called, aroused vigorous protests all over the country; and even *The Times* felt moved to declare:

The crimes which called for punishment were not proved – the crime brought home to the prisoners did not justify the sentence.

An enormous procession of trade unionists, all carefully marshalled behind their respective banners, marched through the streets of London to present a petition to Lord Melbourne at the Home Office. The demonstration had no immediate effect, but it set a pattern for peaceful political agitation in the metropolis.

This, however, was the prelude to a rapid decline of the 'Grand National' and of unionism in general. The 'Grand National' began to break up owing to its inability to provide adequate support for sections of its membership who were on strike. This was especially unfortunate at a time when the very principle of trade unionism was so much on the defensive. Taking advantage of the public alarm about the spread of unionism, many employers tried to eliminate it from among their own employees. In the London building trades, for instance, a good opportunity occurred when some craftsmen employed by Messrs Cubitt were locked out owing to having boycotted beer supplied by a non-union brewery. All the London building contractors united to demand that their employees should sign 'the document' – a pledge not to join or belong to a trade union. In the Leeds area, as we have seen, the same practice was being adopted; in fact, it was common form in trades where the small master was no longer predominant. Owen, who had not previously been a member of the 'Grand National', after the Dorchester trial accepted the office of president, but he could not hold the union together, and its final collapse came at the end of the year, when the treasurer absconded with most of the remaining funds. The Builders' Union faded away at about the same time. The Dorchester labourers were given a free pardon in 1836, and gradually made their way back to England; but this concession was probably due more to the change of Home Secretary – it was now Lord John Russell – and to the greater dependence of the Whig government on Radical support in the Commons, than to any extra-Parliamentary pressure. In the collapse of their high hopes of general organization and cooperative manufacture, and in the worsening trade conditions of 1837, the skilled artisans fell back where they could on the local clubs and craft societies which had existed within or outside the 'Grand National'. They had learnt their lesson from the failure: henceforward we hear comparatively little of cooperative production or of the industrial union of all trades, and even less of secret oaths and ritual.

It may at first sight seem surprising that the twenty years after the collapse of 'general unionism' saw a steady if unspectacular growth of unionism of a cautious town-by-town and craft-by-craft type. For these were also the years of Chartism – a political movement which, confused and inchoate though it was, nevertheless had ambitious national aims based upon a belief in the identity of interests of the entire working class. The fact is that while Chartism increasingly drew its support from the casualties of the industrial changes of the period, trade unionism developed either among craftsmen who were little affected by such changes, as for instance those in the service trades of London, or among workers who had actually benefited from change, as in the case of the new engineering tradesmen, the boilermakers, and so on. There was also a certain alternation of interest by the main body of miners and factory workers, depending upon whether or not they were regularly employed. In times of slump, such as 1838–42 and 1847–8, they tended to join the political agitation; but when they got their jobs back they gave new impetus to unionism.

The direct links between the unions and the Chartist movement are therefore rather tenuous. At Manchester in 1838 many local societies and clubs turned out with banners for a Chartist demonstration; and four years later we hear of union 'delegates' attending a Chartist meeting. But the so-called 'Plug Plot' riots, when the plugs were removed from the cotton-factory boilers, thus forcing them to stop work, seem to have had little to do with Chartism or for that matter with the unions. Some unions ruled the discussion of politics out of order, and at least one society in Lancashire laid it down that no member could claim out-of-work benefit as a result of participating in 'any Political or Popular Turnout'. Many unionists must have come to realize that Chartism was a distraction from their own movement. Sir James Graham, the Home Secretary in the Tory government which took office in 1841, was probably going beyond the evidence at his disposal when he sought to prosecute the Manchester Trades Conference on the grounds that 'a blow struck at this Confederacy goes to the heart of the evil'. On the contrary, in so far as Chartism tended towards violence of word and deed, it increasingly separated itself from the support of the trade unions as such.

In any case, the later years of the so-called 'hungry forties' were not so bad as they have sometimes been painted. After 1842 economic progress was rapid, and Chartism was never as strong again as it had been. In the rapidly growing industries of the North we can discern the gradual development of a new type of unionism, markedly different from that of the artisans' clubs and societies. Among the miners, the cotton-spinners, and the engineering trades, in particular, large-scale organization began to appear, not always surviving for long, but evolving all the time a new pattern of industrial and political action. It is significant that a body founded in 1845, with the title of the National Association of United Trades for the Protection of Labour, turned out to be, in spite of its name, not a revival of the grandiose aims of 'general unionism' but a more practical and limited piece of machinery to enable fully autonomous unions to combine occasionally in the succeeding years for lobbying at Westminster on behalf of particular industrial reforms such as shorter hours or an alteration of the law of combination.

Within each industry there were inevitably considerable variations in union progress and structure due to differences of circumstance of one sort or another. In the widely scattered mining areas conditions of work varied enormously. Many of the pits employed only a few men, and often the natural leaders of the mining communities were the 'butties' or subcontractors. A few attempts at organization were made in Scotland as early as the 1820s, but these were weakened, as they were to be throughout the century, by the rivalry between the indigenous pitmen and the immigrant Irishmen who competed for their jobs. With or without formal union organization, however, the men in the Scottish coalfields managed to impose on their employers a policy of restriction of output by the 'darg' or stint. In South Wales signs of unionism appeared in areas contiguous to England, but for much of the early nineteenth century the only form of common action by the miners took the form of intimidation of over-zealous workers by a secret society called the 'Scotch cattle'. The Northumberland and Durham coalfields, already developed on a large scale in the eighteenth century, provided a better arena for open trade unionism. In 1831 we find that a collier called Tommy Hepburn was able to form a union, to hold the men together through a two and a half months' lockout, and to secure a reduction of hours of work for boys from fourteen to twelve, as well as other concessions. Hepburn became a paid organizer for a time, but the union collapsed in the face of a determined counter-attack by the employers, who introduced non-union labour to replace the strikers, and forced Hepburn himself into destitution.

But the rapid growth of the coal industry ensured the revival of unionism; and in the 1840s we hear of county unions in Durham, Northumberland, Lancashire, Yorkshire, and Staffordshire, as well as fresh attempts to organize in Scotland. At a conference at Wakefield in 1842 delegates from these areas formed a Miners Association of Great Britain and Ireland, which in two years' time was able to claim to represent some 70,000 miners, or about a third of the total labour force in the industry. Already we begin to hear of miners' demonstrations with bands and banners – the fore-runners of the annual Galas which have long been a feature of mining unionism.

Under the lead of a Newcastle publican who had worked in the pits, Martin Jude, and with the aid of a Bath solicitor, W. P. Roberts, who became famous as 'the Pitmen's Attorney-General', the Miners Association fought hard for better wages and conditions for its members. It eschewed any high-flown ambitions, and would have nothing to do with the Chartist movement. Its object was to raise the living standards of its members by raising the price of coal, which it sought to do by a national restriction of output. But in 1844 it became involved in a bitter four-months' strike in its principal strongholds, Northumberland and Durham – a strike which was defeated by the onset of a depression in trade and the importation of non-union labour, much of it Welsh or Irish. The struggle was marked by an impressive solidarity among the native colliers, led by their Primitive Methodist preachers, who, unlike the ministers of the parent sect of Wesleyan Methodism, sympathized warmly with trade unionism. A contemporary accounts tells us that

there was a curious element of religion in the strike, on the side of the men. Many of the local preachers were its most active sup-porters. Prayers for its success were offered up in the chapels; and it was no uncommon thing for a wayside crowd to join in supplicating the assistance of heaven, and to request that the men who were brought from a distance to work in a colliery – the 'blacklegs' as they called them – might be injured.

The defeat of the strike was followed by dismissals and by eviction from tied cottages; but not long afterwards the employers dropped the yearly contract or bond system, the renewal of which had been the occasion of the strike, and replaced it with a monthly notice. The Miners Association, though considerably weakened, continued to exist for a few years, and began to develop what was to be an important aspect of future national miners' organization, namely, the petitioning of both Government and Parliament for improved safety measures in the mines and the appointment of inspectors. But the Association gradually lost ground and collapsed altogether in the renewed economic slump of 1847–8.

Nevertheless, mining unions survived in several counties, and the movement spread again in the 1850s. In 1852 there was much activity in the north-east coast and in Scotland, and in 1859 an unusually able leader of the Scottish miners, Alexander McDonald, sought to revive a federation for the whole of Britain. Born in 1821, McDonald had been a miner at the age of eight, but in his twenties he attended Glasgow University for a time. His own Scottish union survived a severe defeat in a strike of over three months, but he persevered in his plans, which in 1858 resulted in the formation of the National Miners' Association, a body whose urgent concern was with the promotion of legislation for the improvement of conditions in the mines. Clearly in an industry which was so dangerous to life and limb the miners could expect to receive sympathy and assistance from humanitarian feeling in Parliament; and they had already had an early success in the enactment of the Coal Mines Regulation Act of 1860, which, besides improving the inspection of pit safety measures, enforced the practice of appointing checkweighmen, to ensure that the miners were not cheated in the payment for the coal that they had dug. The checkweighmen were chosen and paid by the men, and so naturally they became a convenient focus of trade unionism in each pit.

In the cotton industry, as in mining, unions developed somewhat intermittently in this period, and tended to be localized rather than centralized. What central organization there was came into existence for the purpose of securing Parliamentary action on reforms which the workers were apparently unable to secure by industrial action. To begin with, though, the cotton workers had a separate means of supporting political action, namely the Short Time Committees, which pressed for the passing of the Factory Bill proposed by Lord Ashley (afterwards Lord Shaftesbury) and later carried by John Fielden in 1847. The weakness of the cotton unions in this period was caused by the variety of skills and functions in the trade and by the fact that a high proportion of the workers were women. The initiative in effective unionism was taken by the mule-spinners, whose occupation was the most skilled, and who were all men. By the 1850s there were district societies of mule-spinners at each of the principal centres of the trade – Ashton, Preston, and Stockport. Of these, the Preston society was said to have existed since the 1830s and to have built up considerable reserve funds. In 1853 these societies were loosely knit together by the formation of what was called the Amalgamated Association of Operative Cotton Spinners. But the term 'Amalgamated' was for some time a misnomer for a body which had little power and only a very limited income; and disputes continued to be handled entirely by the district societies.

In other ways, too, 1853 was a key year for the Lancashire and Cheshire Cotton industry. Prices were going up, the industry was prosperous, and demands for higher wages were made in almost every town. A strike of 7,000 spinners took place at Stockport, and with the aid of financial support from other districts it proved successful. Encouraged by this, the Preston operatives determined to press their own demands, both spinners and weavers being involved. Most of the Preston masters refused to give way, and in October some 18,000 operatives were thrown into idleness. The masters had an effective association of their own, but the strikers could match them in organization and in public relations, and altogether over £100,000 was raised for the support of those thrown out of work, contributions being generously provided by trade societies all over the country. The strike dragged on into the new year, and in February the masters began to bring in men and women from the agricultural districts and from Ireland. This led to bitter reactions among the strikers, but their leaders constantly appealed for the maintenance of order, and few disturbances took place. In March the strike was already failing when the masters persuaded the local magistrates to arrest the strike leaders on charges of 'molesting and obstructing' some of the imported labourers, whom they had persuaded to return to their homes. In May the strike finally collapsed, and the charges which were due to be heard at the autumn sessions were dropped.

The Preston operatives had thus been defeated; but the memory of a strike lasting seven months was enough to deter any group of employers, however well-organized, from challenging their workers if they could avoid it. When in 1859 the Padiham master weavers found themselves involved in a dispute with the newly formed East Lancashire Power Loom Weavers Association they secured the assistance of masters in neighbouring districts, but the latter gave their support only on the understanding that the dispute was 'not a mere question of wages, but one of dictation'. There was room, therefore, for compromise with any union whose wage demands were not unreasonable; and it hardly seemed necessary in this particular case for the strike to drag on for twenty-seven weeks before the Blackburn masters induced their Padiham colleagues to pay the same list of prices as was current in the Blackburn area.

Among the weavers, if not among the spinners, unionism was a general movement not restricted to the highly skilled. Nevertheless it was well-disciplined and free from violence except under considerable provocation. It is true that both at Preston in 1853 and at Padiham in 1859 there was some intimidation of operatives who refused to join the strike or who would not make contributions to the upkeep of the strikers. The 'balance-sheets' published weekly by the Padiham strike committee contained many comments such as the following:

> Shame on Shot family; Shot lives next door but one to the Factory Gate. That great hobbling lad on 196 won't pay – shame!
> Nan o' Sutting Nan's won't pay – shame!
> If Bill o' Petts's won't give over persuading weavers not to pay, Punch will deprive him of his top lip.

But all this was a long way from the vitriol-throwing of the Glasgow spinners in the early years of the century, and there were few reports of actual violence in any Lancashire strikes of the 1850s. By the end of that decade it was clear that the cotton workers had acquired the discipline and training in trade-union principles to enable them to bring consistent and effective pressure upon their employers.

The struggles of the miners and cotton workers for some time had only a limited impact in London, the centre of the older unionism of craft clubs and societies. This was because the mining and cotton industries were concentrated in regions far removed from the national capital. But the new engineering industry, which was also a product of the Industrial Revolution, although very largely developed in the North of England, nevertheless had ramifications in the London area. The new type of unionism evolved by the workers in this industry was to be a pattern for the older crafts to imitate, especially after 1851, when the largest union in the industry was established with headquarters in the metropolis.

Ever since the repeal of the Combination Laws there had been a variety of societies of millwrights, machinists, and so on, either local or regional in scope. The strongest of them was the Journeymen Steam Engine Makers, founded at Manchester in 1826 and later usually known as the 'Old Mechanics'. This society prospered, and after a dozen years of existence it set an example of union technique by accepting the principle of financial centralization. This did not, however, seem to be sufficient for the successful organization of the engineering shops, which often contained quite a range of trades; and in the later 1840s it became an aim of many workers in the industry to unite all the engineering trades in one union, so that if any one trade were involved in a dispute with an employer 'the whole of the trades in that shop shall strike'. This still did not include the unskilled labourers, whose numbers in each shop the tradesmen were in any case anxious to limit. But the main object of the tradesmen was to end a practice in the industry whereby an employer before recruiting a new skilled man demanded to see his 'quittance paper' from his previous employer, giving details of his ability and character.

In 1850–1 a number of young society members in the industry took a lead in negotiations for the creation of a national union, to be formed by the fusion of local and sectional bodies. The most prominent in the group were William Allan of Crewe, a taciturn and methodical Scotsman who was now secretary of the 'Old Mechanics', and William Newton of London, a member of the same society who was a powerful and ebullient orator if less able as an administrator. The organization that they founded was called 'The Amalgamated

Society of Engineers, Machinists, Smiths, Millwrights, and Pattern-makers', and became generally known as the Amalgamated Society of Engineers. It had from the start a high rate of contributions and a generous scale of sickness, superannuation, and funeral benefits. Although its district committees were permitted a considerable degree of autonomy, the bulk of the funds were centralized at the headquarters in London, under a full-time general secretary, who was supervised by an Executive Council elected from the branches in the metropolitan area. By the end of 1851 the membership of the new society was already almost 12,000.

Although many of the apparently novel characteristics of the Amalgamated Engineers were borrowed from the 'Old Mechanics', and similar features were to be found elsewhere, such as in the Friendly Society of Iron Moulders, yet the foundation of the new society in 1851 is usually and rightly regarded as a landmark in the history of trade unionism. Sidney and Beatrice Webb hailed it as a 'new model', and we may agree that its establishment with London headquarters and its rapid rise to a five-figure membership and a position of great financial strength did make it a model for other unions both in Britain and abroad. Its high fees and exclusiveness, however, could be copied only by societies of craftsmen, and not by unions comprehending a wider range of workers, including the semi-skilled, as was the case with the miners and cotton weavers. Yet at the same time there were elements in the Engineers' constitution that looked back to the ideals of the 1830s; and Newton, who was a member of the Executive Council of the new union, was still an advocate of cooperative workshops as a solution of the problem of unemployment.

In January 1852, only a few months after the foundation of the Amalgamated Society, the Engineers became involved in a desperate struggle with their employers both in London and in Lancashire. The employers, working in concert, locked out their tradesmen when they refused to accept an increase in the number of unskilled men in the shops. The union was strongly criticized for its attitude by the press, and particularly by *The Times*, and not even the levies on men still at work, amounting to over £12,000, nor the generous

donations from individuals and from other societies, totalling
almost as much again, could save it from defeat. The employers forced their men to sign 'the document'; and the
membership of the Amalgamated Engineers slumped far
below its peak figure of 1851. As soon as the strike was over,
Newton was active in urging the adoption of his plans for
cooperative workshops. Discussion of this idea continued for
some years, but nothing was done officially: it was perhaps
fortunate for the Society that its general secretary was not
Newton, but the more cautious Allan, who gradually built
up the funds on conservative lines.

In the course of the 1850s the Amalgamated Engineers
gradually won recognition from the employers, and the
membership figures once more rapidly increased. At a time
when regional loyalties were still very strong it was impressive that Lancashire men and Scotsmen could accept the
leadership of Londoners. A Manchester employer complained with obvious disgust:

Before 1851–2, we knew almost every workman in the place by
name and dealt with him individually. Since that we have always
had in our eye at a distance the controlling influence of a club that
sits in London.

It was difficult, of course, not only to win respect for decisions made so remotely but also to secure the efficient conduct
of business by local branches, so that central records and
statistics could be properly kept. That the necessary discipline was successfully imposed seems all the more remarkable when we realize that Delegate Meetings were rarely
held – only twice in the years between 1854 and 1874. The
smooth running of the central office in this period forms a
notable tribute to the efficiency of William Allan, who
conducted it for the most part without any full-time assistance, although during the strike of 1852 he engaged an office-
boy at six shillings a week.

The success of the Amalgamated Engineers made itself
felt upon the older type of society in the course of the next
great crisis of London unionism – the strike in the building
industry in 1859–60. For some years the building trade
societies had been agitating for the reduction of working

hours from ten to nine a day; and when a strike of masons broke out against Messrs Trollope of Pimlico owing to the dismissal of a unionist who had served on a deputation to the management, the strike was joined by the other building tradesmen, who also demanded the nine-hour day. When Messrs Trollope refused to give way, the other master-builders of the metropolis decided to support them by locking out their workmen and undertaking not to employ anyone who refused to sign 'the document', which ran as follows:

I declare that I am not now nor will I during the continuance of my engagement with you become a member of, or support, any society which, directly or indirectly, interferes with the arrangements of this or any other establishment, or with the hours or terms of labour, and I recognize the right of employer and employed individually to make any trade agreement on which they may choose to agree.

This was a challenge to the very existence of unionism, yet it received strong support from the principal organs of opinion. *The Times*, for instance, comparing 'the document' with the constitution of a trade union, said:

The question lies between one document and another, the only difference being that a Union document binds a man to one of the most unjust and mischievous codes ever devised, depriving him, for example, of the use of his hands for an hour, while the master's document binds him to nothing at all but to be his own master.

Harriet Martineau, the well-known exponent of Manchester economics, took a similar line in leaders in the *Daily News*. On the other hand, trade societies all over the country rallied to the cause of the London building workers, making what contributions they could either from their funds or from special levies. By far the most impressive support came from the Amalgamated Engineers, which made three separate donations of £1,000 each – an unheard-of sum for any one organization to afford. The money that was raised enabled the strikers to carry on their struggle, and eventually, in February 1860, after they had been out for six months, they came to a compromise with their employers. The nine-hour issue was dropped, and so was 'the document'.

The struggle of 1859–60 had a great effect on the leaders of the small societies in London and elsewhere. In London many of them still had great difficulty in surviving, and usually represented only a small minority of the workers in their trades. Henry Mayhew, in his *London Labour and the London Poor*, suggested that 'the society men of every trade comprise about one-tenth of the whole'; and he drew a sharp contrast between the living conditions of the two groups, the society and the non-society men – a contrast which only underlines the perilous position of the former. But if the engineers had acquired such strength and stability from national organization, perhaps other trades would be well advised also to follow the same course. And perhaps, too, there was a case for more permanent machinery to ensure the collaboration of the different societies in the metropolis.

Developments in both of these directions followed the London builders' strike. In June 1860 there was formed a new union called the Amalgamated Society of Carpenters and Joiners, which as its name implied was designed on the pattern of the Amalgamated Engineers. Robert Applegarth, who became its general secretary in 1862, later acknowledged this:

The London lock-out induced a number of our trade to hold an inquest on the system of 'localism', and their verdict was, 'the thing won't do'. They then decided to follow the example set by the Amalgamated Engineers, and a start was effected with eleven branches and about 350 members; but as for funds . . . in fact, they started without funds.

Such was the humble beginning of what was to be in time, like the Amalgamated Engineers, one of the strongest unions in the country.

The London builders' struggle also precipitated the formation of the London Trades Council, which was set on foot at a conference called by the builders' strike committee in May 1860. For the previous dozen years there had been occasional meetings of 'the Metropolitan Trades Delegates' at the Bell Inn, Old Bailey, to consider matters of interest to all London unionists. Now there was to be a permanent body to act as a medium for mutual help and guidance among London unionists, and to counter the influence of propaganda hostile to unionism. The first executive of the Council was elected in July, and Tom Jones, secretary of the Tinplate

Workers' Society, was appointed secretary. Of Tom Jones it was said that 'he was never seen out of doors without a tall silk hat'. Thus, however downtrodden the great bulk of the labouring population of London still remained, the 'aristocracy' of the trades at least was making a bid for middle-class recognition.

The generation after the repeal of the Combination Acts saw the predominance of combinations of a limited and localized type. In all the ups and downs of utopian Socialism, general unionism, cooperative production, and Chartism, it was the small trade societies and clubs which survived; and as with Siéyès in revolutionary and post-revolutionary France, so with working-class organizations in early nineteenth-century Britain, to have survived was something of an achievement. For although the Combination Laws had been repealed, trade unions still had no legal status; their funds had to be held in private hands, yet they could not sue if they were defrauded. Their main object, to improve the wages of their members, was regarded as impracticable by the exponents of economic theory, who held that wages were inevitably determined by the laws of supply and demand. Indeed, according to the theory of the wage fund, which was popular among economists at this time, if any group of workers obtained advances in wages through collective pressure it could only be at the expense of the legitimate reward of other workers. It is not difficult to see why unionism was therefore regarded in middle-class circles as being not merely mistaken but positively wicked. Even Charles Dickens, who was often critical of Manchester economics, felt that union leaders were self-seeking agitators and that the noblest of the workers was the man who, like Stephen Blackpool in *Hard Times*, was 'sent to Coventry' for refusing to join a union.

After the mid point of the century, however, the horizons of unionism began to extend. The continued expansion of the scale of industry, and the widening of the market both for labour and for goods – caused especially by the building of railways and then by the beginnings of steam shipping – were all factors making for an expansion of the scope of unionism. If the small master gave way to a large employer, and if the large employer chose to frame a common policy towards his employees in association with other employers throughout the country, then the only salvation for the workmen was in combination on an equally large scale. Better communications enabled working men to move around the country more easily; it encouraged the wider circulation of radical newspapers and the improvement of contacts between artisans with similar interests. With these changes, the old type of local independence in the trade-union movement gradually became obsolete. The growth of national organization also received special encouragement from two changes in the law, both of which at least appeared to favour the extension of unionism. One was the Friendly Societies Act of 1855, which gave legal protection to societies with benefit functions, and therefore presumably to trade unions; the other was the Molestation of Workmen Act of 1859, which, in an attempt to clarify the law as laid down in 1825, specifically exempted peaceful picketing in trade disputes over wages and hours from the penalties for 'molestation' and 'obstruction'.

It is true that even the new national unions, with their full-time secretaries and comparatively centralized financial structures, still had to accept the fact that travel about the country was expensive and inconvenient for the employed artisan, although no longer slow. A national executive, meeting regularly to supervise the secretary's work, was therefore impracticable as yet. Many unions of at least regional size had already adopted the system of appointing a particular branch as the 'governing branch' of the union, to supervise the work of the secretary; and this system was at first retained by the national unions. Some unions made a point of transferring the 'seat of government' every few years, to prevent any hard feelings arising from local prejudice; others, including the Engineers, preferred to stay in one place.

At the same time there was now little advantage to be gained from encouraging the artisan to go 'on tramp'. The widening of the market tended to iron out the local and regional variations of boom and slump. Consequently, as Henry Broadhurst of the Stonemasons and Robert Applegarth of the Carpenters both found by personal experience in the slump of 1857–8, it became increasingly difficult to find a job by the old method of 'tramping'. The Amalgamated Engineers published information about the state of trade in different parts of the country, and also paid unemployment benefits to members in their own branches; the Carpenters undertook to provide railway fares to take unemployed members to distant places where jobs were to be had. Another expedient was emigration. Among the pioneers in this field were the Potters, who adopted a scheme in the 1840s when they were worried about the possibility of labour-saving machinery being introduced into their craft. They set up an Emigration Society to transport members and their families to the United States, where a tract of land was acquired for farming purposes in Wisconsin. But 'Potterville', as it was called, was never a success, partly because the machinery scare proved to be a false alarm. Other unions had their own schemes, normally much more modest than this one; and the Carpenters put the encouragement of emigration high among their objects, describing it as the 'natural outlet' for 'surplus labourers and mechanics' produced by the 'prolific character of the Anglo-Saxon race'.

Yet in spite of the growth of population and the apparently permanent existence of an unemployment problem, the standard of living of the artisans continued to improve. And this improvement stimulated among many of them a moral earnestness akin to that of the Victorian middle class, a willingness to eschew intemperance and a desire to engage in 'self-improvement'. The spread of literacy as well as of national unionism led to the growth of a trade-union press: the weekly *Potters' Examiner*, for instance, and the *Flint Glass Makers' Magazine*, both of which set a high standard in the quality of their articles. It is perhaps not surprising that the Bookbinders and the Compositors, the most literate craftsmen of all, should establish libraries for their members; the spread of the habit to other unions, such as the Scottish United Operative Masons, is more noteworthy. The temperance movement, encouraged by the nonconformist sects, exerted an increasing influence on unionists, and the practice of holding union meetings at public-houses began slowly to decline. The Glasgow Coopers were probably not entirely untypical in their course of evolution in the 1850s:

Fines and footings, which hitherto had been exacted from strangers procuring work, or from apprentices entering the trade and passing from one stage to another, and which had led to habits of drinking, were abolished. In their stead were introduced annual soirees, pleasure excursions, vocal and instrumental concerts, etc., open to all comers, whether members or not.

Increasingly, too, the middle-class exponents of Manchester economics began to find that the ablest of the unionists could argue with them on their own terms, and could present a powerful case for the existence of unions. Thus, in 1860 Thomas Dunning of the Bookbinders published a pamphlet entitled *Trades Unions and Strikes*, in which he maintained that it was only by combination that workmen could put themselves on a basis of equality for negotiation with their employers. Dunning also maintained, contrary to the popular view, that as unions depended on 'public spirit ... for a perfectly legitimate purpose', they always comprised 'not only the best workmen, but best men in the moral sense that are to be found in the trade'. This vigorous apologia so impressed John Stuart Mill that he wrote of it:

> Readers of other classes will see with surprise, not only how great a portion of truth the Unions have on their side, but how much less flagrant and condemnable even their errors appear, when seen under the aspect in which it is only natural that the working classes should themselves regard them.

Dunning's advocacy of unionism also helped to colour the report on trade unions which was drawn up by a committee of the National Social Science Association for its 1860 Congress. The detailed character of the report, and its generally favourable tenor, were both portents of a new age in which social problems were to be carefully investigated and working-class institutions more sympathetically treated. The report in fact evinced approval for trade unionism 'as an essay in self-government', and declared that

> leaders of a strike, where there is no regularly organized society, are likely to prove more unreasonable and violent than where there is.

With ideas such as these at last beginning to shape the public opinion of the upper class, the trade unions could hope to consolidate their still tenuous legal status and respectability.

CHAPTER FOUR

◆◆◆

THE FORMATION OF A
PRESSURE GROUP, 1860–80

UNTIL the 1860s it could not be said that there was any national leadership of the trade unions. The National Association of United Trades for the Protection of Labour, which as we have seen had had a shadowy existence since its foundation in 1845, operated only on special occasions, such as when the Molestation of Workmen Bill was being drawn up. We do not know how much support the National Association could claim in the country at large: it can hardly have had very much. But the formation of the London Trades Council in 1860 seemed to put matters on a different footing. Although London was only part of the whole country, it contained a large proportion of existing unionism, and was also the headquarters of a number of the national unions. The full-time secretaries of the latter formed a group which dominated the London Trades Council in its early days, and could claim in some sense at least to be representative of national union opinion.

The dominating figure among this group was Robert Applegarth, who became secretary of the Amalgamated Carpenters in 1862. Although aged only twenty-eight at that time, Applegarth had plenty of confidence, probably derived in large part from three years lately spent in America; and by a combination of shrewdness and good humour he rapidly won the confidence of William Allan, the cautious secretary of the Amalgamated Engineers, and Edwin Coulson, a tough and determined man who was secretary of the Operative Bricklayers Society. Another close colleague was George Odger, a shoemaker still working at his trade, who had succeeded Tom Jones as the part-time secretary of the Trades Council itself. Odger's brilliant oratorical gifts and grasp of political as well as industrial questions went far to make up for the fact that he was unable to devote all his time to the Council's affairs.

This group of leaders developed a common policy on a number of questions of current concern to trade unionists. Since most of them were secretaries of national unions, no longer working at their trades but principally involved in building up the finances of their societies, it was natural that they should take a conservative attitude towards strikes, urging their avoidance whenever possible, so as to prevent any inroads upon union reserves. This was not so much a policy of weakness as one of long-term prudence: they wished to fight only from a position of strength. As Applegarth put it:

> Never surrender the right to strike, but be careful how you use a double-edged weapon.

The group therefore advocated industrial conciliation wherever possible, and favoured the arbitration of disputes. Sometimes they refused to allow the 'credentials' of the London Trades Council to be given to support applications for financial assistance for strikes which they thought undesirable.

This cautious attitude was not universally popular. It particularly aroused the hostility of George Potter, a young carpenter who belonged not to the Amalgamated but to a local society in London, and who had made a reputation as the leader of the London builders' strike in 1859–60. Potter was now running an influential labour paper in the metropolis, entitled the *Bee-Hive*. His more aggressive policy was one that suited the temper of the members of the small old-fashioned autonomous trade societies, still quite numerous in the London area; and he often clashed with Applegarth's group as a result.

On the need for political action, however, there was some common ground. Allan was apparently inhibited by his union's declared opposition to politics; but Applegarth, Odger, and Potter were all agreed that it was important for the unions to influence public opinion on the questions of the day, especially on the question of the extension of the franchise. If their members were to get the vote, they reasoned, it would be very much easier for the unions to secure such alterations of the law as they needed to safeguard their funds and to give them a fair chance of conducting strikes without having their members prosecuted on some criminal charge or other.

In these years before the passing of the Second Reform Act it was only a minority of union members who were within what Gladstone called 'the pale of the constitution'. In some constituencies a fair proportion of artisans had long had the freeman franchise, and before the 1832 Act this sometimes gave them an important influence, as at Liverpool, where the Shipwrights Society as early as the 1790s was assiduously courted by the rival candidates. After 1832 the freemen lost weight in the determination of elections, but there were a few constituencies, of which Sheffield was perhaps the most notable example, where a large number of artisans became qualified under the £10 occupation franchise. At the same time it was always the case that a strong demonstration of support for a particular candidate, even by non-electors, could have some influence at the hustings, for the voting took place in public. Thus, even before 1867, if the unions chose to take a definite stand at an election there was a chance of their doing so to some purpose.

In 1852 William Newton of the Engineers stood as a Radical candidate for the Tower Hamlets division of London: he polled over a thousand votes, but this did not bring him anywhere near success. The contest deserves mention, however, as it was the first time that a distinctively trade-union candidate fought a parliamentary election, albeit without the support of his organization. Although various other workingmen sometimes fought elections, it was not for another sixteen years that a trade-union leader stood again. In the early 1860s, however, a number of factors brought union officials into politics. They had already been drawn into an unprecedented public debate about the merits of unionism at the time of the London builders' strike, which revealed the existence of a number of potential allies of trade unionism among the professional classes. There were, for instance, Christian Socialists such as J. M. Ludlow and Thomas

Hughes, who were both barristers, and there were Positivists, that is, adherents of the positive social philosophy of the Frenchman Auguste Comte, such as Professor E. S. Beesly of University College, London, and another barrister called Frederic Harrison. Several of these men had been involved in the preparation of the report on trade unions presented to the 1860 meeting of the National Social Science Association. Contact with such sympathizers, and the desire to reciprocate their support by helping them in any parliamentary elections that they chose to fight, were no doubt factors pulling Applegarth and his colleagues more fully into the political arena. But in any case, the union leaders felt not only that they could benefit from political activity but also that they had a right and a duty to participate. This view was clearly expressed in an *Address to the Trade Unions* published by a newly founded body called the Manhood Suffrage and Vote by Ballot Association, and actually written either by Applegarth or by George Howell, a young bricklayer who shared his views:

We do not wish you to relax one iota of your efforts in reference to the amelioration of our social condition. . . . Nor do we wish to turn our trades societies into political organizations, to divert them from their social objects; but we must not forget that we are citizens, and as such should have citizens' rights. Recollect also, that by obtaining these rights we shall be able more effectually to secure our legitimate demands as Unionists.

For Applegarth and his colleagues, therefore, the distinction between industrial and political action was not easily drawn; and in the course of these years we find them participating in a multitude of different public causes. Several of them were on the reception committee when Garibaldi visited London in 1864; they were to be found supporting the Northern cause in the American Civil War; and the names of some appear among the early members of the International Working Men's Association, better known as the First International, which for a time seemed to show promise of securing united action between trade unionists of all countries. In 1865 the Reform League was founded, to win the franchise for the working man; and most of the London union leaders took a full part in its activities. The general election of that year saw unprecedented trade-union influence at the polls. Thomas Hughes put up as a Radical at Lambeth, and was much helped in his campaign by a committee of trade-union supporters; he was elected. John Stuart Mill, at Westminster, also had unionist backing, and was elected in spite of – or because of – his famous remark at an election meeting, that working men were generally liars. Odger was present at this meeting, and helped to turn the remark to good account by saying that the working classes wanted friends and not flatterers. Outside London, unionists also gave their support to friendly candidates, and Joseph Cowen, the Newcastle Radical, owed his success in part to the help of John Kane of the National Association of Iron-workers.

The result of the 1865 election was a marked strengthening of the Radical element in the Commons, which had the effect of bringing the question of franchise reform to the point of decision. Great meetings began to be held in London and elsewhere to demand manhood suffrage, the sponsors usually being either the Reform League or the middle-class National Reform Union. At the end of 1866, after the so-called Adullamite revolt and the defeat of Gladstone's Bill, even William Allan urged support for the movement, and carried a resolution to that effect at a meeting of the London Trades Council – though the resolution carried a proviso: 'While advising the great bodies of trades unionists thus to act, we have no desire to make our societies channels for political agitation.' The actual passing of reform was achieved in the end by the subtle Parliamentary tactics of Derby and Disraeli; but the pressure of the unionists, both at the 1865 general election and in the subsequent campaign of popular demonstrations, had played a vital role.

If it was the leaders of the London Trades Council who took the most prominent part in the working-class agitation for the widening of the franchise, it was the Glasgow Trades Council – founded in 1858, or two years earlier than its London counterpart – which largely deserved credit for a reform of the Master and Servant law. The existing law bore heavily upon the employee, for he could be treated as a criminal for any breach of contract, and could be sent to prison, whereas his employer was liable only to civil proceedings. In addition, magistrates had developed the habit of threatening strikers with imprisonment for breach of contract under this law if they did not immediately return to work. For various reasons connected with the character of Scottish industry and the Scottish legal system, the pressure of this law was felt more keenly in Scotland than in England.

The campaign for reform was led by Alexander Campbell and George Newton, officials of the Glasgow Trades Council, and by Alexander McDonald, the Scottish miners' leader. In 1864 these leaders convened in London a national conference of trade-union delegates to discuss the reform that they desired, and at this conference – a unique occasion, for so many prominent leaders of unions from all over the country had never assembled before – arrangements were made for the introduction of a Bill into the House of Commons, and for the formation of local committees to lobby for its support. The Bill made no progress, but the agitation secured the appointment of a Select Committee, which in 1866 came under the chairmanship of Lord Elcho, the heir of a Scottish peer, the Earl of Wemyss. Elcho was quite liberal-minded on this sort of issue, and his committee reported in favour of limited reform. As a result, a measure was enacted in 1867 to remedy the grosser defects of the existing situation. It did not entirely satisfy the unions, however, because it still permitted criminal actions against workmen for breach of contract in 'aggravated cases', whatever they might be.

But the final stages of the campaign for the reform of the Master and Servant law were heavily overshadowed by a sudden crisis which threatened the very existence of trade unionism. This was precipitated by three events: the period of bad trade in 1866–7, the 'Sheffield outrages' of 1866, and the decision in the case of *Hornby* v. *Close*. The bad trade was only temporary, being occasioned more than anything else by a banking panic in the City; but it provided an opportunity for a number of publicists to denounce the unions for weakening the competitive position of British goods by their insistence on higher wages than foreign workmen obtained. This line of argument could only be pursued while trade actually was bad, and so it was more or less abandoned after a year or two; but it was to be heard again in the future, for it had the advantage of being more easily stated than disproved.

The 'Sheffield outrages' were the culmination of a long series of acts of violence directed against non-unionists in the Sheffield cutlery trades. The practice of 'rattening', or removing the wheel-bands or other tools of workmen who were not in good relations with the union, had long been employed as an arbitrary method of discipline in an industry with many small firms and much competition. But this was by no means all: for several years there had been occasional incidents of violence, and these culminated in October 1866, when a workman's house was blown up by gunpowder. Immediately the newspapers of the whole country were attributing this crime, not so much to a special local situation at Sheffield, but to the institution of trade unionism generally. The result was the appointment of a Royal Commission to investigate the whole subject of unionism, and in particular to trace the outrages to their source. In order to secure information, those actually responsible for criminal acts were promised an indemnity if they came forward with a complete testimony.

The respectable leaders in London and elsewhere were naturally very anxious to persuade the public that what had happened at Sheffield had nothing to do with them, and perhaps nothing to do with trade unionism at all. Their anxiety to stand well with public opinion was heightened by the criticisms which they had already encountered as a result of the trade depression, and also by their recognition that something needed to be done to alter the law as laid down in *Hornby* v. *Close*. This was a case in which the Boilermakers Society sued the treasurer of its Bradford branch, in order to recover £24 which he owed the society. The Boilermakers' officials, like those of other unions, had thought that the Friendly Societies Act of 1855 would provide protection for their funds and enable them to secure redress from defaulting officers and members just as if their organization was no more than a friendly society. In this belief, they had deposited a copy of their rules with the Registrar of Friendly Societies.

But the Lord Chief Justice and three other judges declared in their judgment that trade unions were outside the scope of the measure, being still illegal, although not criminal, organizations, owing to their tendency to act 'in restraint of trade'.

The crisis demanded effective leadership on the trade union side, and it was at this time that the so-called 'Junta' emerged as a sort of 'cabinet' of the movement. The term 'Junta' was not used at the time, but was coined by Sidney and Beatrice Webb to describe the group of five men who assumed the title of 'Conference of Amalgamated Trades' and began to meet weekly in London, often with professional advisers but always in secret. The five men were Applegarth, Allan, Coulson, Odger, and Daniel Guile, the secretary of the Friendly Society of Iron Founders. Their aim was to ensure that the Royal Commission conducted its hearings in a way as favourable to unionism as possible; and they therefore demanded that at least two trade unionists should be appointed as Commissioners. To this the Government demurred, on the ground that nobody should be a judge in his own case; but it was agreed that the unionists should nominate a member of the Commission whom they regarded as likely to be sympathetic to their cause; and also that an expert trade unionist should be present during the examination of witnesses. The nominee of the Junta for the membership of the Commission was Frederic Harrison; and as Thomas Hughes was appointed to the Commission in his capacity as an interested Member of Parliament, there was a guarantee of two friendly members out of a body of eleven Commissioners. In addition, Applegarth acted as the Junta's expert trade unionist in attendance.

It is true that for a time the leadership of the Junta was challenged by a rival group led by George Potter, which secured substantial support in the provinces. Potter's group summoned a Conference of Trades, which met in London in March 1867, and appointed a committee to act on behalf of union interests. This committee was allowed to nominate a representative to attend the hearings of the Royal Commission, but the unionist nominated was excluded after a brief period of service because he made a public attack on one of the Commissioners. As a result, Potter and his friends were obliged to leave the campaign almost entirely to the Junta – or rather, to Applegarth and Harrison, with a certain amount of help from Hughes, who missed a good many of the hearings.

The main strategy of Applegarth and Harrison was to concentrate the attention of the Commission on the large Amalgamated unions, of which Applegarth's own was a conspicuous example. He himself appeared as the first witness and did much to present unionism in a favourable light. He, Allan, and Coulson in their evidence built up a picture of the unions as sober insurance societies whose affairs were business-like and entirely respectable. As Coulson put it, pointing to his rule-book:

> Everything is above board. We think as Englishmen that everything we do shall see daylight, and therefore every rule of the Society is in that book.

Applegarth was very definite in asserting that the industrial role of his union was limited to matters of wages and hours of work, in disavowing any interest in the regulation of the number of apprentices, and in declaring that the union's attitude to the non-unionist or to the 'blackleg' must be one of moral suasion only. Allan took a different line on the apprenticeship question, but his impressive statistics about the size of his union (33,000 members in 1867) and its financial resources (£140,000) largely made up for this. The Commissioners were impressed; but those of them who were most hostile to unionism, and in particular J. A. Roebuck, M.P. for Sheffield, tried to overcome the effect by calling on actuarial experts to show that the union benefits could not in the long run be maintained. Such tactics were erroneous, for Applegarth and Allan were only too happy to discuss this sort of question.

The course of further evidence, however, brought out a good deal of evidence about restrictive practices in the building trades, especially among masons and plasterers. Even Harrison was rattled by this: he wrote privately:

> If the unions cannot get over it, some of them and certainly the Masons deserve all that was ever said of them and are as mere

organs of class tyranny. My God! Think if I were to publish a formal recantation. But I keep my counsel as yet.

But such things were not as startling as the result of the investigation into the 'Sheffield outrages', for the special investigators sent to take evidence on the spot elicited a frank confession of guilt from William Broadhead, secretary of the Grinders Union and landlord of the George Inn. By this time, however, Harrison was regaining his strength in the union cause:

I am not going to cave in now. The unions have serious faults but I still believe them necessary as I do Railways, and capable of improvement.

One of the things that sustained him in later hearings was the testimony of A. J. Mundella, the Nottingham hosiery manufacturer, who was a strong supporter of unionism and had encouraging observations to make about a system of industrial conciliation that he had introduced in agreement with the union in his own works.

When the Commission came to draw up its report there were fierce arguments between those broadly hostile to unionism and those favourable to it. In general, Roebuck and the employers on the Commission were hostile; Hughes and Harrison were favourable; and the peers – Lord Elcho and the Earl of Lichfield – were undecided. Fortunately for Hughes and Harrison, the investigating committee at Sheffield found that the outrages there had been steadily declining in intensity during the decade, and were confined to a small group of local unions. Elsewhere in Britain, similar acts of violence appeared to be confined to the brickmaking industry in the neighbourhood of Manchester.

As a result, although the Commission started with a draft report that was very critical of unionism, Harrison was able to whittle away its criticisms until its tone was entirely altered. Then, to the exasperation of their colleagues, he and Hughes refused to sign the Report which they had so drastically altered, and brought in a Minority Report of their own, which only the Earl of Lichfield joined them in signing.

The Majority Report held that some measures ought to be taken to legalize trade unions. For this purpose, it recommended that they should register their rules with the Registrar of Friendly Societies, but that the Registrar should have powers to reject rules having 'objectionable' clauses, such as restrictions on the employment of apprentices, on the use of machinery, or on the introduction of piece-work. They also recommended that the benefit and strike funds of unions should be separated. The Minority Report had no such recommendations for the supervision of the unions: it simply urged the legalization of trade unionism, and a complete repeal of the criminal sections of the 1825 Act, so that questions of intimidation and the like could be dealt with under the ordinary criminal law. It was the Minority's view that trade unions should be given the protection of the Friendly Societies Acts, and that their rules should be registered with the Registrar; but that he should have no powers to reject any set of rules, unless he felt that they were incomplete or fraudulent. If this became the law it would mean that the unions would gain in two ways: they would have the protection of the law to the extent of being able to recover damages from their officers, but they would not be under any State supervision nor be so formally recognized by the law as to be themselves liable to be sued.

The publication of the Commission's Reports resulted in a remarkable change in the public attitude to trade unionism. People recognized that the great bulk of the work done by unions was of a character that was entirely beneficial. A leader in *The Times* in July 1869 acknowledged the transformation of opinion, and declared that it could not be due to anything but the work of the Commission. That this had come about was the greatest tribute to Harrison's skill as an advocate and to the quality of the evidence given by the leaders of the Amalgamated unions, especially Applegarth. It owed something, too, to the influence of John Ruskin, whose *Unto This Last*, with its attack on classical political economy, was published in 1862; and it was accompanied by the gradual abandonment of the wage-fund theory by the economists themselves, especially after the publication in 1869 of W. T.

Thornton's not unsympathetic study of trade unionism entitled *On Labour*. The change occurred in spite of memories of the 'Sheffield outrages', kept alive at the time by Charles Reade's bitterly anti-union novel, *Put Yourself in His Place*, which was serialized in the *Cornhill Magazine* in 1869–70 and then put on as a play.

Meanwhile the trade unions had been gradually moving towards the re-establishment of a permanent national forum for their deliberations. Ever since 1860, when the National Social Science Association paid the unions the compliment of close examination, the more publicity-conscious unionists had in their turn taken an interest in the Association's Congresses; and in 1865 William Dronfield, a journeyman printer who was secretary of the Sheffield Association of Organized Trades, was bitterly disappointed when a paper which he had delivered at the Social Science Congress that year was not published in its Report. A fellow-printer who was a friend of his, Sam Nicholson, the President of the Manchester and Salford Trades Council, at once said 'Why not have a Congress of our own?' In 1866 Dronfield did summon a national congress, but it was for a more ambitious purpose – to establish

a national organization among the trades of the United Kingdom, for the purpose of effectually resisting all lock-outs.

This body was duly set up, under the title of United Kingdom Alliance of Organized Trades; and an attempt was made to raise funds to support member unions engaged in defensive disputes. But the unions could not be persuaded to pay their levies regularly when they did not expect to obtain early benefit from the fund, and so by the end of 1867 the Alliance had collapsed.

In 1868, however, Sam Nicholson reverted to the simpler idea of having a Congress for the sake of discussion and publicity. He and William Wood, the secretary of his Trades Council, issued invitations for a Congress which they hoped would serve as a platform for the opinions of the unionists in the same way as the Social Science Congresses did for the middle and upper classes, but from which as they said 'the artisan class are almost entirely excluded'. They suggested that at the proposed Congress

... papers, previously prepared, should be laid before the Congress on the various subjects which at the present time affect Trades Societies, each paper to be followed by discussion upon the points advanced, with a view of the merits and demerits of each question being thoroughly ventilated through the medium of the public press.

The invitation was sent at first only to trades councils and 'federations of trades societies', but it was later widened to include all societies. The thirty-four delegates who attended the Congress, held in Whit week, 1868, were mostly from provincial trades councils, eleven of which were represented. There were, however, some delegates of national societies and some of local societies; but altogether only two of the delegates came from London – one of them being George Potter. The London Trades Council was not represented, as the Junta evidently thought that the meeting was a renewed attempt to deprive them of their position of leadership. But the Congress did open the way to reconciliation with them, by pledging itself to help them 'in their laudable attempt to secure the legal protection of trade societies' funds' and 'in their endeavours to alter the third section of the act of the 6th of George IV, cap. 128' – i.e. the clauses of the 1825 Act referring to intimidation.

The 1868 meeting is always regarded as the foundation of the Trades Union Congress, but no formal organization was set up on that occasion, and the only indication that there would be any continuity was to be found in the passing of a resolution declaring it 'highly desirable' that annual congresses should be held. The Birmingham Trades Council was deputed to convene the next one. But the year which intervened before the Birmingham Congress improved the prospects of permanence, for it was marked by a long-overdue reconciliation of the rival groups in London. George Potter, troubled by the falling circulation of the *Bee-Hive*, was in the mood to come to terms, and at a joint meeting of his own following and that of the Junta in April it was agreed to concert measures for the support of a Parliamentary Bill based on the Minority Report of the Royal Commission. At the beginning of the following year three members of the Junta – Applegarth, Odger, and Coulson – joined the managing committee of the *Bee-Hive*.

The second annual Trades Union Congress met at Birmingham in August 1869. It was attended by forty delegates representing societies with a total membership of some quarter of a million. Among them, this time, was the London Trades Council. Naturally the delegates spent much of their time discussing the Reports of the Royal Commission and the proposed legislation. The novelty of the occasion, however, was a decision to appoint a committee to 'prepare a statement to go out to the world, to the trades unions and legislators, as to the reasons why we hold the opinions therein contained'. Yet this committee was still not a permanent body, and again the arrangements for summoning the next Congress were left to local unionists, this time those of London. For the London Congress, the idea was that the delegates would be able to spend some of their time lobbying M.P.s at Westminster; and for this reason the Congress was not convened until the Government's trade-union Bill was introduced, which was not in 1870 at all but in February 1871.

The Government Bill was only in part satisfactory to the unionists. It gave legal recognition to trade unions and enabled them to protect their funds by registering under the Friendly Societies Act without any difficult conditions or division of funds between those for benefit purposes and those for strike purposes. But it still left unionists liable to criminal prosecution under the 1825 Act. The intention of the third Congress, therefore, which actually met in March 1871, was to lobby M.P.s for the amendment of the Bill. To ensure that the political pressure was maintained after the Congress was over, a small 'Parliamentary Committee' was appointed by the delegates. The most that was secured by the 1871 lobby, however, was the separation of the criminal clauses into another Bill, so that two acts were passed – the Trade Union Act and the Criminal Law Amendment Act. The unionists would in future be able to concentrate their efforts on the alteration or repeal of the latter, while accepting the former. The Criminal Law Amendment Act was all the more to their displeasure because it had been strengthened in the House of Lords so as to prohibit even the most elementary form of picketing by 'watching or besetting', which had been legalized by the Molestation of Workmen Act of 1859.

The passing of the Liberal Government's legislation, in spite of its shortcomings, was the signal for the dissolution of the Junta. Clearly an important phase in relations between the unions and Parliament had ended. The Parliamentary Committee appointed by the Trades Union Congress could provide a more truly representative leadership; and, furthermore, the driving force of the Junta, Robert Applegarth, was lost in May 1871, when he resigned his office as secretary of the Amalgamated Carpenters. He had been appointed as a Commissioner on the Royal Commission on Contagious Diseases – the first trade unionist ever to receive such an appointment – but the members of his union refused to allow him to attend the Commission's meetings during office hours. To be forced out of the movement in this way was a sad fate for a man who had contributed more than anyone else to making unionism acceptable to the public opinion of the upper classes.

The Parliamentary Committee of the T.U.C. was reconstituted by successive Congresses and thus became a permanent institution; but it had certain limitations as a leadership for the trade unions. Just on account of its representative character, it was less homogeneous than the Junta had been; and because its membership was drawn from all over the country, it could not meet anything like so frequently. Its secretary from 1871 to 1875 was, however, a man of no little ability – George Howell, who had proved himself as an organizer for the Reform League. During Howell's secretaryship, although there were a large number of issues with which the Parliamentary Committee concerned itself, varying from legislation against truck* to the admission of working men to juries, there were two demands which stood out as main points in the T.U.C. programme. One, of course, was for the alteration of the criminal law; the other

* 'Truck' is the payment of wages in kind.

was for some further improvement in the state of the Master and Servant law. But the general law dealing with conspiracy was also brought to the forefront of agitation as a result of the Gas Stokers' Case of December 1872, when some London gasworkers who had gone on strike to prevent the victimization of unionists were found guilty of breaking their contracts, and also of conspiracy to do so, and were sentenced to twelve months' hard labour, which was a punishment well beyond the maximum permissible directly under the Master and Servant Act of 1867. In 1873, furthermore, there was a remarkable exercise of the criminal law when at Chipping Norton sixteen women, who were the wives of agricultural labourers on strike, were sentenced to hard labour – admittedly, only for a few days – for 'intimidation' of blackleg workers.

The failure of the Liberal Government to take any further action to alter the law encouraged the Parliamentary Committee to take a more independent line at the 1874 election than had been possible in 1868. The only practicable policy in the hurried election of 1868 had been the support of Liberals who were friendly to the unions – a policy which had its successes here and there, for instance in the replacement of Roebuck at Sheffield by the friendly A. J. Mundella. But in 1874, with the Parliamentary Committee in being, and with rather more time for preparation, it was possible to pick and choose among the candidates of the rival parties by submitting to them all a series of 'Test Questions'. In cases where the Conservative gave the more favourable replies, unionists were encouraged to vote for him. Furthermore, about ten distinctively working-class candidates stood in various constituencies against both Liberal and Conservative opposition, and although none was elected, several secured good polls.

This independent attitude of the Parliamentary Committee has been obscured by the fact that two trade-unionist candidates who actually won seats in Parliament were fighting with Liberal support in straight contests against Conservative candidates. They were Alexander McDonald, the miners' leader, who was put forward at Stafford on the recommendation of the Labour Representation League (the successor of the National Reform League); and Thomas Burt, a Northumberland miner, who was elected for the Parliamentary borough of Morpeth, which contained several mining villages. Thus the first trade unionists to enter Parliament did so as Liberals; they were to be the forerunners of many more of the same political complexion – the 'Lib–Labs' as they came to be called.

One of the first acts of the new Conservative Government was to appoint a Royal Commission on the Labour Laws. Frederic Harrison, regarding this as just a way of avoiding the immediate need for legislation, refused to serve, but both Thomas Hughes and McDonald consented to appointment. The Parliamentary Committee agreed with Harrison and decided to boycott its proceedings. The result was that the work of the Commission was ineffective and its recommendations of little help. Yet Disraeli and his colleagues were at least free from the dogmatic individualism so common among the Liberals; and R. A. Cross, who was the Home Secretary, had responded favourably to the Parliamentary Committee's 'Test Questions' at the election. Consequently, when in 1875 the Government's proposals for legislation were published the Parliamentary Committee found to its surprise and gratification that they were very much to its taste. There were only a few amendments to be made in order to make the measure entirely satisfactory. These amendments were for the most part accepted by the Government; and the result was the enactment in the course of the same year of both the Conspiracy and Protection of Property Act and the Employers and Workmen Act. By the first of these measures the law of conspiracy was henceforward not to apply in trade disputes unless the actions concerned were criminal in themselves; and peaceful picketing was expressly legalized. Questions of intimidation and violence were left to be dealt with by the ordinary criminal law. By the Employers and Workmen Act – a significant change of title from Master and Servant – the penalty for breach of contract was limited to payment of civil damages.

The Parliamentary Committee was now satisfied. 'The work of emancipation', it announced, was 'full and complete.' Its secretary, George Howell, retired from his post, feeling that his work was done and that the Parliamentary Committee had no further purpose to serve. According to one report of the ensuing Congress:

Mr Howell thought the legislation with respect to Trade Unions was then so perfect that the natural time had run for the existence of Trade Union Congresses so far as Parliamentary action was concerned.

Other union leaders, however, were less sanguine, and the Congress proceeded to elect a successor to Howell. The choice fell upon Henry Broadhurst, the Stonemasons' leader, who was seeking to turn his union into an Amalgamated Society of the same type as the Engineers and the Carpenters, but who was not a member of the old London Trades Council clique.

Before going on to consider the 'Broadhurst era' of T.U.C. history, it would be well to take a glance at the general development of trade unionism in the 1860s and early 1870s. As G. D. H. Cole has pointed out, it is too easy to suppose that the Amalgamated unions centred in London entirely dictated the characteristics of the period, so far as structure and industrial attitudes were concerned. After all, unions of the centralized pattern of the Engineers catered for only a minority of workers in a minority of trades. They suited the artisans in industries where the competition of less-skilled labour was a constant threat, and where the employers had to be induced to respect a favoured section of the workers by accepting restrictions on apprenticeship or some other device to keep the 'non-society' or 'illegal' men at bay. In the two staple industries of the country, however – in textiles and in mining – such sharp competition between the artisans and other sections of the labour force did not exist.

Thus, in the cotton industry, as we have seen, the Amalgamated Association of Cotton Spinners, although limited to skilled workers, was to start with only a loose federation, and so it remained until the end of the 1870s; and the Weavers Amalgamations were both general in their recruitment and loosely federated in structure. In the 1860s and early 1870s the cotton unions continued to be highly localized in character, and as in earlier decades, representatives of all the Lancashire textile workers came together only for purely political purposes. In 1872, for instance, delegates of local societies established a Factory Acts Reform Association, to work for a reduction of the maximum legal weekly hours from sixty to fifty-four. It was an agitation fought, as one of their leaders later admitted, 'from behind the women's petticoats', for the proposed legislation was to apply solely to women and children, and was thus designed to win humanitarian sympathy, although its terms would inevitably also affect the hours of the men. An Act reducing hours to fifty-six and a half was in fact passed by the Conservative Government in 1874.

Among the miners there could be no question of separate unions for the different grades of men who worked in the pits. The mining community was an effective unit, welded together by isolation from other trades, by the hazards of the work, and by a common hostility to the owners. The ferocity with which some of the early struggles of the miners had been conducted could not easily be forgotten. Like the cotton workers, the miners placed high hopes on governmental regulation; and when Alexander McDonald founded the Miners National Association and held a conference of delegates at Leeds in 1863, his object was primarily to secure new legislation by Parliament. We have already mentioned McDonald's role in securing the amendment of the Master and Servant law in 1867; five years later he secured a Mines Regulation Act, which went further in the development of safety precautions and inspection. But for industrial purposes the county unions retained full independence; and in 1869 McDonald found himself faced by a rival organization, the Amalgamated Association of Miners, which developed a good deal of strength in Lancashire – where it was founded – and in Wales and the West Midlands. The Amalgamated Association was a centralized union, designed to provide mutual assistance between widely scattered coalfields and to help to develop unions in areas where, owing to heavy immigration of labour, the owners seemed to have the whip hand.

In the early 1860s, when coal was dear and all the pits were rapidly expanding their output, both national organizations prospered; and in 1873 each could claim about a hundred thousand members. In West Yorkshire the annual Demonstration and Gala of the miners' assocation reached a peak of splendour, with forty-seven brass bands on one occasion and as many or more 'banners, most nine foot by seven, and costing anything from £30 to £60 each'. As the price of coal seemed to be destined always to rise, many of the county unions agreed to a sliding scale for wages, based on this price. But in the later 1870s the price fell heavily, and the miners suffered considerably from their adherence to the principle. The Amalgamated Association was swept out of existence altogether before the end of the decade; and the Miners National Association survived only in Northumberland and Durham and to a limited extent in Yorkshire, where a good deal of union money had been lost in attempts to run cooperative collieries.

Finally, we may turn to the experience of those workers who had as yet virtually no means of enforcing an artificial scarcity upon their employers. They were not necessarily unskilled: it was just that they were, for one reason or another, difficult to organize. Yet many of them were feeling the impact of the organizing spirit of the time, and the extension of the franchise to the urban workers, coupled with the comparative prosperity of the period, encouraged them to organize themselves in imitation of the artisans. Thus, unions of gasworkers, builders' labourers, agricultural labourers, dockers, and railwaymen all made their appearance in the early 1870s.

The gasworks, it is true, did have some history of attempted organization. In 1834 there had been a strike in London which had plunged Westminster into darkness for a time, and attracted some unfavourable notice in upper-class quarters. It is doubtful, however, if any of those who began to form a union at the Beckton Gasworks at East Ham in 1872 had ever attempted such a thing before. They began to agitate for shorter hours – many of them were working as much as eighty hours a week – but although they won some concessions, their leaders were victimized by the manager and foremen and thrown out of work. The result was that the men came out on strike, thereby breaking their contracts with their employer, the Gas Light and Coke Company. The Company thereupon prosecuted them under the Master and Servant Act, and also, as we have seen, indicted a small number of them for conspiracy, securing a conviction and a twelve-months' sentence for each of the latter. London trade unionism as a whole was deeply stirred by the conspiracy charge, and a Gas Stokers' Defence Committee was formed, with Henry Broadhurst as secretary, in order to raise a fund for their defence and for the relief of their families. The Committee also memorialized the Home Secretary on their behalf, and secured a reduction of the sentence to only four months. But although the long-term result of the case was an amendment of the law, the Gas Stokers Union had completely disintegrated, and could not be restored.

It was natural that the builders' labourers should begin early to take an interest in unionism, in view of the rapid growth of the skilled unions in their industry. A Builders Labourers Union came into existence at the time of the builders' strike of 1859, and was reported to have some 4,000 members; but it did not last long. In 1872, during another London builders' strike, a fresh attempt was made by Patrick Kenney, an Irish labourer, and he got some assistance from Applegarth in establishing his union's finances on Amalgamated lines. Its title was the General Amalgamated Labourers Union, and it soon secured some 5,000 members. But again it proved difficult to retain the membership, and Kenney seems to have taken financial assistance from Conservative Party sources, and appeared at the 1881 T.U.C. as an agent in the cause of 'Fair Trade', which meant the reintroduction of tariffs. Some years later he was sent to prison for attempting to steal some spoons at a trade-union conference dinner which he attended at the Holborn Restaurant; and after that his union, or what was left of it, altogether disintegrated.

A third and much larger category of previously unorganized workers who now began to take an interest in unionism were the agricultural labourers. Like the gasworkers, they had in some cases attempted to organize in the 1830s, as we may recall from the story of the Dorchester labourers; but since then there had been virtually no trace of unionism. In 1868 a Church of England clergyman, Canon Girdlestone, drew public attention to the plight of the farm workers, and recommended combination as a remedy; but the initiative for the formation of a union came from the labourers themselves in widely scattered parts of the country. In 1871 a union was started at the village of Leintwardine in Herefordshire; a year later it claimed some 30,000 members in six counties. Then early in 1872 a group of labourers near Leamington persuaded one of their number, a Primitive Methodist lay preacher called Joseph Arch, to organize a union for them. Within a few weeks he had established the Warwickshire Agricultural Labourers Union, with the following paragraph in its rules:

Its object is to elevate the social position of the farm labourers of the county by assisting them to increase their wages; to lessen the number of ordinary working hours; to improve their habitations; to provide them with gardens or allotments; and to assist deserving and suitable labourers to migrate and emigrate.

In no time at all the movement was, as Arch put it, 'flowing over the country like a spring tide'. It is true that it did not spread outside the southern half of England, where the number of labourers was high in proportion to the number of farmers; but there was agitation or strike action taking place throughout this area, from Dorsetshire to Norfolk and Kent, and hundreds of pounds were contributed to their funds by other unions and by wealthy individual sympathizers.

By the end of May Arch's union had been put on a national basis under the title of the National Agricultural Labourers Union; eighteen months later, by the end of 1873, it had over a thousand branches and a membership of 72,000. A weekly journal of support called the *Labourers' Chronicle* was selling 30,000 copies an issue. In addition, there was a completely separate Kent and Sussex Labourers Union, and a Lincolnshire Labour League, both of them with headquarters and weekly journals of their own. The movement was in no way damaged by an indiscreet remark of the Bishop of Gloucester, Dr Ellicott, who suggested that union agitators should be ducked in the village horse-pond. The more that agricultural unionism was attacked by the Church, the more the nonconformists rallied to its support; and at the end of 1872 it won approval from the opposite end of the religious spectrum when Archbishop (later Cardinal) Manning joined a group of Liberal M.P.s on the platform of a meeting in London in support of Arch's union. The Chipping Norton intimidation case, which has already been described, occurred in the following year.

With the decline of British agriculture in the 1870s, however, there was not much prospect of the unions winning strikes against determined opposition; and in the course of 1873 Arch felt obliged to look to the prospects of a programme of emigration. He himself visited Canada, and his union then arranged for the emigration of several thousand men, mostly to Canada but also to Australia and New Zealand. As the years went by and the agricultural depression deepened, things became more and more difficult for the labourers' unions. But Arch's union was able to play a major part in the agitation for an extension of the Parliamentary franchise in the counties, and shortly after that was attained he himself was elected to Parliament for a Norfolk constituency.

The problems of organization among the railwaymen were in their way almost as great as among the agricultural labourers – from whom, incidentally, the railway labour force was mostly recruited in the first instance. Many of the grades of railway labour could, of course, be regarded as skilled, but except for some abortive efforts made about 1865 to organize individual grades, and the formation of an Engine Drivers and Firemen's United Society in 1866, there was no railway unionism until 1871. There were three main reasons for this: the considerable number of grades of labour in the industry caused disunity and enabled the companies to play off one class of worker against another; the labour policy of the companies was in any case paternalistic, and provided special benefits for the workers in the form of company schools, company churches, and so on; and at the same time the managers of the various companies ran their lines with a virtually military discipline, which found expression many years later in the remark of one of them to a Parliamentary Select Committee:

> You might as well have a trade union or an amalgamated society in the army, where discipline has to be kept at a very high standard, as have it on the railways.

All the same, a union came into existence at the end of 1871, under the name of Amalgamated Society of Railway Servants. The founder, to all intents and purposes, was M. T. Bass, a wealthy brewer who had become Liberal M.P. for Derby, where he had many railwaymen among his constituents. Bass apparently financed the first organization in London and also the establishment of a weekly journal to advocate the union's aims; no doubt it was also his influence that secured the inclusion of a clause 'to prevent strikes' among the declared objects of the society. Bass was invited to become President, but he refused; another middle-class man, however, Dr Baxter Langley, was elected Chairman; and it seems clear that the intention of the officials was to establish the organization as little more than a friendly society in the first instance, inducing railwaymen to join for the sake of the accident and superannuation benefits, and for the rest confining their activity to agitation for Parliamentary measures to reduce hours because of the risk of accidents.

In fact, a number of railway strikes did take place in 1872, over which the society's officers had virtually no control; and some improvements were won in the pay and conditions of the senior grades. For several years the finances of the society were in a hopeless state of disorder, owing to the inefficiency of the first general secretary; and anything less like the smooth-running Amalgamated Engineers under Allan, or the Carpenters under Applegarth or his successor John Prior, would have been difficult to imagine. The membership total was in the neighbourhood of 17,000 in 1872; three years later, however, it was down to less than 14,000, and with the economic depression at the end of the decade it dropped to half that figure. None of the railway companies was willing to recognize the union as a bargaining agent; and in short, while it had some of the appearance of being modelled on the pattern of the great Amalgamated societies, it had very little of the reality of their strength and status.

We have surveyed a wide range of industries and unions, and have noticed how in almost every case the early 1870s were a period of prosperity and expansion, while the later 1870s saw a marked decline and a weakening or collapse of the efforts at organization. The two obvious exceptions to this were the greatest of the Amalgamated societies, whose fortunes we have yet to trace; but their progress was less obviously due to 'Amalgamated principles' than to other more accidental circumstances. The Engineers were pursuing their accustomed cautious policy under William Allan, when suddenly the growth of mining trades unionism in the North-East and its success in reducing hours infected the engineering and iron workers in that area. Under the leadership of John Burnett, a member of the Engineers, a Nine Hours League was set on foot, and a strike took place. Both society and non-society men readily joined in, and regular financial assistance was paid by the Northumberland Miners Union. The employers began to import labour from the Continent in order to break the strike, but this only strengthened the strikers' resolve not to give in, and the Northumberland Miners increased their aid. Discontent among the German and Belgian blacklegs, fomented by union agents, combined with the hostility of the community to force the employers to give way after a resistance of five months. The whole movement had been initiated without the support of Allan and his executive, who thought that it would fail. But now it rapidly spread to other areas; and in 1875, after Allan had died, Burnett was elected general secretary. It fell to him to fight a difficult defensive action on behalf of the nine hours; and in 1879, a year of bad trade and unemployment, the society had to pay out more strike pay than in all the preceding twenty-six years put together. But 1879 was the only year in which the membership total showed some decline. The engineering industry was continuing to expand, and Burnett's firm policy constantly won new members.

The success of the Carpenters was won by less honourable methods. For many years the Amalgamated had faced the competition of the General Union of Carpenters and Joiners, an older organization with a less centralized system. In 1878 Prior declared war against the General Union, which had just lost a strike in the Manchester area, and in the words of one of his colleagues he 'used Prussian methods' on them. Members of the Amalgamated entered lodges of the General Union in order to sow dissension and to bring their members over in batches; and the entrance requirements of the Amalgamated were temporarily waived. The result was that about half the membership of the General Union was won over, and five-sixths of the remainder abandoned trade unionism altogether. But the Amalgamated had gone up from 16,000 members to 23,000, so it could be said that 'Prior's War' ended in a victory of sorts. Before it was over, however, he had resigned from his secretaryship in order to become a government inspector.

It is against this background of structural variety and economic vicissitude that we must set Broadhurst's work as secretary of the Parliamentary Committee from 1875 onwards. He himself was a fervent Liberal, who played a leading part in the Eastern Question agitation of 1878, and when he was elected to Parliament for Stoke in 1880 there was no more determined Gladstonian in the House than himself. For a few months there were three 'Lib–Lab' M.P.s, but in 1881 Alexander McDonald died and the number returned to two. The weakness of the labour interest at Westminster, now that the main objects of the Parliamentary Committee had been secured by the legislation of 1871–5, could not be concealed.

Certainly the circumstances of the period did not encourage Broadhurst to take a wide view of his responsibilities as secretary of the Parliamentary Committee. Action meant expense, and the Committee's funds were of Lilliputian proportions. Broadhurst was lucky to have for some time an assistant who had a private income, otherwise he could hardly have attended both to his Parliamentary responsibilities and to his duties as the Committee's secretary. At a time when bad trade was reducing the number of those represented at Congress from a peak of almost twelve hundred thousand in 1874 to less than half that total in the period 1879–84, he could hardly propose any course which would have involved an increase in the unions' affiliation fees. Nor could Broadhurst look for any immediate expansion in the authority of the T.U.C. itself within the labour movement. When it was suggested at the 1878 Congress that something should be done to prevent demarcation disputes between unions – a growing problem as the unions expanded their membership – he firmly replied

that the less their annual Parliament interfered with the differences arising between trade and trade, and industry and industry, the better would it be for the success of their great undertaking.

It is true that Congress continued to have a parliamentary programme. The most important proposal on the agenda in the late 1870s was a demand for an Employers Liability Act, which should enable workmen or their families to obtain adequate compensation from their employers for industrial injuries or death if negligence was involved. This was a matter in which the miners and the railwaymen were especially interested. A parliamentary Select Committee of 1876–7 reported against framing as comprehensive a Bill as the T.U.C. desired, but the new Liberal Government elected in 1880 put forward a measure which the Parliamentary Committee was willing to accept, and which was passed into law as the Employers Liability Act, 1880. But the T.U.C. leaders were still not satisfied, as it allowed employers to plead freedom from liability if the injury was caused by a fellow-workman 'in common employment' with the injured. They also thought it undesirable that workmen should be permitted to 'contract out' of the terms of the Act. Other reforms for which the Parliamentary Committee pressed were (apart from the extension of the parliamentary franchise) an increase in the number of factory inspectors and the limitation of summary jurisdiction by magistrates. In response to the enthusiastic advocacy of the Liberal M.P. Samuel Plimsoll, they also demanded the application of the Employers and Workmen Act to seamen.

But these reforms were, after all, of very limited scope; and some of them seemed to have more relevance to the administrative problems of trade-union officialdom than to the general condition of the working class. Meanwhile, the unskilled labourers and the workers in the 'sweated' trades remained outside the scope of the Parliamentary Committee's continuous field of interest; and when a few middle-class ladies appeared at annual Congresses in the late 1870s and early 1880s to voice the grievances of working women, whom they were trying to organize, Broadhurst worked to secure their exclusion, not only on the grounds that they were not *bona fide* workers, but because

He doubted even the wisdom of sending women to these congresses, because under the influence of emotion they might vote for things they would regret in cooler moments.

But if we can understand the impatience with Broadhurst that the keener reformers must have felt, we must also recall the remarkable advances that had taken place in the status of the unions as a result of the pressure-group tactics that he inherited from his predecessors as secretary of the Parliamentary Committee. His role was primarily to maintain, in a less favourable period, what had been won in years more suitable for political progress. In the circumstances of the 1870s and early 1880s he served the unions well.

PART TWO

THE CONSOLIDATION OF LABOUR

THE SETTING

THE years from the 1880s to the 1920s, which are now to be considered, form a much shorter period than that which we have surveyed in the preceding four chapters. But they saw a great growth of unionism, as well as many changes in its character which remain important today. They must therefore be examined in some detail.

It is true that the rate of growth of industrial production was already slowing down in the last quarter of the nineteenth century, the years of the so-called 'Great Depression'. There was a rapid growth of competition in international trade, owing to the industrialization of the United States, Germany, and other countries, and British manufacturers were faced with declining profits and the need to search for fresh markets. But although agriculture suffered a real decline in these years, industry as a whole was able to find new outlets for its products, often in the remoter parts of the world that were now for the first time being colonized or developed. The early part of the twentieth century was a period of fair prosperity and expansion for British industry, although in the development of new inventions and processes it was clear that other countries were often in the lead. It was only after the First World War, in the 1920s, that the staple export trades of coal and cotton fell into continuous difficulty, and serious unemployment became a constant feature of the economy.

It is in these years of the late nineteenth and early twentieth centuries that we can most safely speak of a comparatively homogeneous 'working class', as indeed contemporaries were now willing to do. This was to some extent a result of the further growth of the factory system, which now tended to reduce the differential of skill and to demand large numbers of semi-skilled workers, employed in factories by the hundred or thousand. Developments in the mining industry – the sinking of deeper shafts and the increase in the size of pits – moved in the same direction; and this was the period of the dominance of the miners' unions in the counsels of the T.U.C. and its Parliamentary Committee. In part, the growth of working-class cohesion was due to the effect of better transport facilities and to the constant expansion of the cities and towns by migration from the countryside. In part also it owed something to the gradual improvement in living standards, especially in those of the unskilled labourer, who benefited in the years of the 'Great Depression' from the declining price of foodstuffs if not from money-wage increases. State education, introduced in 1870 and made free in 1891, gradually assured a general minimum of literacy and gave the children of all manual workers a common background of early experience and training which was not shared by the children of the middle class. The Reform Acts made all alike conscious of their political opportunities, and encouraged some of the politicians to look with more favour on the extension of unionism to the unskilled. The result was, from the 1880s, the permanent establishment for the first time of unions of unskilled workers, which in due course rose to equal and to surpass in size the societies of the artisans.

But while the working class was becoming more homogeneous, in many ways the social distance between its better-off elements, on the one hand, and the middle class, on the other, grew wider than before. The diverse effect of the system of education was one factor; another was the growth in the scale of industry and commerce in many of its departments. More and more family firms were converted into limited-liability companies, in which the old personal contact between employer and worker was lost. So too, as cities and towns grew in size and as local train and tram services improved, there developed an increasing separation of the classes by residential area: those who could afford the housing costs and the fares moved to 'select' suburbs, where they were out of sight of industry and manual workers alike. To an increasing degree, their knowledge of working-class conditions, if they had any, was derived at second hand from the reports of social investigators.

In spite of the formal legalization of unions in the 1870s, therefore, the union leaders found that they had to wage constant struggles in order to retain their place in a society which regarded their exclusion from all places of responsibility as natural and inevitable. Although there were always exceptions, in general the political parties, the civil service, and the legal profession could not as yet understand working-class aspirations or recognize that trade unions demanded more than the mere right to exist – that they sought to play a major role in the country's future. Even if it had not been for the existence of a new generation of union leaders influenced by Socialism and impatient with the old political parties, the hostility of the law to trade-union claims might well have impelled the unions to form a political party of their own. As it was, the Labour Party represented a powerful combination of social forces which, after it had come into existence, could not be prevented from gradually causing the disintegration of the existing structure of Parliamentary politics. In the meantime, while this process was taking place, the unions showed their growing strength in ever larger and more extensive strike action, on several occasions in the new century threatening a virtual disruption of the economic life of the country.

The First World War showed even more clearly the reality of the unions' industrial power; temporarily, it won their leaders some of the national recognition that they had long been claiming. It also caused an immense extension of the machinery of government, which required the close cooperation of the unions to ensure smooth working. But the end of the war brought a rapid dismantling of this machinery, and the reversion of the unions and their political arm to a role of opposition and hostility to the government of the day. The short-lived Labour Government of 1924, heavily defeated at a general election after only a few months, could hardly do anything to ease the general sense of frustration in the union ranks. The industrial power of the unions, increasingly easy to mobilize but unharnessed to constructive purposes, was bound to come into conflict with the State. The result was the General Strike of 1926 – which showed once and for all that the only alternative to social revolution lay in a more effective partnership between the unions and the Government, whatever its political complexion.

CHAPTER SIX

NEW UNIONISM AND NEW POLITICS, 1880–1900

THERE is no doubt that the early 1880s saw a considerable change in the climate of political opinion – a change that was due in part to the effect of the 'Great Depression', with its apparent threat to the future of Britain's industrial supremacy, and in part to the rise of Marxian Socialism on the Continent and to the recognition of social problems at home. But the emergence of Socialism in Britain was to begin with on a very small scale, and the movement derived much of its influence from a tiny group of well-to-do supporters in London. Among the organizations founded at this time was the Fabian Society, which never became more than a forum for a few hundred intellectuals, influential though their ideas were to be.

The most immediately important of these little Socialist bodies, and also the first to be founded, was the Social-Democratic Federation, whose moving spirit was H. M. Hyndman, a City man who was converted in 1880 by reading Marx's *Capital* in a French translation (it was not available in English until 1887). Hyndman, never a tactful man at the best of times, uttered not a few disparaging remarks about the value of the trade unions; but his organization succeeded in recruiting or influencing many of the abler young artisans in London, and it took the lead in the great unemployed demonstrations of 1886 and 1887. As early as 1883 the S.D.F. (as we may call it) was advocating a law to establish the eight-hour day.

One of the young artisans who had joined the S.D.F. was Tom Mann, a member of the Amalgamated Engineers who had already worked both in England and America and had suffered severe spells of unemployment in England. In 1886, at the age of thirty, he published a pamphlet entitled *What a Compulsory Eight-Hour Working Day Means to the Workers*. In spite of its rather clumsy title, the pamphlet conveyed an entirely new conception of the responsibilities of trade unionism, as may be seen from the following extract:

> To Trade Unionists, I desire to make a special appeal. How long, *how long* will you be content with the present half-hearted policy of your unions? I readily grant that good work has been done in the past by the unions, but, in Heaven's name, what good purpose are they serving now? All of them have large numbers out of employment even when their particular trade is busy. None of the important societies have any policy other than of endeavouring to keep wages from falling. The true Unionist policy of *aggression* seems entirely lost sight of; in fact the average unionist of today is a man with a fossilized intellect, either hopelessly apathetic, or supporting a policy that plays directly into the hands of the capitalist exploiter.

The vigour of Mann's demand for a new policy for the trade unions inspired a number of his fellow-Socialists. Among them was John Burns, a fellow-member of the Amalgamated Engineers two years younger than Mann, who had already come to notice as an effective open-air speaker and as one of the S.D.F. leaders tried after the riots of the London unemployed in 1886. Another was H. H. Champion, who had also been on trial with Burns, but who was a very different type of person – an ex-army officer who owned a printing-press where he not only printed Mann's pamphlet but introduced the eight-hour day for his employees. In 1887 Champion broke off from Hyndman and in the following year started publishing his own weekly paper, the *Labour Elector*, to advocate a policy of forming an Independent Labour Party.

Meanwhile the same militancy and criticism of the existing leaders of trade unionism was being expressed by a young Scottish miners' leader, James Keir Hardie. Hardie's views were shaped as much by his own difficult struggle to organize the Ayrshire miners as by the Socialist literature that he read. In Ayrshire the miners, weakened by heavy immigration and by unemployment, had never secured union recognition from their employers, and a state of open class warfare prevailed. This made Hardie all the more bitter against socially accepted leaders like Henry Broadhurst, who in addition to having served many years as secretary to the Parliamentary Committee had acquired extra dignity from a brief term as under-secretary at the Home Office in Gladstone's third ministry – the first working man ever to become a Minister of the Crown. Hardie felt that Broadhurst, who had so many political friendships among the Liberal employers, was virtually collaborating with the enemy: so at the 1887 T.U.C. he launched an attack on him, specifying, in particular, his electoral support of John Brunner of the chemical firm of Brunner, Mond, whose workers, according to Hardie, suffered under exceptionally harsh conditions of employment. Personal censure of this kind was not likely to weigh very heavily in the scales against Broadhurst's long record of service to unionism; and after Broadhurst's reply Hardie's motion was overwhelmingly defeated. But the sharp, militant tone he had introduced into the proceedings of Congress was not to be stifled; in succeeding years it was to grow yet more insistent.

That the unskilled workers were becoming steadily more willing to respond to the call of unionism in the mid-1880s was illustrated by the strange story of the growth of the Knights of Labour in Britain. The Knights were an American organization, of a primitive type corresponding more closely to Owen's Grand National than to anything that had since been seen in this country. The 'Order', as it was called, had a masonic ritual, much of it supposed to be secret, and a hierarchy of officers with grandiose titles from 'General Master Workman' downwards. In the United States many of the local branches or 'assemblies' catered for men of all trades or none; but others were craft societies of an exclusive type, whose members seem to have paid only lip service to the more general aims of the organization. Among the latter was the Window Glass Workers, which with a membership of about two thousand included nearly all the craftsmen in the industry within the United States. The leaders of this little body, seeking to extend their influence to the European

85

centres of the industry, and thus still further to control the supply of labour, in 1884 sent missionary organizers to various countries of Europe, including England, to win the window-glass workers for unionism. This was to go against what one might call the prevailing wind of unionism: men tended to migrate westward across the Atlantic, and in some cases – the Engineers, the Carpenters – they took their union membership with them and founded branches in America. But now an American union was seeking to proselytize in Europe.

The attempt to organize the European window-glass workers was a failure, and not least in England. Messrs Pilkington's of St Helens, the largest window-glass manufacturer, resisted all efforts; and Hartley's at Sunderland was only temporarily won. But the astonishing thing was how a temporary success at the Chance factory at Birmingham led to a spread of the idea of general unionism among other workers in the area. However limited the glass workers' aims, the gospel of the Knights was a broad one; and as its membership expanded to hundreds of thousands in the United States in 1886–7, so it spread in the Black Country and elsewhere and recruited thousands into 'mixed assemblies', each of which was given an official number by the General Master Workman in Washington. At their peak in 1888–9 the Knights in Britain had at least ten thousand members; but it was difficult for the Registrar of Friendly Societies to see his way to register a body which claimed to have its headquarters in the United States; and by the time that the British leaders had decided to establish themselves independently from Washington, there had been an unfortunate case of embezzlement and an unsuccessful prosecution to recover lost funds. The membership began to dwindle, and by 1894 there was nothing left of the Knights except for one small benefit society. Among its offshoots, however, were the National Union of Stove Grate Workers, formed at Rotherham, and possibly also some of the dockers' organizations at Liverpool and Glasgow.

The Knights were not the only body to anticipate the great spread of general unionism at the end of the 1880s. On Tyneside, where the Nine Hours League of the early 1870s

had shown what could be done by united action of both
society and non-society men, a union called the National
Federation of Labour came into existence in 1886, assisted
by Edward Pease, a Fabian Socialist from London. Tyneside
was a good area for unionism, owing to its strength among
the miners and the metal workers; even the Amalgamated
Society of Railway Servants was quite militant there in the
early 1880s. It was there too that a revival of unionism among
seamen was set on foot by a young man called Joseph
Havelock Wilson. Wilson's union rapidly spread to other
ports, and he was able to claim a membership of 65,000 at
the time of the 1889 T.U.C.

Thus the great spread of unionism in the London area in
1889 and the immediately following years, which is usually
regarded as the main phase of the 'new unionism', had been
widely anticipated outside the metropolitan area. In London,
a small but significant harbinger was the 1888 strike among a
few dozen women match workers of Messrs Bryant and May,
to whose miserable conditions Mrs Annie Besant, the Free
Thought and Fabian lecturer, had drawn attention in her
weekly paper the *Link*. With the help of Mrs Besant and other
Socialists, the women were successful in their strike, and
they formed a little union of their own. The assistance
provided by Socialist leaders both in publicity and in organization was to be a feature of the foundation of the new
unions.

In March of the following year, 1889, Will Thorne, a young
Birmingham-born Irishman who was working at the Beckton
Gas Works at East Ham, began to organize a union among
his fellow-workers. Almost completely illiterate himself, he
was a member of the Social-Democratic Federation; and on
founding his union he received a good deal of clerical assistance from Eleanor Marx, daughter of Karl Marx. Within
four months the union had some 20,000 members; and
Thorne felt sufficiently strong to present demands for a
three-shift system of working at the gasworks instead of
two shifts. This meant a cut in the basic working day from
twelve hours to eight. The South Metropolitan Gas
Company conceded the demand at once, and the other gas
companies followed suit. This was a victory which, as Tom

Mann said, 'put older and larger trade unions to shame'.

In the warm summer of 1889, in conditions of unusually full employment, the success of one group of workers made other groups restive and anxious to strike. The dock labourers in the Port of London, who were the comparatively unskilled men employed in unloading cargoes and in warehousing, had much in common with the gasworkers. Often, indeed, men worked at the gasworks in the winter, when port traffic was slack, and then became dockers in the summer months. The dockers had plenty of grievances against their employers: they were paid only fourpence or fivepence an hour, and even at this wage it was only a minority of them who could secure permanent rather than casual employment. The 'casuals' worked whenever they could, but this was often only very intermittently, and at other times they had to 'hang about the docks and starve', as a witness explained to the Royal Commission on Labour a few years later. The stevedores, who undertook the more skilled task of loading vessels, had their own union since 1872 and worked under distinctly better conditions.

After the success of the gasworkers in July, the slightest incident was enough to make the dockers revolt against their employers. On 12 August Ben Tillett, the secretary of a little society of tea warehousemen which had existed since 1887, found himself besieged by men insisting that he should formulate immediate demands to be sent to the employers. He claimed an advance of wages to sixpence an hour, with eightpence for overtime and a minimum employment period of four hours. This done, he hastily summoned to his side as many able union organizers as he could secure – among them Tom McCarthy of the Stevedores, and Tom Mann and John Burns.

The strikers at once set about advertising their cause to their fellow-workers. Processions of them, led by bands, toured the docks to bring more men out on strike. Stevedores, lightermen, coal porters, and others came out in sympathy – some of them formulating their own demands upon the employers. After a few days a combined committee was chosen to conduct the strike from headquarters at Wade's

Arms, Poplar. The excellent weather helped the open-air propaganda, and day after day mass meetings were held on Tower Hill and addressed by Tillett, Mann, and Burns among others. Burns was the most effective speaker, and the straw hat that he constantly wore singled him out as the cynosure of the vast crowds. Each day after the meeting he led the strikers on a march through the City, and the sight of this enormous but completely orderly host of determined men, walking five abreast, impressed public opinion and won many generous contributions to the strike funds. A Joint Committee of employers, formed belatedly to fight the strike, could make little headway in putting the dock companies' case. An observer who saw the dockers' marches taking place has left us a vivid description of them. By no means all the marchers were 'unmistakable casuals with vari-coloured patches on their faded greenish garments'; there were also their better-off sympathizers such as the watermen, who paraded 'in long scarlet coats, pink stockings and velvet caps, with huge pewter badges at their breasts, like decorated amphibious huntsmen'; and there were various emblems carried by the marchers in order to drive home the moral of their struggle:

the dockers' cat and the sweaters' cat, the dockers' dinner and the sweaters' dinner, the dockers' baby and the sweaters' baby, diminutive and ample respectively; Sir Hardwood (a gentleman understood to be connected with the Joint Committee), attired in mortarboard, gown, and mask, gravely saluted the bystanders and bowed low in front of the Dock House. The bass dressers, locked out for forming a union, brought up the rear, carrying their bass brooms like lictors.

After two weeks, however, the situation began to look desperate. Blackleg labour was being imported on a large scale, and the strikers' funds were running short. The Joint Committee made an offer of a fivepenny rate, but the strikers turned it down. On Tom Mann's initiative, it was decided to issue a call for a general strike of all the London trades. But suddenly, at the end of August, astonishingly large contributions to the dockers' funds began to flow from Australia – the one part of the world where labour was already better organized than in England, and where fraternal feeling for their kinsfolk in Britain was especially strong. The total aid sent to the dockers from Australia amounted to about £30,000 in all; but the first sums were decisive in giving the strikers fresh confidence and inducing them to withdraw their appeal for a general strike – a desperate measure that might easily have resulted in a fiasco. The withdrawal was also due in part to the intervention of Cardinal Manning, who was concerned on behalf of the many Catholics among the dockers. Soon, however, the Lord Mayor of London established a committee of conciliation at the Mansion House, and with his and Manning's aid, and after the struggle had lasted five weeks, the dock directors were persuaded to make more generous concessions. They gave the dockers their sixpence an hour – as Burns called it, 'the full round orb of the docker's tanner'; and they also conceded the demand for eightpence overtime. But they insisted that the blackleg labourers whom they had imported to take the place of strikers should not be displaced from their jobs. The strike committee agreed to this, but later succeeded in persuading over a thousand of them to accept a gratuity and retire. A dockers' union was established on a permanent basis, with the title of Dock, Wharf, Riverside, and General Labourers Union; Tillett became its full-time secretary, and Tom Mann was at first its President. By the end of November it claimed a total of 30,000 members.

The autumn and winter of 1889–90 saw the spreading of the unionist enthusiasm through the industrial areas of England, Wales, and Scotland. The gasworkers everywhere sought to secure the eight-hour day, and in several towns bitter strikes took place. The fiercest struggle was at Leeds, where on the initiative of Will Thorne a procession of blacklegs guarded by police and soldiers was bombarded by brickbats and other missiles as it passed under a railway bridge. To the disgust of many of the leaders of the older unions, Thorne positively boasted of his part in this affray, and said that he would willingly do it again. He was pleased when Friedrich Engels presented him with a copy of Marx's *Capital*, addressed to 'the victor of the Leeds battle'. Thorne's union also enrolled a good many workers in trades which had nothing to do with gas – for instance, woollen workers in the West Riding.

The London dockers' union was much less successful than the Gasworkers in expanding throughout the country. Even in the Thames basin there were other unions catering for dock labourers, notably the South Side Labour Protection League, whose secretary was Harry Quelch, a leading member of the Social-Democratic Federation. It is true that Tillett's union secured support in some other ports, including Bristol; but elsewhere it had to contend with the competition of another new union, the National Union of Dock Labourers, which developed in Glasgow and spread to Merseyside and to the Irish ports. The secretary of this rival body for many years was James Sexton, a Liverpool docker of Irish origin. On Tyneside the National Federation of Labour was, as we have seen, already in existence; but a new body called the National Amalgamated Union of Labour grew up in successful competition with it. Meanwhile Havelock Wilson was busy going round the ports organizing the seamen; and there was also a revival of agricultural labourers' unions, including Arch's union and a new body called the Eastern Counties Labour Federation. A General Railway Workers Union was founded to cater for the casual railway labourers and others whom the Amalgamated Society of Railway Servants, with its substantial subscription of fivepence a week, could not recruit. These were perhaps the most significant of the new unions; but there was hardly a single occupational group, from laundresses and waiters to post office sorters, which was not brought into the movement.

All these new organizations shared, to a greater or lesser degree, new characteristics: it is not surprising that they were spoken of collectively as the 'new unionism', and that their novel features were regarded as marking them off from the older, established unions. The 'new unionism' appeared to differ from the old both in tactics and in organization. Catering largely for unskilled and poorly paid workers, the new unions tended to have low entrance fees and subscriptions, and depended not on benefits but on aggressive strike tactics to win concessions from their employers and so keep their members satisfied. Furthermore, they were willing to recruit workers without distinction of type of employment, as was indicated by the word 'general' which was often to be found in their titles. The leaders of the older unions were inclined to doubt whether such tactics could prove successful in the long run. They seemed suitable only for periods of good trade, when labour was comparatively scarce; given a depression, there would be ample supplies of unemployed labour to take the place of any unskilled men who came out on strike.

Events proved that the older unionists were at least partly right in their estimate of the new unions' future difficulties. Their successes were soon followed by defeats, and much of the ground that they took in the first flush of their progress was lost within a year or two. As early as the winter of 1889–90 the Gasworkers were again in conflict with the South Metropolitan Gas Company, and by the following spring there were hardly any union members in its employ; an attempt to organize the postmen failed, partly owing to the hostility of the Government and partly because of ineffective organization by the leaders; at Hull, after temporarily winning control of the port, the unions were soundly defeated by a well-organized counter-attack by the employers. The agricultural labourers' unions were in constant difficulty and appear to have broken up altogether in the 1890s.

Nevertheless, the 'new unionism' survived. It did so because many of the so-called unskilled labourers in fact had a real degree of skill which gave them scarcity value and so bargaining strength. It is true that many of their unions' aspirations to 'general' organization had to be abandoned. Tillett's London Dockers had become somewhat exclusive in their attitude almost as soon as they had won their 1889 strike; and the same tendency spread to the other unions. In the West Riding the Gasworkers Union fell back more and more on its membership among the gasworkers and dyers. On the north-east coast the National Amalgamated Union of Labour retained its shipyard workers, but lost most of its general branches. In some cases, indeed, the new unions became largely dependent on their hold on the employees of a few large firms with a friendly or timid attitude towards unionism.

By the early 1890s, therefore, the 'new unionism' was already developing in the direction of the type of unionism that already existed. Its 'general' aims, if retained, seemed remote and impracticable. Yet its leaders were still very different men from the leaders of the old unions. For one thing, they were often a whole generation younger, and their youth as well as their success in their early struggles made them militant and aggressive. Furthermore, they had been strongly influenced by the Socialists, who had assisted their organizing work in its early stages and given them help with publicity and other matters. Many of them were Socialists themselves: Thorne was to be a member of the Social-Democratic Federation throughout his life; Tillett and Sexton were both Socialists of a sort; and the same was true of many of the other new union organizers and the secretaries of many of the local branches. Nor was this Socialism simply due to a feeling of gratitude for help received from Socialists: the idea of Socialism appealed to men who wanted to buttress their industrial gains by legislative enactment. Above all, they wished to see the establishment of the eight-hour day by Act of Parliament. Much could also be done through municipal politics: and the 'new unionists' were eager to see the extension of trades councils to towns where they still did not exist. According to the Webbs, some sixty new councils were established in the years 1889–91, which must have resulted in more than doubling the total. The Gasworkers, as might be expected, were especially interested in municipal politics; it was largely through their efforts that West Ham became in 1898 the first local authority to be controlled by Labour.

Thus if the 'new unionists' soon found that their unions would have to develop the same sort of industrial strength as all unions before them had needed, that did not mean that there were not many differences between the new and the old. The new men first appeared in strength at the 1890 T.U.C.; and John Burns has given us an amusing account of the first clash of 'labour' with the 'trades', which he saw as much in terms of a physical contrast as anything else:

Physically, the 'old' unionists were much bigger than the new.
. . . A great number of them looked like respectable city gentlemen;
wore very good coats, large watch chains, and high hats and in
many cases were of such splendid build and proportions that they
presented an aldermanic, not to say a magisterial form and dignity.
Amongst the new delegates not a single one wore a tall hat. They
looked workmen; they were workmen. They were not such sticklers
for formality or court procedure, but were guided more by common
sense.

But it must not be supposed that the old unions remained
entirely unaffected by the new spirit. In the first place, they
increased their membership considerably in these years,
partly because the temporary prosperity favoured their
efforts to organize just as much as it did the new unions;
partly because the success of the new unions stimulated non-
society craftsmen to join the bodies for which they were
eligible. The Amalgamated Engineers, for instance, jumped
from 53,740 members at the end of 1888 to 71,221 at the end
of 1891. At the same time, the old unionists' attitude to the
less-skilled workers began to change. In some industries
increasing mechanization was threatening the status of the
craftsman and upsetting the existing structure of wages and
conditions. This was true of considerable sections of the
engineering industry, as well as of lesser industries such as
printing and the manufacture of boots and shoes. Among the
Engineers there were, of course, active young militants such
as Mann and Burns, who when they had their time free from
other commitments agitated vigorously for a change of policy
by the Engineers' officials. The policy they demanded was
put in a nutshell by Burns in 1890 when he said:

Labour-saving machinery is reducing the previously skilled to
the level of unskilled labour, and they must, in their own interests,
be less exclusive than hitherto.

In 1891, when the existing general secretary, Robert Austin,
died at the age of sixty-five, Tom Mann became a candidate
for the office, and he fought a strenuous campaign for a
policy of opening the society to less-qualified workers. He
was narrowly defeated by John Anderson, the assistant secretary, who took a more conservative view. But the campaign
had its effect: at a Delegate Meeting in 1892 the union's

structure was considerably altered. The number of full-time officials was increased from four to seventeen, and the entrance barriers were reduced, so that a larger proportion of workers in the industry could join. In future, Delegate Meetings for the revision of rules were to take place regularly every four years. These changes in the foremost of the Amalgamated unions showed more clearly than anything else that 'new unionism' had had a profound influence on the old unions as well.

Perhaps of greater importance, however, owing to their numerical weight, was the shift in policy of the miners' unions. For many years they had been tied to a sliding scale, so that wages rose and fell with the price of coal; but in the 1880s this proved disastrous to their fortunes, as the price of coal fell heavily. The county unions lost many of their members, and by 1887 the prospects for mining unionism seemed grim. In 1888, however, Ben Pickard of Yorkshire rallied as many county unions as he could for an overall ten per cent wage demand, and was surprisingly successful. The result was the foundation in 1889 of the Miners Federation of Great Britain, a body to which most of the miners' unions of the country except Northumberland, Durham, and South Wales adhered, and which pledged itself to secure the eight-hour day for the miners. Here was a strong block of potential support at Trades Union Congresses for at least some part of the legislative programme that was favoured by the 'new unionists'.

Even at the 1890 T.U.C. – when, as we have said, the 'new unionists' first appeared in strength – there was clearly sufficient support for their views from some of the old unions to prevent any appearance of a split in Congress along the lines of new against old. The Miners Federation of Great Britain supported the eight-hour day by legislation, and so did the cotton unions; but the strongest opposition came from the Northumberland and Durham Miners, whose members had already won a reduction of hours to seven, and who naturally feared that this advance would be endangered by any general legislation. This Congress was also marked by the resignation of Henry Broadhurst from the post of secretary of the Parliamentary Committee, ostensibly on grounds of ill-health; but no significant change of policy ensued, for his successor was Charles Fenwick, a Northumberland miner who had been a Liberal M.P. since 1885, and who fully shared the views of his union on the undesirability of eight-hours legislation. It is therefore a mistake to suggest, as the Webbs and G. D. H. Cole have done, that Socialism was already triumphant at the first Congress of the 1890s.

The immediately following Congresses saw constant warfare between the supporters and opponents of the statutory eight-hour day, and between those who favoured and those who disapproved of a more vigorous and independent policy of political action. In 1891 the supporters of the eight-hour day put forward a motion calling for a Bill with an optional clause, to allow trade unions hostile to its enforcement to opt out; the debate was intensely earnest and the successful result was read out 'amidst a flourish of hats, umbrellas, walking sticks, and the handkerchiefs of . . . the women delegates'. The following year Fenwick was attacked for failing to support the eight-hour day in Parliament, although it was now official T.U.C. policy; but he was easily re-elected secretary of the Parliamentary Committee. Exactly the same happened in 1893; but in 1894, after Fenwick's vote against the second reading of a Miners' Eight Hour Bill had helped to turn the scales against it, he was defeated for re-election as secretary by another miner, Sam Woods of Lancashire, who was in favour of the eight hours.

Meanwhile the more 'advanced' delegates at Congress had been urging the Parliamentary Committee to secure more effective labour representation in Parliament. The unions had benefited from the extension of the franchise in 1884, but not so much as they might have done. The number of unionists in the House of Commons had been two at the dissolution in 1885; after the election it was eleven, six of them miners. All these eleven sat as Liberals, but it was not at all clear that the Liberal Party as a whole was more likely to espouse the labour cause than the Conservatives. In 1891, in fact, the Conservative Government did perform one major service for labour by accepting a 'fair wages' resolution of the House of Commons whereby it was agreed that in the awarding of government contracts every effort should be made 'to secure the payment of such wages as are generally accepted as current in each trade for competent workmen'.

It was only after the following general election, in 1892, that a few Labour M.P.s of more or less independent views appeared. In that year Keir Hardie, Havelock Wilson, and John Burns won seats which they had contested as independents; and there were also ten others, including five miners, who were elected as Liberals. Of the three supposed independents, Wilson and Burns soon showed that they were willing to make their peace with Liberalism; but Hardie, whose attitude remained as militant as ever, advocated the formation of a new political party for labour. At the 1892 T.U.C. he carried a resolution instructing the Parliamentary Committee to draw up a scheme for a labour representation fund; but the Committee was very lukewarm and made no real effort to find general approval for a practicable proposal. Although the 1893 Congress reaffirmed its interest in the idea, the Committee continued to stall, no doubt expecting the economic depression of the time to damp the ardour of any union officials who were likely to think of contributing.

One reason why the members of the Parliamentary Committee must have had doubts about a labour representation scheme is to be found in the passing of a resolution in 1893 urging the unions to support only candidates pledged to 'the collective ownership and control of the means of production, distribution, and exchange'. This resolution was a great victory for the Socialists on the floor of the Congress: it did not, however, reflect the views of the leaders of the large unions who dominated the Parliamentary Committee. The Socialist resolution was again carried in 1894; but the Socialists were unable to change the composition of the Parliamentary Committee to their liking, and Tom Mann, who was the candidate of the Socialists, ran third in the contest for the secretaryship.

The strength of the Socialists in 1893 and 1894 was due in large part to the foundation and rapid growth of the Independent Labour Party (I.L.P.), which was the product of the growth of Socialism among certain sections of the working class. This in turn was one of the results of 'new unionism' and the part that the Socialists had played in forming the new unions. The I.L.P., in which Keir Hardie rapidly became the leading personality, had the bastion of its strength in the woollen area of the West Riding, which had hardly been unionized at all before 'new unionism'. Its local branches set about the task of influencing trade-union branches and trades councils in the direction of Socialism, and sending delegates to Congress pledged to Socialist aims: their success was evident in the voting at Congress.

But it was at this point that the majority of the Parliamentary Committee decided that the time was ripe for an alteration in the system of representation and voting at Congress. So far it had been customary for the voting to be done by show of hands, which meant that there was no allowance for the number of constituents represented by each delegate. Trades councils were allowed to send delegates on an equal basis with unions, and there was much dual representation as a result; and it was a well-known fact that the Socialists had a degree of control in the trades councils which was out of proportion to their strength in the unions. Reform therefore seemed not unjustified; and a sub-committee of the Parliamentary Committee, under John Burns's chairmanship, recommended that in future representatives of unions should have one vote for each thousand members, or fraction thereof; that trades councils' delegates should be altogether excluded, owing to the duplication of their membership with that of the unions; and that nobody should be entitled to act as a delegate who was not working either at his trade or as a permanent paid official of his union. The proposals were carried at a full meeting of the Parliamentary Committee only by the casting vote of the chairman, David Holmes of the Amalgamated Weavers.

It is clear enough why men like Sam Woods and David Holmes supported these changes. Their own unions, the Miners Federation and the Amalgamated Weavers respectively, were the 'big battalions' which would benefit from a more effective counting of heads represented at Congress. Burns, on the other hand, seems to have had nothing to gain from the changes, except the satisfaction of damaging the prospects of the I.L.P., which he had refused to join. His *rapprochement* with Liberalism was a decade later to make him the first working man ever to enter the Cabinet. An older Liberal, Henry Broadhurst, who since his retirement from the secretaryship had been re-elected to the Parliamentary Committee, strongly opposed the changes as they would mean his own exclusion from Congress. Hardie, who was also to be excluded, suggested that they join together in fighting for the *status quo*, but nothing came of this. The new Standing Orders were applied by the Parliamentary Committee in its summons for the succeeding Congress, and the *coup d'état* was accepted and approved by the delegates who had survived it. Socialism and the plans for independent labour representation had received a severe setback; but, as Tom Mann wrote in Hardie's weekly paper, the *Labour Leader*: 'Both the cause and the men will continue to make themselves felt.'

Tom Mann's prediction was justified by various important changes which were taking place in the general environment of the trade-union movement. Although public opinion had supported the dockers in their 1889 strike – or at least in the earlier stages, until the introduction of blackleg labour caused greater ill-feeling and gave rise to charges of 'intimidation' – the dislocation of industry and the violence which often accompanied later 'new unionist' organizing led to a hardening of middle-class attitudes. At the same time, many employers in industries most directly affected by the impact of 'new unionism' began to concert plans to recover their lost independence of action in the field of employment. The shipowners – notoriously bad employers of labour – in 1890 formed a Shipping Federation which introduced its own register of seamen, and the men were offered jobs only if they undertook not to refuse to work with non-union men. In the succeeding years the Federation's agents supplied blackleg labour for ships or dockside tasks at ports throughout the country, and the unions' strength – and particularly that of Havelock Wilson's union – was gradually weakened. This activity culminated in a fierce struggle at Hull in 1893, when thousands of labourers were brought in under military protection in order to take the place of men on strike.

The success of these efforts to counter the strength of maritime trade unionism led in 1893 to the formation of a body with more general aims, the National Free Labour Association, whose secretary was a former omnibus driver and transport union organizer called William Collison. Collison, a man of intelligence and determination, was largely supported to begin with by the Shipping Federation, but in later years the railway companies seem to have supplied most of his funds. The object of his organization was to supply 'free' or blackleg labour to take the place of unionists on strike. It also took part in public agitation and in lobbying at Westminster and Whitehall in opposition to the unions. But Collison's tactics were not uniformly successful: when it came to breaking strikes not among seamen or dockers but inland, at places where there could be no effective isolation of the blacklegs from the community as a whole, 'free labour' caused more trouble to employers than it was worth. The resulting bitterness often had the effect of prolonging strikes, rather than the contrary; and there were serious problems involved in securing the protection of the blacklegs. Naturally Collison urged the strictest possible interpretation of the law concerning intimidation and picketing.

The unions, for their part, supposed that their legal position was guaranteed by the Acts of 1871 and 1875. Peaceful picketing was expressly provided for by the 1875 Act; and in addition, union funds were protected from liability for damages in cases of tort, as trade unions were not considered to be corporations in the eyes of the law. But in both these respects the legal position of the unions was undermined in the course of the 1890s. On the question of picketing, judges were apparently influenced by concern about the violence which often took place in strikes when blackleg labour was introduced; on the question of the liability of trade-union funds, legal opinion was perhaps affected more by the evolution of the 'representative action' as a means of enabling unregistered companies to be sued; though the very size of the unions and the extent of their influence disposed judges to the view that they ought to be held legally responsible for their actions. The force of the latter argument was felt particularly strongly when a trade union inflicted injury upon a third party not involved in a dispute with it – as often happened in boycott cases. An instance of this was the case of *Temperton* v. *Russell* (1893), in which the Court of Appeal held that an action was maintainable against the three unions involved. A further extension came in 1896, when the Court of Appeal allowed Messrs Trollope and Sons to recover damages from the London Building Trades Federation, which had included them on a 'black list' of 'unfair' employers. On the other hand, *Allen* v. *Flood* (1898) contradicted the tendency: in this case, two carpenters employed in a shipyard sought redress for discharge against the secretary of the local branch of the Boilermakers after a demarcation dispute; but the House of Lords decided that the Boilermakers' action was not an offence in law at all. The confusion on the question of the unions' legal liability could not have been more complete.

On the picketing question, however, the unions suffered a clear setback in the case of *Lyons* v. *Wilkins*. Lyons was a leather-goods manufacturer, and Wilkins was the secretary of a very small union called the Amalgamated Trade Society of Fancy Leather Workers. When early in 1896 the society struck against Lyons and picketed his premises, he applied for an injunction to prevent this, and although there was no question of violence or threat of violence, an order was accordingly made. The society thereupon appealed, but the Court of Appeal upheld the injunction. The case was heard again in 1897–8, and again went against the society, both in the High Court and in the Court of Appeal. The Parliamentary Committee of the T.U.C. had been very interested in the case because of its importance as a precedent, and would have taken the case to the House of Lords had not a solicitor's error allowed the opportunity to lapse. If the judgment were to be accepted as determining the law it would mean that henceforth even the most peaceful picketing was illegal – a state of affairs not contemplated by those who had drawn up the Conspiracy and Protection of Property Bill over twenty years earlier.

Officials of unions now began to realize that when they ordered their members out on strike they no longer stood on firm statutory ground but on a quicksand of conflicting or adverse legal interpretation. It was with more than usual apprehension, therefore, that they saw the strengthening of the national employers' associations at this time, and a development of agitation against the very existence of trade unionism. In 1896 a body called the Employers Federation of Engineering Associations was founded, obviously to counter the Amalgamated Engineers. The union's militancy had continued to grow, and was marked by the election of George Barnes, a sympathizer of Tom Mann's and an I.L.P. member, to the general secretaryship in the same year. In 1897 the Federation intervened in a strike in the London area, where the Engineers, in concert with other unions, had struck for the eight-hour day at several workshops. The Federation, determined to match strength with strength, ordered a national lock-out, and a struggle ensued which lasted for six months – from July 1897 to January 1898. This conflict, the first major national strike or lock-out in British history, was accompanied by a great debate in the press on the merits of the two parties, and indeed on the whole question of trade unionism. The employers complained that the strength of trade unionism damaged the country's competitive position in foreign markets and even in the home market. Colonel Dyer, the leader of the Federation, went so far as to say that the purpose of himself and his colleagues was

to obtain the freedom to manage their own affairs which has proved so beneficial to the American manufacturers as to enable them to compete . . . in what was formerly an English monopoly.

Barnes and other union leaders and sympathizers replied, not without effect, as may be seen from the following excerpt from a letter to *The Times* by John Burns:

The real test of effective industrial competition is not hours worked or wages paid; the determining factor is the cost per ton, the price per horse-power, and invariably the most successful competitor is he who harnesses short hours and high wages to skilled supervision, good design, economic working, utilitarian and varying demand of customer.

With the aid of the National Free Labour Association, some of the employers kept their works going: in the case of Yarrow's works on the Isle of Dogs, the blacklegs were quartered on a steamer moored near by. The other unions rallied to the support of the Engineers, and some £169,000 was raised by voluntary subscription. But the total cost to the union itself was £489,000. Expenditure on this scale could not last, and by the end of 1897 the strain was becoming unbearable. Although a national conference of unions summoned by the London Trades Council offered further help by means of a general levy, the Engineers' executive decided to sue for terms. The demand for the eight-hour day had to be withdrawn, and the employers insisted on the spelling-out of certain rights which they had claimed, such as the right to determine what class of workman should be employed on new machinery. It was a humiliating setback for a union which was still regarded as the foremost in the country, indeed in the world.

The effect of the defeat of the Engineers on the trade-union world was to give fresh impetus to the idea of forming a federation of unions for mutual financial support. The 1897 Trades Union Congress accepted a resolution approving the idea in principle, and it established a special committee to draw up plans. The committee recommended to the 1898 Congress that a special conference of unions interested should be held to launch the scheme, and this took place at Manchester in January 1899, when a General Federation of Trade Unions was established. The Federation belied its name: it was not a federation but simply a committee controlling a fund, and it never became general, for many unions (including all the miners) refused to join, arguing that they could never get their money's worth of strike benefit in return for their contributions. At the outset, it secured the adhesion of only forty-four unions with a total membership of 343,000 – little more than a quarter of the total membership represented at Congress.

But in any case the foundation of such an organization could not solve the problems raised by the adverse legal decisions; and the need for some sort of determined political action by the T.U.C. seemed all the more urgent in view of the

establishment in 1898 of a new general employers' organization, the Employers Parliamentary Council, which was
evidently designed to counter the influence of the T.U.C.
Parliamentary Committee at Westminster. There were,
indeed, so many employers in the House of Commons that
it seemed that they could easily have things their own way
if they were effectively marshalled against the interests of
the unions. The Employers Parliamentary Council devoted
itself not only to exerting influence on Members of Parliament but also to publicizing the advantages already accruing to employers from recent legal decisions. It published
a book entitled *The Case Against Picketing*, by W. J. Shaxby,
which pointed out how easy it was to prevent picketing
under the terms of *Lyons* v. *Wilkins*. All in all, it looked as
if the unions were in for a difficult time if they did not
strengthen their political arm as quickly and as decisively
as possible.

Meanwhile Hardie and the other leaders of the I.L.P. had
been working hard to overcome their double defeat of 1895 –
in the general election of that year and in the revision of the
T.U.C. Standing Orders. The failure to elect a single M.P.,
and the decline in the party's membership that took place
afterwards, made them feel that some sort of an alliance with
the trade unions was essential if rapid progress was to be
made. In spite of the conservatism of the older union leaders,
the possibility of such an alliance did not seem to be too
remote. In the first place, there was a growing concern among
many union leaders about the need for a stronger voice in
Parliament. Secondly, the new unions, such as the Gasworkers and the Dockers, had no inhibitions about collaboration with the Socialists. Thirdly, members of Socialist
societies were beginning to win key positions in some of the
old unions. Barnes of the I.L.P. had, as we have seen, become
general secretary of the Engineers in 1896; and in the same
year a member of the S.D.F., James Macdonald, was elected
secretary of the London Trades Council. The London
Society of Compositors and the Boot and Shoe Operatives
also had active Socialist factions in their ranks. Keir Hardie
worked hard to bring all these elements together: in 1896 he

spoke of the need for a conference to which 'all Socialist organizations, together with all Trade Unions and Cooperative organizations' should be invited. In 1897 the matter was discussed at the I.L.P. annual conference, and a paper was read proposing a 'labour representation conference'. By this time local branches of both the I.L.P. and the S.D.F. had had the experience of collaboration with trades councils and union branches for purposes of municipal elections. In 1898 Hardie was advocating 'the same kind of working agreement nationally as already exists for municipal purposes in Glasgow'. With this in mind, the I.L.P. executive made a formal approach both to the Parliamentary Committee of the T.U.C. and to the corresponding body of the Scottish T.U.C., which had just come into existence.

The Scottish T.U.C. was a body formed by the Scottish trades councils in 1897, as a result of their exclusion from the annual Congresses of the T.U.C. by the Standing Orders of 1895. For geographical reasons, trades councils formed a much stronger element of Scottish trade unionism than of English. The Scottish Congress of April 1899 proved willing to act on the I.L.P. suggestion, and its Parliamentary Committee, which had an actual majority of I.L.P. members, made the arrangements for a special conference of trade unions, Socialist societies, and cooperative societies in January 1900. At this conference a body called the Scottish Workers Parliamentary Elections Committee was set up.

It was not likely to be so easy for Keir Hardie and his colleagues to persuade the United Kingdom organization to act as its Scottish offshoot was doing. But they had many enthusiastic supporters working for them in local union branches and on union executives. There was no union more politically minded, for instance, than the Amalgamated Society of Railway Servants, which had by now given up the passive attitude to industrial action which had marked its early days, but which had still not secured recognition for its bargaining role from the railway companies. Since the railways constantly required fresh legislation on all sorts of matters, it was evident to the Railway Servants that parliamentary representation would have great benefits for themselves. But such representation, owing to the scattered nature of the membership, could only be secured in association with other trades: there were no obvious railwaymen's constituencies, as there were mining constituencies. By 1899 there was already a strong I.L.P. element within the union; and it was one of the leaders of this element, Thomas R. Steels, a former member of the lay executive, who got his local branch at Doncaster to forward a resolution for the T.U.C. along the lines of Hardie's plan for a labour representation conference. The resolution was endorsed by the union's executive and proposed at the 1899 T.U.C. by James Holmes, the union's West of England organizer.

Most of one afternoon of the 1899 Congress was spent debating the resolution proposed by Holmes. It called on the Parliamentary Committee to join with the Socialist societies and the cooperative societies in summoning a special conference on the subject of labour representation. As was to be expected, the resolution was supported not only by the Railway Servants but by representatives of most of the new unions. The Engineers would no doubt also have given their approval, but owing to the allegedly unsympathetic attitude of the Parliamentary Committee to a demarcation dispute of theirs, they had temporarily withdrawn from the T.U.C. In the course of the debate, Sexton of the Liverpool Dockers argued that the existing state of affairs led to 'disgraceful confusion' of labour candidatures, because labour men often opposed each other as Liberals or Conservatives. Margaret Bondfield of the Shop Assistants, a union founded in 1889, pointed out that small organizations like her own could not expect any labour representation except by cooperation with other unions. Against the motion, there were spokesmen of both the miners and the textile workers. Confident of the miners' ability to elect their own M.P.s, W. E. Harvey of the Derbyshire Miners could argue for individual self-help by the unions. Thomas Ashton of the Cotton Spinners opposed for a different reason: he knew that the Lancashire workers were deeply divided between Conservatism and Liberalism, and he maintained that 'if their society were to intervene in politics, it would go down immediately'. By 'politics' he meant 'party politics': in point of fact the Lancashire textile workers had an effective pressure-group system in operation on the Lancashire M.P.s of both parties through their federal organization, the United Textile Factory Workers Association, which existed for no other purpose.

Still, the conference proposed by the Railway Servants was to be a voluntary affair. Many of the delegates must have felt that there could be little harm in allowing it to take place, as it would not commit any union which did not attend. Consequently, when the card vote was taken on the motion 546,000 were deemed to have voted in favour and only 434,000 against, with about a sixth of the total voting strength abstaining. The supporters of the motion greeted the result with enthusiasm, climbing on to their chairs, waving their hats, and cheering. This was the victory which some of them had expected to gain two or three years earlier, if it had not been for the imposition of the new Standing Orders; but as it was, it indicated a big swing in union opinion, no doubt as the result of the changes in the external environment which we have discussed.

Now it was for Keir Hardie and his colleagues to make the best alliance that they could out of the mixture of Socialist sympathizers, moderate and extreme, and trade unionists, cautious and militant, who met at the special conference that the Parliamentary Committee summoned in London in February 1900. Out of this conference, attended by delegates representing less than half the strength of the unions belonging to the T.U.C., and by no cooperative delegates at all, a new organization was born, calling itself rather shamefacedly the Labour Representation Committee. It was clearly not yet a Labour Party; but as a writer in the Socialist weekly, the *Clarion*, put it at the time, it was

a little cloud, no bigger than a man's hand, which may grow into a United Labour Party.

The preceding sections of this chapter have concentrated on the changes in trade unionism in the 1880s and 1890s, to the exclusion of what was carried on unchanged from earlier periods of development. It is easy to exaggerate the importance of the changes. It is true that the period was one in which Socialist influence grew, and in which more and more union leaders became interested in forming a political party of their own; but this did not make the British movement, by contrast with those in foreign countries, either markedly Marxist or even markedly concerned with any type of party politics. In most of the countries of Europe trade unionism was much weaker than in Britain, but frequently it was unionism of so strong a political kind that there had to be different unions to cater for different political standpoints. Only in the United States was there a movement at all comparable to that in Britain: this was not the Knights of Labor, which collapsed quickly after its mushroom growth of the 1880s, but the American Federation of Labor, which was consciously modelled on the T.U.C. by its President and moving spirit, Samuel Gompers. Gompers in 1894 instituted an annual exchange of 'fraternal delegates' between the American Federation and the T.U.C., and thereafter some part of the time of the Congresses of both bodies was taken up by their speeches and by the presentation of suitable gifts. But for many years the American Federation was by far the weaker of the two bodies.

In relations with trade unionists on the Continent British union leaders were inclined to go slow, not only because of language difficulties but also because they did not as a rule like the degree to which Continental unionists were tied up with Marxist politics. Attempts were made at the end of the 1880s to revive the links which had existed, in however rudimentary a form, at the time of the First International. But the Second International, which was founded in 1889, was so obviously a political rather than an industrial organization that most of the leaders of the T.U.C. would have nothing to do with it. It is true that there was plenty of support in Britain for the first international eight-hour-day demonstrations, which were timed for the First of May 1890. The great meeting which was held in Hyde Park, not on May Day but on a Sunday three days later, seemed to Friedrich Engels to have enormous symbolic significance. 'On May 4th, 1890,' he wrote in an Austrian paper, 'the English working class joined up in the great international army.' And it is true that from that date onwards May Day has been regarded in this country as elsewhere as the Festival of Labour. But it was only a minority of British union leaders who retained ties with the Second International; and when in 1896 its conference was held in London, the senior ranks of the British movement were disgusted by what they saw or read of the disorder of its proceedings, which presented a sharp contrast with the normal quiet dignity, as they regarded it, of the sessions of the T.U.C.

Most British union leaders of this period prided themselves that their approach to industrial problems was of a practical and not of a theoretical character. Among the old unionists, of course, there was a good deal of distrust of the middle-class Socialists, and a fear that they were out to capture the unions for their own ends. Edward Cowey, of the Yorkshire Miners, was warmly applauded at the 1889 T.U.C. when he said:

> The Socialists told them that trade unionism was played out. What did they want there, if trade unionism was played out? The simple fact was, they wanted a house that had been built by someone else.

But even leaders of the 'new unionism' could share a good deal of the scepticism about what Tillett called on one occasion the 'hare-brained chatterers and magpies of Continental revolutionists'. Out-and-out dogmatic Marxism of the S.D.F. type was very much a minority creed in Britain; and the moderate Socialism of a rather larger proportion of unionists did not prevent their unions from adopting highly conservative policies on many issues.

In a period which was so much influenced by the growth of 'new unionism', it is also important to remember that numerically it was the old unions which gained and retained by far the greatest strength. If we take the county unions of the Miners Federation and the components of the United Textile Factory Workers Association each to be separate unions, we find that in 1900 only one 'general' or 'all-grade' union (the Gasworkers) was among the ten largest unions in the country, and that there were only two more among the next ten largest. Only five such unions had more than 10,000 members each. The South Wales Miners Federation had more members than all these five 'new' unions put together; and although this Federation itself was in fact even 'newer' in life, having been founded only in 1898, it had few of the characteristics of 'new unionism' as we have described them. It was, as its name implies, a federal union; its leaders were Liberals; and although it was affiliated to the Miners Federation of Great Britain, its wage structure remained tied to the sliding scale.

Furthermore, there still existed plenty of examples of the small, more or less localized, craft union of the type which had been predominant early in the century. The Industrial Revolution, which had already transformed some industries by 1800, had hardly touched others by the end of Queen Victoria's reign. At that time the London silk-hat manufacture, for instance, was still carried on in tiny workshops, and the Journeymen Hatters Fair Trade Union maintained a seven-year apprenticeship and enforced workshop rules which Benjamin Franklin would have recognized as familiar. It was by no means only the 'sweated' trades which were conducted on a small scale; in Birmingham and the Black Country, as well as in London, masters and men were not infrequently working side by side at inherited and highly traditionalized crafts.

If the 1880s and 1890s appear from the preceding narrative to have been a period of constant strikes, it must be remembered that, as the Webbs pointed out at the time, strikes and lock-outs were costing 'much less loss of working time in the year than our laudable custom of treating Good Friday and Christmas Day as Sundays'. The growth of unionism may have led to a temporary increase in the number of industrial disputes, but it held out the prospect of their diminution in the future; as was stated in the Final Report of the Royal Commission on Labour, 1891–4: 'Peaceable relations are, upon the whole, the result of strong and firmly-established trade unionism.' Furthermore, the idea of arbitration or conciliation gradually spread, as employers came to realize that the unions in their industries were here to stay. The schemes initiated by a few enlightened pioneers in the 1860s and 1870s, such as Mundella's Conciliation Board in the Nottingham hosiery industry and Sir Rupert Kettle's arbitration in the Wolverhampton building trades, often did not survive the enthusiasm of their original sponsors. But the ideas spread easily from one industry to another, if conditions were favourable.

Conciliation proved effective on a permanent basis in iron and steel, following Sir David Dale's introduction of Mundella's scheme into the Northern iron trade as early as 1869. In the north-east generally, strong unionism in heavy industry encouraged the employers to make the best of their situation and to devise conciliation boards for mining, engineering, and shipbuilding. The national lock-outs in the boot and shoe industry in 1895 and in the engineering industry in 1897–8 were both concluded with national agreements between the parties and with the establishment of machinery to deal with disputes which arose in the operation of the agreements. The same was virtually true of the 1893 cotton strike, which was terminated by the historic 'Brooklands Agreement' hammered out in an exhausting overnight session of negotiation. In 1893 also a sixteen-week strike by the Miners Federation ended, after mediation by the Foreign Secretary, Lord Rosebery, in the establishment of a board of conciliation. This board continued in intermittent operation until after the turn of the century, and by that time all the important areas of mining in England, though not of Wales or Scotland, were covered by conciliation boards.

On the whole, the unions believed more in conciliation than in arbitration: that is to say, they were more willing to negotiate a settlement of their own accord, perhaps with the help of expert negotiators, than to trust any supposedly impartial person to impose a settlement on both parties. Their experience of the law courts in the 1890s did not encourage them to believe in the impartiality of the 'judicial mind'; and in any case, the complexity of industrial negotiations was such that those without practical knowledge of the industry concerned often had difficulty in understanding the issues. In the cotton industry, in particular, wage negotiations were so intricate that the unions had introduced competitive examinations for the selection of their officials; and the Home Office's choice of one of these officials, Thomas Birtwistle of the Weavers, for appointment as a factory inspector was dictated by his exceptional experience of the issues involved.

The Consolidation of Labour

It was one of the recommendations of the Royal Commission on Labour that a public department should have power to appoint suitable persons as arbitrators or conciliators in industrial disputes at the request of the parties concerned. This was in fact the only proposal of the Commission which led to legislative action: by the Conciliation Act, 1896, the necessary powers were conferred on the Board of Trade, which for some years had had a department concerned with labour statistics and information. The Act had hardly had time to prove its value by the turn of the century, but there was no question of its becoming a dead letter on the statute book. If the last two decades of the nineteenth century saw a notable widening of the area of trade union organization, they also saw a strengthening of the desire on the part of both union officials and employers for the avoidance of industrial disputes through methods of orderly negotiation.

CHAPTER SEVEN

FROM TAFF VALE TO TRIPLE
ALLIANCE, 1900–14

WE have seen that the leaders of British trade unionism ended the nineteenth century with feelings of some concern about the security of their legal rights. It did not take more than a few months of the twentieth century for these feelings to turn into a definite anxiety and an insistence upon political action to remedy the situation. The change was caused by the decision of the House of Lords in the Taff Vale case in July 1901 – a case which had more far-reaching effects for trade unionism than any other which the courts had ever been called upon to decide.

The case arose from a strike in August 1900 on the Taff Vale railway in South Wales. After the alleged victimization of a signalman who had led a movement for a pay rise, the men went on strike and secured the official support of the Amalgamated Society of Railway Servants. The general secretary of the union, Richard Bell, went down to Cardiff and organized picketing to prevent the company from importing blackleg labour, which it had arranged to do through the agency of the National Free Labour Association. The company's general manager, Ammon Beasley, a man who according to an impartial observer (G. R. Askwith) 'loved litigation for its own sake', was in close touch with the Employers Parliamentary Council, and he knew that he could expect to secure an injunction and damages against the Amalgamated Society for the picketing activity of its leaders. An injunction was accordingly applied for and duly granted; and although the strike was settled by mediation after only eleven days, the case went on, the Court of Appeal reversing the initial decision, and the House of Lords restoring it. The decision of the House of Lords was of great importance, because it determined that the funds of a trade union were liable for damages inflicted by its officials. A consequent case to determine the damages against the union resulted in its having to pay £23,000 to the Taff Vale Railway Company, together with its own costs, which brought the total to about £42,000.

It did not take union leaders in general very long to realize the crippling effects of this decision on their own prospects of successful strike action in the future. It is true that there were a few who thought that some good might come from the recognition of trade unions as legal corporations, for they would presumably be able to enter into legally enforceable agreements with their employers. But the great majority at once concluded that the disadvantages outweighed the advantages, especially when coupled with the crippling restrictions placed upon picketing by the decision of *Lyons* v. *Wilkins*. Another House of Lords decision, in a boycotting case known as *Quinn* v. *Leathem*, followed the Taff Vale pronouncement by only two weeks and re-emphasized the liability of union funds for damages.

The reaction of the great bulk of union leaders to this state of affairs was naturally very hostile. One result was that they gave a much warmer support to the Labour Representation Committee than had appeared likely immediately upon its foundation in 1900. The Committee in its first year of working secured the affiliation of unions and trades councils representing only 353,070 members; and this in spite of the fact that the subscription was only ten shillings per thousand members. Consequently it could do little in the 1900 election, on which it spent a total of only £33; and it was largely a matter of luck that two of the fifteen candidates that it endorsed, Keir Hardie of the I.L.P. and Richard Bell of the Railway Servants, were elected to Parliament. Even after two years the affiliated industrial membership was only 455,450. But many fresh affiliations followed, including that of the United Textile Factory Workers Association; and the total rose to 847,315 by early 1903. In addition, the annual conference of the organization in that year decided to raise a fund for the payment of Labour M.P.s by means of a compulsory levy on the unions, and it laid the foundation for a distinct disciplined party in Parliament by declaring that its candidates must 'strictly abstain from identifying themselves with, or promoting the interests of, any section of the Liberal or Conservative Parties'. Thus, 1903 was the year in which, as a result of the Taff Vale decision, the principle of an independent political party really secured the support of a large body of unions.

At the same time the Parliamentary Committee of the T.U.C. was slowly working itself to the pitch of formulating proposals for legislation to put matters right. At the Trades Union Congress of 1901 much alarm had been expressed, and John Hodge, the secretary of the Steel Smelters, had declared melodramatically that he had 'made over his little possessions to his wife by deed of gift'. But no constructive policy at first emerged. On the one hand, the Socialists uttered gloomy forebodings about the growth of trusts on the American model in various branches of British industry, and predicted that they would attack the trade-union movement with the same ferocity as had been displayed in labour conflicts in the United States. *The Times* seemed to provide confirmation for these views by publishing a series of articles in 1902 on 'The Crisis of British Industry', in which it was argued that trade unionism and the restrictive practices it encouraged were responsible for the weakened competitive position of British industry compared with American and German. On the other hand, some members of the Parliamentary Committee seemed to feel little sense of urgency about the unions' plight after Taff Vale, and were disposed to accept the Conservative Government's offer of a Royal Commission on the subject.

It was not until after a Commons debate had taken place in May 1902, when the Liberal Opposition pressed but failed to carry a motion for legislation, that the Parliamentary Committee as a whole came round to accept the need for the detailed formulation of a Bill which would restore the *status quo ante* Taff Vale. The introduction of such a measure, though defeated when first proposed in the Commons in 1903, was carried in 1904 and again with a larger majority in 1905 – gestures which reflected the approach of a general election, but gestures only, for the Bill was so altered in committee on each occasion that it was abandoned by its sponsors. The Government had meanwhile gone ahead with its suggestion of appointing a Royal Commission, but it appointed no trade unionist as a member, and so Congress recommended its affiliated bodies not to give evidence.

There was a danger that the T.U.C. and its two offshoots, the General Federation of Trade Unions and the Labour Representation Committee, would find themselves at cross-purposes if they all took a part in politics – as even the G.F.T.U. was inclined to do to some extent. In February 1905, therefore, a conference was held at the Caxton Hall in Westminster to arrange for effective liaison. An agreement was made which became known popularly as 'the Caxton Hall Concordat': by its terms, all candidates at the forth-coming general election who were formally approved either by the Labour Representation Committee or by the Par-liamentary Committee were to be supported by both bodies. The Parliamentary Committee's list, of course, contained candidates standing as Liberals; but Ramsay MacDonald, the secretary of the Labour Representation Committee, had already in 1903 made a secret agreement with the Liberal whips for the coordination of candidates, so there was no difficulty in accommodating these so-called 'Lib–Labs'. When the election came there were forty candidates put forward by unions or trades councils affiliated to the Labour Representation Committee; ten candidates under the same banner who were sponsored by the I.L.P.; an additional fifteen, mainly miners' candidates, who had the formal ap-proval of the Parliamentary Committee; and also a few other 'Lib–Labs' standing without the formal backing of any national organization.

January 1906, when the election actually took place, found the Conservatives in considerable disarray. The issue of tariff reform had disrupted their ranks, and as a result their Liberal opponents were triumphant in all parts of the country, except for Chamberlain's Birmingham. In this general swing, almost all the Labour and 'Lib–Lab' candidates did well: it was reckoned that altogether fifty-four of them were elected, of whom twenty-nine were members of the Labour Repre-sentation Committee. This body now changed its name to the simpler one of 'Labour Party', and its M.P.s constituted themselves as a parliamentary party with officers and whips. The Parliamentary Committee of the T.U.C. suddenly found that of its thirteen committee members, nine were M.P.s, six as members of the Labour Party. The 'Lib–Labs' included W. C. Steadman, secretary of the tiny Barge Builders' Union, who had been elected secretary of the Parliamentary Committee when Sam Woods retired in 1904.

During the election the report of the Royal Commission set up by the Conservatives had been published. It advocated, not a return to legal immunity for the trade unions, but on the contrary, a statutory recognition of them as legal entities, together with provisions for the separation of their benefit funds from their general and strike funds, so that the benefit funds could be declared immune from action for damages. The Commission also recommended changes in the law, to restore the right of peaceful picketing. The new Liberal Government accepted the report as the basis for legislation, and a Bill on these lines was accordingly drawn up.

The Parliamentary Committee might have been wise to agree to the Liberal Bill, for a clear legal status would have had many advantages for the unions in the long run. But its members still feared the courts, and they knew well that in the course of the election campaign the vast body of Liberal M.P.s had pledged themselves to the measure which had already been debated by the previous Parliament. The Government was therefore forced to give way, and the Parliamentary Committee's Bill was accepted and passed into law before the year was out, the House of Lords in its political capacity deeming it inexpedient to offer any resistance. Thus, the unions had secured from the ballot-box the respect for their privileged position which had been denied them in the courts.

The Labour Party, as we have seen, was in large measure a weapon of the trade-union leaders devised for the reversal of the Taff Vale decision. After playing its part in that cause, it seemed for a time thereafter to have lost its sense of purpose. Unable to influence the Government significantly on general social questions, it lost prestige in the country, and its members tended to divide into hostile factions – some of the Socialists trying to take the lead with an aggressive policy, and some of the trade unionists objecting to almost any distinctive tactics. The latter were strongly reinforced in 1909 as a result of the decision of the Miners Federation to affiliate to the Labour Party: the Federation's M.P.s formally became Labour instead of Liberal, but it did not make much difference to their attitude to the issues before Parliament at the time. The legislation for which they most deeply cared – a measure for the limitation of work in the pits to eight hours a day – was passed with Liberal support in 1908. But their adhesion to the Labour Party did at least have the effect of breaking up the remnants of the 'Lib–Lab' group in the Commons.

The real initiative for social reform in the period of Asquith's premiership – from 1908 onwards – came from Lloyd George, the Chancellor of the Exchequer, ably assisted by Winston Churchill at the Board of Trade. They got little help from John Burns, the President of the Local Government Board, who seemed to be dominated by his departmental officials; but they soon showed that they could manage without him. Although the T.U.C. had approved a list of reforms not very different from those which the Liberal Government undertook, the Parliamentary Committee found itself giving rather hesitant consent to a series of measures which neither it nor the Labour Party had actually initiated, and which sometimes seemed to threaten State appropriation of responsibilities which the unions had previously undertaken.

Generally speaking, Lloyd George and Churchill took care to placate the unions, because they wanted the support of their M.P.s in the Commons debates and the continued backing of the trade-union vote at future general elections. Thus, when in 1909 Churchill introduced a bill for the establishment of labour exchanges – a reform suggested to him by the Webbs and worked out by W. H. (later Sir William) Beveridge – the union leaders were afraid that the exchanges would become agencies for the supply of blackleg labour; but Churchill took care to consult the Parliamentary Committee on the administration of the

Act, and appointed a number of union officials, among others, to supervise the exchanges.

The same sort of problem arose in a much wider field when the Government introduced its schemes for health and unemployment insurance; for the unions did not wish to see their benefit arrangements replaced by a uniform State-controlled system. Lloyd George sensibly decided not to attempt to weaken or destroy the existing pattern of friendly-society and trade-union benefits, but to make the societies and unions the agents or 'approved societies' for the operation of the state system. The result was that when the system came into operation there was a rapid expansion of the membership of the 'approved societies': union membership, and especially membership of unions catering for the lower grades of worker, increased markedly. The total of members represented at the 1911 T.U.C. was 1,661,000, which was only about ten per cent more than in 1901; but by 1913 it had jumped to 2,682,000 – an increase of sixty per cent in two years. The Workers Union, which had been founded by Tom Mann in 1898 for semi-skilled workers in the engineering industry, showed a remarkable rate of increase: in 1910 it had 5,016 members, but by 1914 it had 159,600. There were other reasons for this rapid growth, as we shall see; but probably none was as important as the integration of the unions' benefit functions into the state schemes for health and unemployment insurance.

The Liberal Government also made a limited advance into the realm of State wage determination – a development not very warmly welcomed by the unions as a whole or by the Parliamentary Committee, but strongly supported by those who had the welfare of the workers in the 'sweated' industries particularly in mind – above all, by the members of the Women's Trade Union League, which existed to promote the sadly retarded welfare of women workers, and also, among M.P.s, by the veteran Liberal Sir Charles Dilke. After the report of a select committee, Winston Churchill in 1909 introduced a Bill, enacted in the course of the same year, for the purpose of setting up 'trade boards' to fix wages in the ready-made tailoring industry and in other industries no-torious for the employment of cheap labour. The reluctant approval given by the Parliamentary Committee to this measure was paralleled by its lukewarm attitude to the Minority Report of the Poor Law Commission of 1905–9, which was drawn up by Sidney and Beatrice Webb. One of the most powerful statements of a positive social policy ever to be published in this country, it was greeted by the Parliamentary Committee with a notable absence of enthusiasm; and neither Congress as a whole nor the Parliamentary Committee endorsed the campaign for the enactment of their proposals which the Webbs launched and ran, without success, in the years 1910–11.

Meanwhile in 1909 the trade unions and the Labour Party, and particularly the Labour Party, had been struck a heavy blow in the law courts. This was the Osborne Judgment, which ranks second only to the Taff Vale decision for its effect on the trade-union movement in both its industrial and its political aspects. Once again it was the Railway Servants who suffered the direct impact at first. It was their Walthamstow branch secretary, W. V. Osborne, who being a member of the Liberal Party decided to bring an action to restrain the union from contributing to the upkeep of the Labour Party. He argued that this form of expenditure was *ultra vires* for a trade union. The case was heard in the High Court in 1908, and Osborne's arguments were rejected; but the Court of Appeal reversed the decision, and the Lords in December 1909 unanimously confirmed the opinion of the Court of Appeal. An injunction was granted restraining the Railway Servants from raising a political levy and from making a contribution to the funds of the Labour Party.

Three of the five judges giving judgment in the House of Lords took the general ground that the legal activities of trade unions were limited by the Trade Union Act of 1871 and by an amending Act of 1876. The support of a political party was not mentioned among the functions of a trade union in the Act of 1876, and so, in the view of the three Lords, it was, as Osborne claimed, *ultra vires*. 'What is not within the ambit of that statute,' said Lord Halsbury, 'is, I think, prohibited both to a corporation and a combination.' He had himself been born only three years after the repeal of the Combination Laws, and as Lord Chancellor in previous Conservtive Governments had always pursued a policy strongly hostile to trade unionism. He and his colleagues now chose to regard trade unions, which were voluntary associations, as being bound by the same rules as restricted the powers of bodies created by statute, such as local government authorities. One of the Lords also held that it was 'contrary to public policy' that candidates for Parliament supported by a trade union should be obliged to promise to obey the Labour Party whip, which was 'subversive of . . . their freedom'. Another argued that it was not within the legitimate objects of trade unionism to apply money for the election and maintenance of M.P.s if those M.P.s were forced to belong to one particular party, as no party could be said to be solely concerned with the interests of labour.

Although there was some substance in the judgments which criticized the Labour Party loyalty pledge, the views of Lord Halsbury, which were much more restrictive in implication, failed to take account of the social changes which had led to the expansion of trade-union functions in the previous generation, and which now included not only political action of an extensive and institutionalized character but also the support of educational projects and various other functions. It is not surprising that union leaders reacted against the Osborne Judgment almost as strongly as they had done against the Taff Vale decision, and that they set about agitating for immediate legislation to reverse it. At the 1910 T.U.C. a resolution to this effect was carried by 1,717,000 votes to 13,000.

It did not prove very easy, however, for the unions and the Labour Party to secure the redress that they desired. Early in 1910 a general election was held, largely on the issue of Lloyd George's reforming budget of the previous year, which the House of Lords had rejected. The Conservatives failed to win the election, but they recovered a good deal of the ground lost in 1906, mainly at the expense of the Liberals, but also to some extent at the expense of the Labour Party, which lost five seats. Although the Liberal Government could continue in office with Irish and Labour support, it had some difficulty in passing fresh legislation in the face of stronger opposition from the Conservatives; and before it dealt with the Labour Party's claims it had to satisfy its larger ally, the Irish Nationalists, with the most contentious legislation of all, an Irish Home Rule Bill. Lloyd George in 1911 introduced the State payment of M.P.s which saved the members of the Labour Party from the embarrassment of a complete loss of income; but even for this concession he extracted a guarantee that the party would actively support his National Insurance Bill. The passing of a measure to restore the unions' freedom to contribute to the Labour Party's upkeep had to wait until 1913.

Nor did the Trade Union Act of 1913 completely restore the *status quo* in the simple way that the Trade Disputes Act of 1906 had done. It is true that unions were henceforth authorized to engage in purposes not mentioned in the 1876 Act. But the right of an individual trade unionist to refuse to pay a political levy was recognized, and unions desiring to raise such a levy were obliged to pay it into a fund quite distinct from their other funds, and to enable members to opt out of payment of the political levy if they so wished. Furthermore, it was laid down that unions could not establish a political levy or make contributions to a political party until they had held a ballot of their membership on the subject, and secured a majority of those voting in favour of such a levy. The Act satisfied the basic requirements of the Labour Party; but its terms annoyed the union leaders, who resented the restrictions it imposed on the use of their funds. And, in addition, it was passed only after the Labour Party had been feeling the effects of the Osborne Judgment for four years – years which had seen an unfortunate weakening of its Parliamentary position and its prestige with the union rank-and-file.

To examine the results of this weakening, however, we must turn back to the industrial history of the decade before the outbreak of the First World War.

The restoration in 1906 of the legal immunity of trade unions, and of their freedom to engage in peaceful picketing, initiated a period of comparative industrial militancy. The tendency was also encouraged by a gradual rise of prices which characterized the period, and which became accentuated towards its close. Between 1902 and 1908 the cost of living rose by some four or five per cent, and between 1909 and 1913 it rose by almost nine per cent again. The pressure on trade unions to seek increases in wages was correspondingly increased.

The first large union to challenge the employers over a broad front after the passing of the Trade Disputes Act was the Amalgamated Society of Railway Servants – the union which had suffered directly from the Taff Vale decision and which was still in the ignominious position of not being recognized by the employers as a bargaining agent for the railwaymen. The only exception was the North-Eastern Railway Company, whose recognition of the union in 1897 was no doubt influenced by its special strength among North-Eastern employees – probably due in turn to the strength of unionism generally in the area, particularly among the miners and metalworkers. Elsewhere things were not the same; but in 1907 Richard Bell, the Railway Servants' secretary, initiated a national 'all-grades' movement, and approached all the companies for negotiations to discuss a rise of wages for all grades of railwaymen. Only the North-Eastern Railway accepted the proposal; and after the refusal of the other companies the union members voted for a national strike.

A national railway strike had never previously taken place, and the Government was naturally extremely apprehensive about its possible repercussions upon essential services and upon the whole industrial life of the country. Accordingly, Lloyd George, who at this time was President of the Board of Trade, intervened and acted with great energy to prevent the strike taking place. He thought that the companies were wrong to refuse to negotiate; and he at once set about cajoling them to do so, although he was conscious of the weakness of his own powers in the crisis as laid down by the Conciliation Act of 1896. The company directors maintained their opposition to direct negotiations with the union leaders; and Lloyd George had to summon the two parties in turn to meet him at the Board of Trade, and act the part of a go-between in the attempt to find a basis for settlement. In the end it was agreed to set up Boards of Conciliation for each railway, and for each grade of employment on each railway, on which both company and employees would be represented; but the employees' representatives were to be chosen by direct vote, and would not necessarily be unionists and still less union officials. In the case of disagreement by any Board there was to be a final appeal to a single arbitrator. The acceptance of this arrangement by the union without recourse to a national strike was due very largely to the personal influence of Richard Bell, the secretary, a man of moderate views who was capable of distinguishing the reality of the concession made by the companies from the appearance of non-recognition which still persisted. He saw that the unions in the industry, and particularly the Railway Servants, would gradually be able to dominate the men's side of the Conciliation Boards.

The following year, 1908, was not an auspicious year for wage advances, for it was a year of depression, and employers were inclined to reduce wages rather than to raise them. The major disputes of the year in fact owed their origin to proposals for wage cuts. The Amalgamated Engineers on the north-east coast, for instance, came out on strike for this reason, against the advice of their leaders in London, but after a seven-month struggle they were forced to accept defeat. In 1909 trade conditions improved, but the main industrial disturbances were caused by the operation of the Miners Eight Hours Act, which dislocated existing practices in the pits without in fact reducing hours very much: 'eight hours' meant, by the wording of the Act, distinctly more than eight hours' work for the miners, for it excluded 'winding time', that is, the time taken to take the miners up and down the mine shafts. At the beginning of 1910 the Durham and Northumberland miners, who had always opposed the idea of eight-hours legislation, were introduced to a three-shift system, which upset their home life; they at once embarked on a strike, which lasted three months before they gave way. Although in the mines, as on the railways, the tendency was towards national regulation of the industry, it was obvious that conditions in different areas varied too much to allow the easy application of nationally uniform agreements.

But the problems of the mining industry went deeper than

this. In many areas output per worker had been falling and costs rising, mainly owing to the greater depth and thinness of the seams. Yet the miners had grown more militant, and their younger spokesmen were beginning to demand a guaranteed minimum wage. The men in South Wales took the initiative: late in 1910 those working in pits controlled by the Cambrian Combine refused to accept new rates offered to them by a Conciliation Board, although the Board included their old and respected leader, W. Abraham, M.P. (known in South Wales as 'Mabon'). The men embarked on a ten-month strike which was marked by rioting, the dispatch of police reinforcements from London, troop movements, and one fatal casualty at Tonypandy. Among those who went down to help and encourage the strikers was Tom Mann, who had lately returned from a sojourn in Australasia, as vigorous as ever, and full of new ideas about syndicalism and the political importance of industrial action.

The growth of syndicalism was due to two main influences, one coming from America and the other from France. In 1905 the Industrial Workers of the World was founded at Chicago, with the intention of reorganizing American unionism industry by industry instead of craft by craft and of conducting a much more militant struggle on the principle that 'the working class and the employing class have nothing in common'. Among those who helped to shape the new body was the leading American Marxist Daniel De Leon, whose propaganda circulated almost as widely in Britain as in the United States. Meanwhile in France Georges Sorel was shaping the philosophy of the general strike, which he conceived as a political weapon, to win control of the State, or – if it failed – at least to solidify the working class.

Almost as soon as he returned to England, Tom Mann had paid a brief visit to France to learn about the new philosophy at first hand; and later in 1910 he started the publication of a monthly pamphlet-journal, the *Industrial Syndicalist*, and formed an Industrial Syndicalist Education League to propagate his views. He also established 'Amalgamation Committees' in various industries, to agitate for the consolidation of sectional or craft societies into one single union for each industry. In November 1910 he achieved at least a partial success with the formation of the National Transport Workers Federation, which included both dockers and seamen, though not railway workers. It was a fortunate coincidence for him that both Ben Tillett, his old colleague in the London Dock strike of 1889, and Havelock Wilson, the secretary of the National Sailors' and Firemen's Union, were feeling the need for a revival of the aggressive tactics of twenty years earlier.

The following year, 1911, was thus destined to be a year of strikes among the dockers and seamen. The first blow was struck by the seamen at Southampton, who held up the new liner *Olympic* and quickly won an advance of pay. The unrest spread to all types of transport elsewhere in the country, and there was rioting, looting, and even bloodshed in some cases: the strength of the reaction took even Mann and Tillett by surprise. A short general strike took place at the London docks, but it was brought to an end by prompt action on the part of the government conciliator G. R. Askwith. The Shipping Federation was at last induced to recognize the Sailors' Union, and improvement took place in the pay of most of the strikers. A more prolonged struggle took place at Liverpool, where Mann organized the dockers and carters so effectively that essential food supplies could pass through the port only with a military escort or by special licence provided by the strike committee. Two men were killed in one incident when troops clashed with rioters.

Meanwhile the leaders of the railway unions, impatient with the slow processes of their Conciliation Boards, united to threaten a national strike once more. Asquith, the Prime Minister, himself intervened to prevent this occurring, but he lacked the conciliatory skill of Lloyd George, and his demeanour only made things worse. The result was that the first national railway strike began on 18 August 1911. Lloyd George took over from Asquith, met both directors and union leaders separately, and played a new and unexpected card – warning of the danger of industrial strife at a time when the country might become involved in war with Germany over the Agadir affair. This tactic worked: a compromise was reached after only two days' stoppage of the railways. A Royal Commission was set up to examine the operation of the

Conciliation Boards; and on its report later in the year, a new scheme was introduced. The railway companies, having been impressed by the response of their employees to the strike call by the unions, at last conceded recognition, although only in a roundabout way: the men's side of each Conciliation Board was empowered to appoint a secretary 'from any source they please', and this usually meant a union official. In 1912 the new Boards were at work, and new agreements were being made. The membership of all the railway unions went up rapidly as a result.

Yet if 1911 had appeared to be a year of strikes, it hardly compared with 1912 in the number of days lost by stoppages. In February the Miners Federation, employing the tactics of the railwaymen, began a national strike to secure a minimum wage – 'five and two' as they called it, or five shillings per shift for men and two shillings for boys. The Government intervened rather belatedly, and a somewhat awkward committee of four Ministers, led by the Prime Minister, heard the views of both sides to the dispute. They soon came up against the reluctance of the owners to pay a definite guaranteed wage at a time of falling output per man. A Bill to establish district minimum wages – but not necessarily the 'five and two' – by decision of local boards with independent chairmen was rushed through all its stages in March. This was not all the Federation leaders wanted, but it clearly established a principle of great importance to them. The result was that after a somewhat inconclusive ballot of their members the miners' leaders ordered a resumption of work in April. The strike had shown the disruptive effect on the nation's whole industrial life which a miners' general stoppage could cause – hundreds of thousands of other workers were thrown out of work – but it also suggested that there were limits to the extent to which, in the face of public opinion, any one union could extort concessions from their employers by putting pressure on the Government.

These limits were shown even more clearly in the London dock strike which took place in May. The Port of London Authority had now been constituted and was the employer of a large proportion of the dock workers; its chairman was a tough and determined man, Lord Devonport. The Authority became involved in a dispute with the National Transport Workers Federation over its right to employ non-unionists. A Cabinet committee of five Ministers intervened, but with singular lack of success; and the Federation took the drastic step of calling a national strike of transport workers. This proved to be a fiasco: the workers in the various ports had little sense of national solidarity, and Bristol was the only one to give an effective response to the call. Many blacklegs were brought in to work in the London docks, and Ben Tillett, addressing a meeting on Tower Hill in a style that caricatured his performances of over twenty years earlier, uttered the bitter prayer: 'O God, strike Lord Devonport dead!' In August the strike collapsed, and the union members had to fight for their jobs against the competition of the blacklegs.

Lord Devonport had stemmed the tide of successful strikes; and although 1913 was a year of continued unrest, no great national conflicts took place. Yet as we have seen, the unions gained many new members as the state insurance system came into operation and obliged the workers in many industries to make a choice of 'approved society' through which to receive their benefits. The most important industrial event of 1913 took place in Ireland – the struggle of the Irish Transport Workers Union against the Dublin employers, which lasted for eight months and excited much interest in Britain. The Irish Transport Workers Union had grown up under the influence of American syndicalist ideas, and its leader, Jim Larkin, was a strong believer in the power of sympathetic strikes. He demanded help of this character from the British unions, and a vocal minority in Britain supported him. The T.U.C., meeting in September 1913, was sufficiently roused to send a delegation to Dublin to attempt mediation; but nothing came of this. The Parliamentary Committee then decided to raise funds for the relief of the strikers, and a total of £60,000 was contributed. But most of the British union officials fought shy of sympathetic action, partly at least because they had little trust in the patently irresponsible leadership of Larkin. The Parliamentary Committee made the gesture of commissioning a steamer to take a supply of food to the Dublin docks, and the ship went into harbour to the cheers of the strikers, as if she were relieving a city besieged by enemy troops. But the strike eventually collapsed in January 1914, and its legacy to Britain was an increase in the existing discord between the older and more sober leaders and their younger and more militant critics.

What were the causes of the pervasive rank-and-file militancy of the years before the First World War? It is easy to regard it as part of a general malaise of Britain at the time, for it coincided with the bitter constitutional conflict between the Liberal Government and the House of Lords, with the campaign of violence by the suffragettes, and with the ever-mounting intensity of the struggle for Irish Home Rule. But there were also more tangible reasons for the so-called 'labour unrest' of the period. It has already been pointed out that prices had been rising for some time; and the pace of inflation increased in the years 1909–13. This in itself generated a considerable pressure for industrial action by the unions. There was also the fact that many workers were disillusioned by the failure of the Labour Party in Parliament – and this at a time when the gospel of Socialism had spread widely among their ranks. Even the I.L.P., which unlike the S.D.F. had maintained its adherence to the Labour Party, had suffered considerable dissension on the question, many of its members seceding in 1911 to join with the S.D.F. in forming a new independent Socialist organization, the British Socialist Party.

In the 1880s and 1890s Marxism had been the creed of a very small minority, largely isolated from the trade unions. In the first decade of the twentieth century, however, it secured a wider influence among industrial workers. This may be illustrated from the early history of Ruskin College, Oxford – a small residential centre for the further education of working men which had been founded by an American philanthropist in 1899, but over which the Parliamentary Committee and other trade-union organizations had assumed a trusteeship. In 1908 many of the students of the College, together with their Principal, Dennis Hird, demanded a re-organization of the syllabus of teaching so that the whole emphasis could be placed on Marxist economics and sociology.

Failing to persuade the trustees, they seceded from the college and set up their own Labour College. To support the new college, which was soon moved to London, a body called the Plebs League was founded, its title being derived from a pamphlet by the American Marxist, Daniel De Leon. Many of the members of the Plebs League belonged either to the South Wales Miners Federation or to the Amalgamated Society of Railway Servants – and these men were largely responsible for the aggressive tactics of their respective unions in 1911–12.

We have already seen how Tom Mann returned to Britain in 1910 and started propagating the ideas of syndicalism. Among the members of the Plebs League he found ready converts to these ideas. In South Wales they formed what was called the Unofficial Reform Committee of the South Wales Miners Federation, and in 1912 this Committee published a pamphlet called *The Miners' Next Step*, which summed up their aspirations. The pamphlet marks the high water of syndicalist influence in British trade unionism. It speaks of the need for the 'elimination of the employer', not by the usual Socialist method of nationalization, but by a process whereby each industry would be

thoroughly organized, in the first place, to fight, to gain control of, and then to administer that industry.

The various industries of the country would be coordinated by a 'Central Production Board', which would leave it to the workers in each industry to devise the methods of producing the desired output.

This would mean real democracy in real life, making for real manhood and womanhood. Any other form of democracy is a delusion and a snare.

It was men professing these views who began almost at once to take over the official posts of leadership in the South Wales Miners Federation.

Yet we must not exaggerate the importance of the new ideas upon British trade unionism as a whole. The 'amalgamation' movement that Tom Mann had launched, and which was the necessary first step of any effective syndicalist movement, did not get very far in these years. The formation of the National Transport Workers Federation had seemed to point the way, but the failure of its call for a national strike in 1912 showed the inadequacy of anything short of a real consolidation of the unions in each industry. The Parliamentary Committee was persuaded in 1912 to supervise a ballot for the amalgamation of unions in the building industry; but the unions concerned rejected the scheme by a vote in which less than a quarter of the total membership involved took the trouble to participate. The 'amalgamation' movement secured only one noteworthy success before 1914, and even that was an incomplete one. In 1913 the Amalgamated Society of Railway Servants united with the General Railway Workers Union, and a smaller body called the United Pointsmen and Signalmen's Society, to form the National Union of Railwaymen. But both the Associated Society of Locomotive Engineers and Firemen and the Railway Clerks Association retained their separate existence, so that it could not be said that an 'industrial' union of railwaymen had been achieved.

If amalgamation was still unattainable, at least the pre-war years showed that the Miners and the Railwaymen could conduct effective national strikes, and that the Transport Workers Federation could bring the Port of London to a standstill. All three bodies had compelled government intervention at the highest level. What if they were to coordinate their activities for mutual support? A proposal to this effect was put forward by Robert Smillie, the Scottish miners' leader and veteran Socialist, who had just become President of the Miners Federation. Negotiations took place between the three bodies on the lines that he suggested, and a tentative agreement was made in June 1914. The idea was that the members of the 'Triple Alliance', as it was called, should arrange that their contracts terminated simultaneously, so that they could threaten the employers and the Government with a disruption of the economic life of the country on an unprecedented scale. But difficulties arose about the precise terms of the Alliance, and it was not brought into being until December 1915, at which time the exigencies of war still further postponed its operation.

It might seem as if the Triple Alliance was not very far from the syndicalists' concept of the general strike for political purposes. It should be remembered, however, that while its object was to bring pressure on the Government as well as on the employers, it did not have any ulterior purpose beyond the immediate improvement of the wages and conditions of the workers concerned. The idea of 'direct action' for revolutionary political purposes might influence some of the Welsh miners; it had little appeal to the great bulk of British union leaders, whose respect for parliamentary methods, though somewhat weakened by such events as the Osborne Judgment, was yet too deeply ingrained to be easily lost. For some of them, a milder theory called Guild Socialism, which was gradually evolved in these years by a number of journalists and intellectuals, proved more attractive. The Guild Socialists believed in workers' control of industry, but unlike the syndicalists they did not attach much importance to the idea of achieving it by 'direct action' on the part of the workers. A. R. Orage and S. G. Hobson, two journalists on the left-wing weekly *New Age* who elaborated the theory of Guild Socialism, conceived of 'National Guilds' which would develop from the trade unions, and which would restore something of the pride in craftsmanship which had characterized the medieval gilds. These ideas, which owed not a little to the writings of Ruskin and William Morris, attracted the interest of skilled workers who felt their crafts to be threatened by the spread of mechanization. But the Guild Socialists had not had much chance to influence the trade union movement before the First World War broke out in August 1914.

In the first decade and a half of the twentieth century the expansion of industry, the increasing interference of the State in the country's economic life, and the sheer growth of their own movement, all made for a greater complexity in the relations of the trade unions with the Government at the national level. Yet the traditions of *laissez-faire* Liberalism combined with the union leaders' rooted hostility to any erosion of their voluntary and extra-legal status to prevent more than the most limited modification of the late-nine-teenth-century pattern of industrial relations.

Throughout the period the number of conciliation and arbitration boards in existence increased rapidly – from sixty-four in 1894 to 162 in 1905 and 325 in 1913. But at the same time, the whole weight of T.U.C. political influence was thrown against any proposals for compulsory arbitration, or for recognition of the trade unions as legal corporations able to sue and be sued as well as merely to protect their funds. Basically, this was due to the union leaders' dislike of the legal system, with its inordinate delays and its heavy expenses, and their complete distrust of the judiciary, which they believed to be ignorant of industrial problems and animated by upper-class prejudices against unionism. This point of view always carried the day at the T.U.C. whenever a resolution was brought forward for the legal enforcement of industrial disputes. At the 1913 T.U.C., for instance, a delegate of the Railway Servants made an allusion which was not lost on his audience when he said that his union 'had considerable experience of judge-made law, and we do not want any more of it': the resolution was defeated by a large majority. As a result, the only type of governmental inter-ference that was tolerated outside the 'sweated trades' (in which unionism was weak) was that provided by the mach-inery of voluntary conciliation established by the Act of 1896.

That this machinery was used frequently and successfully is shown by the activity of G. R. (later Sir George) Askwith, the Board of Trade conciliator, who became involved in negotiations to solve almost every major dispute in the decade before the outbreak of the First World War. In 1911 the machinery was extended by the establishment of the Indus-trial Council, a body consisting of prominent employers and union officials who could be called upon to hear disputes and recommend terms of settlement. But the Council proved to be too clumsy to be very helpful, and it was allowed to die. In cases of a national strike, where there was a threat to the flow of essential supplies or to the continuance of the indus-trial life of the country, Ministers of the Crown were naturally impelled to intervene; but they did not always do so with success, and Sydney Buxton, who was President of the Board of Trade from 1910, became convinced that it was best to rely upon experienced civil servants like Askwith so far as possible. In any case, as Askwith pointed out, the Government had no 'labour policy' as such. It merely responded *ad hoc* to strikes as they took place, and its policy was shaped by external pressures from different directions, including, of course, that of the T.U.C. and of the Labour Party in the Commons.

Nor was the central organization of the unions clearly possessed of more than a very negative policy in this period. The Parliamentary Committee had no control over the trade unions, although it did improve to some extent its control over the proceedings of Congress. Its chairman was given the duty of presiding over the meetings of Congress, and giving the introductory address, which in the past had been given (somewhat to the boredom of the delegates) by the President of the trades council of the city or town where Congress happened to convene. But the administrative efficiency of the Parliamentary Committee was still cruelly restricted by financial stringency: only one clerk was employed to assist the secretary, and the secretary himself, owing to his parliamentary duties and perhaps also owing to duties with his own union, was not really engaged full-time in the service of the Committee. A significant incident at the 1908 T.U.C. will illustrate the weakness of the Parliamentary Committee. It proposed to the Congress that it should be permitted to issue a quarterly report of its activities, so that the unions should know what it was doing at more frequent intervals than were provided by the annual report. The proposal was carried, but only because the senior delegate of the Miners Federation had mislaid his voting card, which prevented the Miners' block vote, amounting by now to over half a million, from being recorded in opposition.

Of course, this treatment of the Parliamentary Committee only reflected the way in which the leaders of the affiliated organizations were themselves treated by their own members. Those who represented federations of unions were almost always on a shoestring – especially the leaders of the Miners Federation, whom R. H. Tawney later described as an 'impossible' body of 'ambassadors refusing to accept responsibility'. Generally speaking, even in the case of national unions, the salaries of full-time officers were determined more by the standard of wages prevalent among the members than by the nature of the responsibilities involved. Furthermore, although some unions built imposing headquarters offices, administrative costs were pared to a minimum owing to the members' constant suspicion of office work. This was a definite disadvantage at times of stress. Harry Gosling of the Watermen noticed during the dock strikes of 1911 and 1912 that the employers always had the advantage of business efficiency in negotiating with the unions:

> When a point came up in private negotiations or in discussions before the public, Lord Devonport and the employers were able to find their documents neatly pigeon-holed for reference. Ours had to be got together somehow, though there were half a ton of them lying in the office. But there was no staff to sort them out or make them available for immediate use.

But in none of the unions was the rank-and-file distrust of the officials so marked in this period as in the Amalgamated Engineers, once the very model of administrative efficiency. The Engineers had always had a complicated constitution, designed to safeguard the members against the usurpation of power; and in 1908 George Barnes, the general secretary, had resigned office rather than see his own policy and that of the Executive Council overruled by the members on the north-east coast. Distrust of the full-time Executive Council continued to build up; and in 1912 a Delegate Meeting of the union, when making new rules, decided to declare all their posts vacant, although their terms of office had not expired and in some cases had only just begun. The Council members refused to accept this decision, whereupon the Delegate Meeting appointed a new provisional Executive to take over the administration. The old Council refused to give way, and barricaded themselves in the head office in Peckham Road; but they were summarily ejected when their opponents broke through the wall from the house next door. The defeated Council members sued for redress, both in the public courts and in the union's Final Appeal Court. In the former they were denied redress; but in the latter they were upheld, and the new Executive was ordered to pay them their wages up to the date of the expiry of their original terms of office. In 1913 there was also an undignified contest for the General Secretaryship which led to a successful libel action by the defeated candidate.

Generally speaking, however, although the machinery of the movement was already old-fashioned, it did work without leading to complete chaos. The trouble was that even with the best will in the world it was often difficult to secure liaison between all the different and overlapping organizations which had come into existence in the previous generation or so. As we have seen, the T.U.C., the Labour Party, and the G.F.T.U. all had functions which needed to be coordinated; but the way in which they were coordinated was by the establishment in 1905 of a so-called Joint Board, which was simply another committee, meeting infrequently with limited authority and without any administrative staff of its own. Such a body could hardly formulate a positive policy of its own.

One of the items in such a positive policy might have been the establishment of a national daily newspaper; but characteristically it was not until such a paper had been founded by left-wing militants – who took over a strike sheet of the London Society of Compositors issued in 1911, under the title of the *Daily Herald* – that the Labour Party and the Parliamentary Committee decided that action in this sphere was desirable. Then they established a paper called the *Daily Citizen*, which appeared belatedly in 1913. The *Daily Citizen*, cautiously pursuing the official policies of the labour movement, was orthodox and dull; the *Daily Herald*, run by rebels, was provocative and interesting. In 1913 George Lansbury became editor of the *Herald*, and his warm-hearted tolerance built up a devoted band of writers ranging from Belloc and Chesterton to G. D. H. Cole and the brilliant cartoonist Will Dyson. Whereas the *Herald* managed to survive the impact of the First World War – although it had to become a weekly – the *Citizen* became a fatal casualty in the early stages.

In the field of working-class education, also, the leadership of the national organizations of the movement was equally weak. We have already seen how Ruskin College came into existence as a result of American philanthropy, and how it was rent asunder in 1908 by the secession which led to the formation of the Labour College. The same dispute also had its effect on the Workers' Educational Association, a body founded in 1903 by university dons and others interested in coordinating and extending extra-mural education for working men and women. Representatives of the T.U.C. were drawn into its counsels, but neither Congress nor the Parliamentary Committee ever considered its work as deserving of any considerable effort on their part to raise financial support. To no small extent this lack of enthusiasm may be accounted for by the hostility of the supporters of the Labour College, who regarded any type of education other than their own Marxist variety as being positively harmful.

Finally, the Parliamentary Committee continued to keep its links with foreign trade-union movements to the absolute minimum. It went on exchanging fraternal delegates with the American Federation of Labor, and extended the same arrangement to certain other bodies, which, of course, meant spending rather more of the time of Congress on what were nearly always purely formal speeches and greetings. As was to be expected, it formed no links with the Socialist International, with which the Labour Party became formally associated in 1908; but it even refused to associate itself with a new body known as the International Secretariat of Trade Union Centres, with which it might appropriately have affiliated. The British affiliate of this organization was the General Federation of Trade Unions, a body still no more representative of British trade unionism as a whole than it had been in the first years of its existence. As a result of pressure from the Miners Federation, whose county unions had never belonged to the G.F.T.U. but whose leaders attached some importance to international links, the Parliamentary Committee was gradually pushed towards a recognition of its responsibilities; and when in 1913 the International Secretariat was reconstituted on a rather firmer basis as the International Federation of Trade Unions, a delegate of the T.U.C. attended the inaugural meeting. But foreigners could be forgiven if they found it difficult to work out whether there was any national authority at the head of the uniquely strong trade-union movement in the most industrialized country in the world. Beatrice Webb had said of the T.U C. in 1902: 'There is no leadership in the Congress . . . but a certain unanimity of opinion among the delegates.' A decade later, the sense of unanimity inspired by Taff Vale had disappeared, and there was still no leadership.

CHAPTER EIGHT

WAR AND THE GENERAL STRIKE
1914–26

THE outbreak of the First World War not only took the trade-union movement by surprise: it also presented it with a whole range of problems for which there was no precedent – for the country had not been engaged in major hostilities since trade unionism had ceased to be illegal.

At first there was a moment of doubt as to whether the bulk of the movement would support the war effort. It was, however, only a moment. The I.L.P. Members of Parliament, led by Ramsay MacDonald, who was chairman of the parliamentary Labour Party, decided to oppose; but the trade-union M.P.s at once refused to go against the steadily rising tide of national opinion. What hesitations there had been had almost all been removed by the German invasion of Belgium. On 5 August MacDonald resigned his chairmanship of the parliamentary party and was succeeded by Arthur Henderson, the secretary of the extra-parliamentary party and for many years an official of the Friendly Society of Iron Founders. With the Socialists thus excluded from office in the Labour Party, relations between its new leaders and those of the trade-union movement became closer and more informal.

At the same time both Socialist and non-Socialist could continue to collaborate in the task of protecting the workers' living standards in time of war. Henderson had already summoned a special conference of delegates from all sections of the labour movement for 5 August, and this conference decided to establish a standing committee which became known as the War Emergency Workers National Committee. This body, representative of Socialist and cooperative societies as well as of trade unions and trades councils, met weekly for the rest of the year and thereafter less frequently. It acted throughout as an important agency for the formulation and expression of an economic and social policy to safeguard the living standards of the workers and their families in the increasingly unfamiliar conditions of wartime.

For some months, the Government showed little recognition of the need to take a firm control of the country's economy. Very few people imagined that the war would last more than a few months; and there was at first no budgeting for future scarcities of either man-power or supplies, no elaborate production planning, no control of prices. The first economic effects of war were in fact a sudden rise in the cost of living, a considerable amount of unemployment in industries not producing munitions, and a heavy voluntary enlistment of men from all types of occupation, whether or not of vital importance for the maintenance of essential supplies.

The trade-union leadership was in general anxious to do what it could to help the Government. On 24 August, at a meeting of the Joint Board – the liaison committee of the Labour Party, the G.F.T.U., and the Parliamentary Committee – a resolution was adopted as follows:

> That an immediate effort be made to terminate all existing trade disputes, whether strikes or lock-outs, and whenever new points of difficulty arise during the war period a serious attempt should be made by all concerned to reach an amicable settlement before resorting to a strike or lock-out.

On 2 September the Parliamentary Committee followed the lead of the Labour Party in expressing approval of the national recruiting campaign. But the steady rise in prices and the distress caused by unemployment in some areas naturally began to cause some concern among both the leadership and the rank and file of the unions. When firms engaged on war contracts began to press for the relaxation of established 'trade practices' – of which the most important was the reservation of certain types of work to skilled workmen – both officials and members began to have doubts about the desirability of making concessions without securing guarantees from the Government and also corresponding sacrifices by their employers.

The problem naturally arose principally in the engineering and shipbuilding industries, which supplied the most important armaments and munitions and which were endeavouring to increase production rapidly in response to the needs of the armed services. In February 1915 Sir George Askwith presided over a small Treasury Committee on Production to examine ways and means of expanding both the supply and the productivity of labour in these industries. As a result of the committee's recommendations, both employers and unions in the engineering industry in March 1915 made the 'Shells and Fuses Agreement' whereby 'dilution', that is, the introduction of unskilled labour, including that of women, on jobs formerly reserved for skilled men, was permitted by the unions in return for solemn guarantees by both Government and employers that the trade practices thereby suspended would be restored without prejudice at the end of the war.

Such concessions by union officials were, of course, worthless unless they were also accepted by the members in the workshops. A danger signal had already been flashed from the Clyde in February, when in defiance of their officials a fortnight's strike of some 8,000–10,000 engineers took place. The strike was led by a 'Central Withdrawal of Labour Committee', an unofficial body consisting of shop stewards – the part-time representatives of the unions on the shop floor. Shop stewards had existed before the war, but they had received little general notice, and their activities were often curbed by intolerant employers; but now they made their appearance with impunity, and often exercised an important role, especially in the large factories of the engineering industry. In the 1915 Clydeside strike they were simply demanding a wage rise to keep pace with the increase in the cost of living; but since they had interrupted the supply of munitions and, moreover, had acted against the advice of their full-time union officials, they were bitterly denounced by the national press, although they won most of the advances which they asked for.

It is not surprising that direct ministerial intervention took place almost at once in order to persuade the unions to make more concessions. Lloyd George, who was still Chancellor of the Exchequer, and Walter Runciman, the President of the Board of Trade, summoned representatives of the Parliamentary Committee and of the unions to a conference in the boardroom of the Treasury, where there was a gilt throne of Queen Anne's time. Lloyd George himself later described the spectacle of

those stalwart artisans leaning against and sitting on the steps of the throne of the dead Queen, and on equal terms negotiating conditions with the government of the day upon a question vitally affecting the conduct of a great war. Queen Anne was indeed dead.

The ministers pressed the union leaders to agree to compulsory arbitration and 'the relaxation of the present trade practices' in all industry regarded as essential for the war effort. All the unions accepted the demand except for the Miners Federation and the Amalgamated Engineers, and the document that they signed became known as the 'Treasury Agreement'. The Engineers were brought in after a few days in return for an undertaking from Lloyd George that war profits of firms would be so taxed as to secure for the State any benefits accruing from the unions' abandonment of their peace-time practices. The agreement signed by the Engineers' leaders was confirmed by a ballot of the members in June. Meanwhile the Committee on Production presided over by Sir George Askwith was constituted on a permanent basis as an arbitration tribunal.

By this time the whole country had grown alarmed by revelations about the shell shortage on the Western Front; and it was clear that the war would last for much longer than a year. In May Asquith decided to establish a Coalition Government, and he offered a place in the Cabinet to Arthur Henderson, which after consultation with his colleagues Henderson decided to accept. He became President of the Board of Education, a somewhat unsuitable post; his real task was to act as Cabinet adviser on labour problems. Two other Labour M.P.s were appointed to junior government office. In the following month a Ministry of Munitions was set up, and Lloyd George became the Minister in charge. He at once drafted a Bill to give the force of law to the terms of the Treasury Agreement. The Bill provided the Government with enormous powers over the munitions industry and its workers: it authorized the compulsory arbitration of disputes and the suspension of trade practices, and it limited the profits of the firms concerned to one-fifth in excess of the pre-war rate. It also introduced a system whereby munition workers could not leave their jobs without the consent of their employer in the form of a 'Leaving Certificate'. The Bill was rapidly passed through all its stages and became law on 2 July 1915 as the Munitions of War Act.

Although the new Act gave the unions some compensation for their sacrifices in the form of a limitation of employers' profits, it certainly embodied an extraordinary degree of State control over labour; and it was not at all clear whether the workers would accept it, or if not, whether they could be forced to accept it. As it happened, the Government's new powers were very soon put to the test. Only a few days after the Act came into force the South Wales Miners rejected a wage award by Sir George Askwith, and Lloyd George promptly issued a proclamation under the Act, making any strike in the South Wales mining industry illegal. Two days later, however, 200,000 South Wales miners came out; and Lloyd George, realizing the impossibility of sending them all to prison, was obliged to negotiate a settlement in the ordinary way and to persuade them back to work in return for the concession of most of their demands. A number of stoppages on the Clyde indicated that in the engineering industry also it was very difficult to enforce the Act if the workers were determined to ignore it. In general, though, it was accepted as a necessary evil.

Soon, however, the unions grew concerned about abuses both of the arrangements for the dilution of labour and of the system of Leaving Certificates. In September they held a special conference to draw up a list of complaints about the operation of the Act, and as a result an Amending Act was passed in January 1916. This declared that unskilled workers employed in the place of skilled workers should receive the skilled men's rate of pay; and it also provided for certain safeguards in the use of Leaving Certificates. If this improved the general conditions of labour in the factories it could not allay the discontent in certain areas. When Lloyd George and Arthur Henderson visited establishments on the Clyde in December 1915 they were received with open hostility by the workers; and early in 1916 various left-wing journals published in Glasgow were suppressed and a number of unofficial strike leaders were arrested and given prison sentences. This had a temporary deterrent effect; but the shop stewards had formed a powerful Clyde Workers Committee, which continued in existence and later helped to form a National Workers Committee Movement, linking up the unofficial leaders in factories throughout the country.

Meanwhile the Government had been forced to introduce conscription for the armed forces. The T.U.C., when it met in September 1915, had passed a curiously ambiguous resolution on this subject, which indicated that there would be no great opposition from the labour movement if Parliament adopted such a measure. The first Military Service Act, applying only to single men, was passed in January 1916. It was followed in May of the same year by a second Act applying to married men. Under both Acts arrangements were made for the exemption of skilled men in key occupations, but unskilled men were called up out of the factories. Friction frequently occurred between the War Office and the unions over individual cases; but for a time in 1916–17 certain skilled unions were authorized by the Government to issue cards of exemption known as 'trade cards' – an unusual delegation of power. Although in this and other instances union officials might enjoy the position of trust with which they were invested by the Government, they had constantly to be on their guard against the danger of estrangement from their own rank-and-file members, which was so clearly threatened by the success of the shop stewards' movement in the engineering industry.

The accession of Lloyd George to the Premiership in December 1916, and the formation of the Second Coalition, marked a new stage in the mobilization of the country's resources for total war. Whatever criticism might be levelled against Lloyd George for the way in which he replaced

Asquith, there could be no doubt that the change led to an increase in the efficiency of government and to a more complete mobilization of resources for the war effort. In forming his government, Lloyd George called for a much fuller participation by the Labour Party, and offered its leaders not only a place in the small War Cabinet but also a number of other senior administrative posts and a wide range of policy concessions along the lines of what the War Emergency Workers National Committee had long been demanding – State control of the mines and of shipping, strict control of food supplies, and the establishment of a Ministry of Labour. The new Premier needed Labour Party support to help consolidate his shaky position in the Commons; but the generosity of his offer must have owed something to his recognition of the close links between the party and the trade-union movement, and his desire to improve the industrial atmosphere by political means. The Labour Party felt that the terms were too good to refuse; and so Arthur Henderson joined the War Cabinet, and John Hodge, the secretary of the Steel Smelters, and George Barnes, the former secretary of the Amalgamated Engineers, took the new posts of Minister of Labour and Minister of Pensions respectively. Several other Labour M.P.s, also former trade-union officials, were appointed to junior offices.

The reconstruction of the Ministry and the appointment of so many Labour men did not prevent the recurrence of industrial unrest, although it helped to keep it within bounds. The continuance of the process of dilution and the calling-up of some skilled workers for military service caused discontent in the factories, and strikes occurred, often led by members of the unofficial Workers Committee Movement. In 1917 the Government appointed a number of Commissions of Enquiry into Industrial Unrest for different regions of the country, and the reports enumerated a wide range of grievances, including the significant point that many union members had lost confidence in their official leaders. The task of summarizing the reports fell to one of the Labour ministers, George Barnes, whose experience as secretary of the Amalgamated Engineers gave him special qualifications on the subject of unrest among the union rank and file. Barnes enumerated a series of 'psychological conditions' making for unrest, which included

> the feeling that there has been inequality of sacrifice, that the government has broken pledges, that the trade union officials are no longer to be relied upon, and that there is a woeful uncertainty as to the industrial future.

One important consequence of the Commission of Enquiry was the abolition of the Leaving Certificate system. But this by itself could not remove the root causes of unrest.

The strain betweeen the union leadership and the rank and file was further intensified by the events of 1917 – and especially by the Russian revolutions of February and October. The first revolution, which set up the Kerensky régime, was greeted with enthusiasm by both Marxist and non-Marxist Socialists, and the leaders of the I.L.P. and the British Socialist Party summoned a special conference at Leeds in June to greet the event. The conference was a great success, for it was attended by delegates not only of Socialist party branches but also of trade-union branches and trades councils. One of the resolutions of the conference actually urged the establishment of Workers' and Soldiers' Councils on the Russian model in Britain; but nothing came of this afterwards. It was a revolutionary gesture and no more, but it signified the weakening of the existing ties of authority within the labour movement.

For the Government, the overthrow of tsarism was a matter of concern, for it foreshadowed the withdrawal of Russia from the war. The War Cabinet decided to send Arthur Henderson to visit Russia and advise on the best means of keeping the new régime in alliance with Britain and France. Much to the disgust of his Cabinet colleagues, Henderson returned to Britain with a firm conviction that the right course was to pursue, in association with Kerensky, the possibilities of a negotiated peace with the Central Powers. In accordance with this view, Henderson favoured the dispatch of delegates from the Labour Party to a proposed International Socialist Congress at Stockholm, at which it was expected that there would be German representatives; and he persuaded a special conference of the Labour Party to agree to this. Henderson was then summoned to a meeting of the War Cabinet, but (in the so-called 'doormat incident') was kept waiting outside the door while the other members discussed his behaviour. On finally being invited inside, he was reprimanded by Lloyd George. He at once resigned his post, but agreed that the incident should be regarded as a personal one between himself and the Prime Minister. The result was that his place in the War Cabinet was taken by George Barnes, and the Labour Party remained in the Coalition Government. But, as we shall see, the change was to have important political consequences.

Meanwhile the Parliamentary Committee of the T.U.C. had decided to seek powers from the 1917 Congress to enable it to play a more active part in the foreign diplomacy of the labour movement. This was a logical development of a decision of the 1916 Congress, when the Miners Federation had succeeded in passing a resolution for the reconstitution of the Joint Board with the Labour Party only, thus excluding the G.F.T.U. It followed that the G.F.T.U. could no longer be regarded as a suitable agency for the representation of British trade unionism abroad. In fact, the G.F.T.U. secretary, W. A. Appleton, was very right-wing in his views, and Henderson with his new policy of peace by negotiation welcomed the initiative of the Parliamentary Committee. He himself received a great ovation at the 1917 T.U.C., shortly after his resignation from the Government, and he said significantly in his speech that

it has been to the impoverishment of international politics that Congress has not taken a larger share in that work in days gone by.

At this Congress the Parliamentary Committee also asked for and obtained powers to increase its secretarial staff, to obtain more ample office accommodation, and to 'levy affiliated societies for the money necessary'. It is probable that much of the initiative for these requests came from Harry Gosling, the Watermen's leader, whose views on the inadequacy of trade-union administration we have already quoted. The existing secretary of the Parliamentary Committee, C. W. Bowerman of the London Compositors, who succeeded Steadman in 1911, was hardly likely to have taken the lead himself. The result was that it was possible to start building up a T.U.C. staff, and in 1918 a special international bureau was set up.

To begin with, the Parliamentary Committee had to leave most of the policy initiative in the hands of Henderson and his Labour Party assistants; but it was consulted at every stage in the preparation of the 'Memorandum on War Aims', which was endorsed by a conference of Allied labour leaders in February 1918. The idea of peace by negotiation was also endorsed by a large majority at the T.U.C. in September 1918. Samuel Gompers of the American Federation of Labor, who had been asked by President Wilson to maintain the fighting morale of the Allied labour movements, chose for a time to regard the G.F.T.U. as more representative of British labour than the Parliamentary Committee; but a visit to the 1918 T.U.C. forced him to recognize his error.

The fact that both the extra-parliamentary Labour Party and the T.U.C. had pledged themselves to a foreign policy which was distinctly different from the Government's undoubtedly went some way to reduce the distrust of union leadership which had manifested itself in the shop stewards' movement and the unofficial strikes. It also provided a basis for reconciliation with the members of the I.L.P., who had opposed the war from the beginning. It is true that there were some union officials who seemed more enthusiastic for the 'knock-out blow' against Germany than Lloyd George himself. Among them were, for instance, Havelock Wilson and his colleagues of the Sailors' and Firemen's Union, whose members had suffered severely from the ravages of unrestricted submarine warfare. But such views commanded only a small minority at Congress or in the Labour Party: it was the block vote of the Miners, the Railwaymen, and the Engineers which determined policy. Consequently, as soon as the war ended in November 1918 the leaders of these unions voted for the withdrawal of the Labour ministers from the Coalition, and the Labour Party prepared for an independent stand at the 'khaki' election of the following month.

The results of the 1918 general election were quite as conclusive as they were expected to be: the Lloyd George Coalition returned with 474 seats, an overwhelming majority; and to oppose them there was a Labour Party of fifty-seven and some twenty-six Asquithian Liberals. All but eight of the Labour M.P.s were trade-union nominees; and Ramsay MacDonald and all the I.L.P. Socialists in the preceding Parliament were defeated, owing to the voters' hostility to the pacifists. In the absence of more competent parliamentarians the party chairmanship fell to Willie Adamson, a Fife miner; and MacDonald, in his exile from the House of Commons, referred contemptuously to the new Labour M.P.s as 'a party of checkweighmen'.

The Coalition Government now had the task of making peace, of demobilizing the troops, and of re-establishing a peace-time economy. One of its first measures after the announcement of the armistice had been to repeal the compulsory arbitration clauses of the Munitions Acts, and to make the existing wage rates enforceable as legal minima for a period. In the course of 1919 a Restoration of Pre-war Practices Act was passed, which obliged employers to accept the return, for a time at least, of the trade practices which had been put aside by the Treasury Agreement or by the Munitions Acts. An Industrial Courts Act set up a permanent arbitration tribunal, known as the Industrial Court, to which disputes could be voluntarily referred by the two parties concerned; but the State could no longer compel the enforcement of the decision. Minimum wages, it is true, were permanently enforceable over a wider range of occupations than before the war, owing to the extension of the 1909 Trade Boards Act by an Amending Act of 1918, and owing to the fact that an Agricultural Wages Board had been set up by the Corn Production Act of 1917. But at the end of 1919 the only industries still under direct State control were the mines and the railways.

For a time it was hoped by the more moderate elements on both sides of industry that the atmosphere of industrial relations after the war would be transformed for the better by the existence of Whitley Councils. These councils, composed of both employers and union leaders, were set up in many industries on the recommendation of the Whitley Committee on the Relations of Employers and Employed, which reported in 1917. The idea was that the popular demand for 'workers' control' might be met if such committees, constituted in each industry both at the national level and at the local and even workshop level, were to discuss not only wages and conditions but also general problems of industrial efficiency and management. In practice, however, the Whitley Councils did not extend very far: some industries, such as mining, cotton, and engineering, failed to establish them at all, largely because the unions were too militant to accept them; and in other industries they were established only at the national level and not in the workshops, because the employers were afraid of interference with their prerogative of management. Whitley machinery did, however, become established in the sphere of government employment – in the Post Office, in the Civil Service, and in the Royal Dockyards.

Fortunately, the return to peace-time conditions was eased by the post-war boom, which caused a heavy demand for industrial goods. There was at first little unemployment, in spite of the demobilization of millions of troops; and although in some industries there were agreements for the reduction of hours, wages retained their levels and if anything, owing to continued inflation, tended to rise. But all this was changed in the summer of 1920 when the boom broke: unemployment grew rapidly, especially in the metal trades and in building, and by June 1921 had reached 17·8 per cent of insured persons, or a total of over two millions.

In the vicissitudes of this period the tone of industrial relations was largely set by relations between the Government and workers directly under its control. Naturally a Conservative-dominated Government, as the Coalition was after the 1918 election, was not likely in peace-time to treat the unions with as much circumspection as the more broadly based governments of the war years had done. Yet this Government had to deal with a situation of greater industrial militancy than ever before. In 1918–19 there were even strikes by the police, the first of which occurred in London in August 1918, before the end of the war. About a year later another police strike which extended to the provinces was directed against the Government's refusal to allow the men to join a union. The strike was a failure in London, but in Liverpool it was more complete and led to rioting and the intervention of troops. The men concerned were dismissed and police unionism was stamped out.

In dealing with the miners the Government had to act very differently. It was faced by a difficult situation as early as January 1919, when the Miners Federation came out with drastic new demands – a six-hour day, a thirty per cent increase in wages, and the nationalization of the mines and minerals. When the Government resisted these demands the Miners Federation balloted its members and they voted six to one for a strike. Lloyd George was then forced to make concessions, and he prevented an immediate strike by agreeing to set up a Commission to consider not only wages but also the question of the ownership of the industry. The Federation was to nominate, in effect, half the members of the Commission, and it was to be presided over by a judge, Sir John Sankey. The commissioners appointed by agreement with the Federation included three miners' leaders (of whom one was Robert Smillie) and also Sidney Webb, R. H. Tawney, the Socialist historian and W.E.A. lecturer, and Sir Leo Chiozza Money, a well-known economist who had joined the Labour Party.

The Commission was required to produce an interim report on the question of wages and hours, before proceeding to the larger issue of ownership. The commissioners could not agree on their interim recommendations, but Sankey urged a scale of concessions which formed a compromise between what the Federation wanted and what the owners were prepared to offer. This was accepted by the Government, and the Federation fell into line and took what was offered – a good augury for the final result of the Commission. Thereafter the Commission's work was devoted to the wider issue, and Smillie with the help of Webb, Money, and Tawney turned the sessions into a sort of grand inquisition into the shortcomings of private enterprise. The fact that the Commission met in the King's Robing Room of the House of Lords made its deliberations seem all the more impressive. In the end, the Federation's six nominees all recommended a scheme put forward by the Federation itself for nationalization of the industry and its control by a National Mining Council, on which the Federation would be strongly represented. The coal owners and employers on the Commission opposed nationalization, but Sankey, who put in his own separate report, tipped the balance in the Federation's favour by recommending 'that the principle of State ownership of the coal mines be accepted'.

Sankey's decision was no doubt painful to Lloyd George; but whether he personally would have accepted it or not, his Conservative colleagues obviously would not. The result was that the Government rejected nationalization outright, and would only accept a more limited plan put forward by one of the other members of the Commission for the consolidation of colliery ownership. The Miners Federation rejected this course, and in the end no structural changes were enacted for the industry. The Federation appealed to the T.U.C. for its support, and late in 1919 the T.U.C. and the Labour Party launched a joint political compaign, under the title 'The Mines for the Nation', in order to win public opinion to their side.

Lloyd George's tactics had postponed an industrial crisis with the miners and had diverted their energies temporarily into what proved to be a completely barren political campaign. Meanwhile, his Government had dealt rather more brusquely with the railwaymen and had had to face a national conflict with them. The President of the Board of Trade, Sir Auckland Geddes, endeavoured to force wage reductions on the men in the industry – hardly a wise move at a time when prices were still rising. The result was a national strike in September 1919, which, of course, led to great inconvenience to the public. A novel feature of the struggle was the effort made by the National Union of Railwaymen, assisted by the Labour Research Department (an offshoot of the Fabian Society), to put its case before public opinion by advertisements in newspapers and even by preparing a film. The Government organized a not ineffective system of food distribution by lorries while the strike continued, but it lasted only seven days in all. Its early termination was largely due to the intervention of a Negotiating Committee appointed by the Transport Workers and other unions affected by the strike: employing a variety of diplomatic devices, not excluding the threat of sympathetic action, this body found a basis for a settlement whereby the Government undertook to maintain the existing wage levels for a further year.

It was inevitable that the year which followed, 1920, should see fresh industrial strife. The cost of living continued to rise for several months, and both the Miners and the Railwaymen had disputes with the Government which had only been embittered by postponement. But the first notable event of the year was the peaceful settlement of a claim by the London Dockers after both employers and unions had agreed to accept arbitration under the terms of the Industrial Courts Act of the preceding year. The Dockers' case was put by one of their national organizers, Ernest Bevin, formerly a Bristol mineral-water roundsman. Now aged thirty-nine, a heavily built but vigorous man, Bevin made a great impression on the court, particularly when he exhibited in evidence the actual amount of food that dockers and their families could buy with their existing wages. As a result, the union got most of what it claimed; and Bevin became nationally known as 'the dockers' K.C.'.

But before the year had proceeded much further, there was an unprecedented demonstration of industrial militancy for a purely political purpose. The Government was helping the Poles in their war against Soviet Russia, and at the East India docks a ship called the *Jolly George* was awaiting a shipload of munitions for their support. The dockers, with Bevin's encouragement, refused to load the ship, and prevented it from sailing. Both the Labour Party and the T.U.C. took up the issue, denounced the Government's policy, and urged industrial action if necessary to prevent any further British assistance to Poland: and a 'Council of Action' was set up to take control of the situation. It is not clear whether this determined stand was in fact responsible for the decision to cease aiding the Poles, for the Polish forces, which earlier had been in retreat before the Red Army, won a victory at the Vistula which at least guaranteed their survival. But it is clear that the Government did make such a decision, so that the first and so far the only instance in Great Britain of 'direct action' by use of the strike weapon for purely political ends appeared to have been completely successful.

Yet neither the trade unions nor the Labour Party had really embraced the idea of 'direct action' as a method of circumventing the normal constitutional processes of government; and the unions did not lose sight of their main purpose, which was to use industrial means for industrial ends. Plans were soon being made to revive the Triple Alliance between the Miners, the Railwaymen, and the Transport Workers, which had been negotiated in 1914 and 1915 but not put into operation owing to the war. The Miners persuaded their partners in the alliance to support them in their demand for fresh wage increases, and when the Miners began a strike on this issue on 16 October the Railwaymen and Transport Workers threatened to follow suit. The Government reacted at once to this unprecedented threat: it quickly passed through Parliament an Emergency Powers Bill, to provide authority for action to ensure the maintenance of essential services; and it negotiated a temporary six-month wage increase for the Miners, which enabled them to call off their strike within two weeks of its start. This was an effective demonstration of the power of the Triple Alliance, but the crisis was in reality merely postponed for half a year. The Government was seeking to gain time while pushing ahead with its plans for the decontrol of both the mines and the railways.

The depression in trade which had begun in the summer of 1920 no doubt reduced industrial militancy in some quarters, but it led to increased bitterness in the Government's relations with the Miners and Railwaymen. The Government first of all decided to decontrol both the mines and the railways on 31 August 1921; but the heavy losses being made by the coal industry led it to advance the date of transfer of the mines by five months. The coal owners for their part could see no alternative to heavy cuts in wages, which of course the Miners refused to accept. The result was that on the day of decontrol, 31 March, the miners were locked out and the Triple Alliance was again invoked. The Railwaymen and the Transport Workers agreed to begin a sympathetic strike on Saturday, 16 April; but shortly before this date a fresh attempt at negotiation began between the Government and the Miners, only to be broken off abruptly by the latter. On Friday 15 April, the day before his union was due to join the strike, J. H. Thomas of the Railwaymen demanded that the Miners should resume negotiation; and on their refusal, he and Robert Williams of the Transport Workers cancelled the sympathetic strike. The Miners stayed out; but they felt that they had been 'betrayed' by their allies, and 15 April 1921 was thereafter known as 'Black Friday'. At the end of June the Miners were forced to give way, accepting heavy cuts in their wages. The Triple Alliance was now dead: it had been killed, not so much by the 'betrayal' by Thomas and Williams as by the inherent difficulty involved in all alliances – the difficulty of securing joint action in a crisis if there is no joint control of negotiations.

Meanwhile even before the collapse of the Triple Alliance the leaders of its weakest component, the Transport Workers, had been turning their minds to the problem of building effective machinery for the coordination of all the unions' industrial action. The successful part played by the Negotiating Committee set up by the Transport Workers in settling the 1919 railway strike suggested to them the need for a permanent national authority for this purpose. Harry Gosling, who had already taken the lead in strengthening the powers of the Parliamentary Committee, in 1919 persuaded his fellow-members on that body to appoint a Coordination Committee to plan such a development. Ernest Bevin, Gosling's colleague in the Transport Workers, submitted proposals for what he called a 'General Council', to replace the Parliamentary Committee and as he put it to 'develop the industrial side of the movement as against the "deputizing" or "political" conception'. The Coordinating Committee reported favourably on this proposal to a special Congress in December 1919, and the broad outline of Bevin's plan was accepted. After further meetings of the Coordination Committee a definite plan proposed by Gosling was adopted at the 1920 Congress.

The result was that there came into existence in 1921 a General Council of some thirty members – considerably larger than the Parliamentary Committee – with powers far beyond those of its predecessor, though still not so large as to infringe the autonomy of the unions. The General Council was to 'coordinate industrial action', to promote common action by the unions on all industrial matters, to seek to prevent inter-union disputes, to help unions in their organizing work, and to enter into relations with trade-union movements in other countries. Clearly, this reconstruction of Congress leadership did not go anything like as far as the advocates of 'industrial unionism' would have liked; but even so, there was a strong minority who thought that it went too far, and Gosling discovered that he could not secure agreement for a proposal to have a permanent chairman for the General Council, who would undoubtedly have wielded great influence. The question was, could the new, rather ungainly General Council take an effective lead in future industrial struggles – so that, as Bevin suggested, 'strikes will be less because of the power of our new organization'? It remained to be seen.

The effect of 'Black Friday' and the collapse of the Triple Alliance, coupled with the trade depression, was that industrial unrest tended to die down in the immediately succeeding years. The unofficial shop stewards movement, which had been in decline since the end of the war, was finally broken by the heavy unemployment of the 1920s, although some of its leaders adapted themselves to the situation and set up what they called the National Unemployed Workers Committee Movement. But all the elements of the pre-war and war-time industrial left wing – the syndicalists, the Labour College movement, the National Guilds League, as well as the Workers Committee Movement – were disrupted by the Bolshevik revolution. Many of the foremost unofficial strike leaders decided to follow the star of Lenin, and Lenin urged them repeatedly to accept the need for political as well as industrial action and to join the Marxists of the British Socialist Party in adherence to the Third International. Thus the Communist Party of Great Britain came into existence in 1920–1 as an amalgam of all these groups – an amalgam, however, that in the following decade was itself never as large as the pre-war British Socialist Party alone.

The National Guilds League, the organization of the Guild Socialists, was also weakened by other factors. Late in 1920 and in 1921 a number of building guilds had been formed under trade-union control, and they had secured important construction contracts from local authorities in the post-war housing boom. Many of these contracts were successfully completed; and while the work was going on, a National Building Guild was formed to coordinate the whole movement. But the collapse of the boom in 1922 and the guilds' inadequate financial backing led to their rapid disintegration. The National Building Guild itself had to go into liquidation at the end of the year. All this was very damaging not only to the Guild Socialists but also to the Left in general. It was not merely a coincidence that in 1922 the *Daily Herald* was obliged to seek a subsidy from the T.U.C. and the Labour Party, which it obtained at the expense of its old independence.

Meanwhile the unions themselves, after many years of rapid gains in membership, were beginning to lose members and were feeling the need for consolidation. Whether owing to apathy or to conservatism, it had proved very difficult for union leaders to persuade a sufficient number of their members to accept amalgamations with other unions under the terms of the 1876 Act, which required a majority in a total poll of at least two-thirds of the qualified members. The process was, however, simplified by the Trade Union (Amalgamation) Act, passed in 1917 on the initiative of John Hodge as Minister of Labour. Hodge's own union, the Steel Smelters, had already negotiated an extremely ingenious scheme to overcome the limitations of the 1876 Act and to create a new union called the British Iron, Steel, and Kindred Trades Association; this scheme was already being brought to fruition in 1917. But in a few years' time there followed various other amalgamations. The most important were: the creation of the Amalgamated Engineering Union (A.E.U.) in 1921, out of a combination of the Amalgamated Society of Engineers and several smaller unions; the formation of the Transport and General Workers Union in 1922 on the basis of the dockers' and carters' unions; and the emergence of the National Union of General and Municipal Workers in 1924 out of several general unions, the principal one being Will Thorne's Gasworkers. Of these amalgamations the most effective strategically and, in the long run, numerically was that which established the Transport and General Workers Union, which soon rendered the Transport Workers Federation unnecessary, and which owed its success to Ernest Bevin. Bevin became the secretary of the new union and continued to build it up by the absorption of smaller unions and by fresh organizing, until eventually it became the largest union in the country.

In 1922 the Coalition Government broke up, owing to the unwillingness of the Conservatives to carry on under Lloyd George; and a new general election took place. The Labour Party, reorganized in 1918 by Arthur Henderson so as to permit individual membership in addition to that of affiliated societies and unions, had developed a degree of popular strength in most constituencies, and it put forward no less than 414 candidates. It won 142 seats, which was twice the number it had at the dissolution. Of these, eighty-five were trade-union nominees – the largest total ever, but a smaller proportion of the party, which also included thirty-two representatives of the I.L.P. The Socialist element in the party had re-emerged in force, and when Parliament met, Ramsay MacDonald was elected chairman of the party. He also became official Leader of the Opposition in the Commons, for the Labour Party was now larger than the fragments of the Liberal Party put together. Although many trade unionists still regarded MacDonald with suspicion, most of them acknowledged his ability; and the movement as a whole began to think that after all Parliament might provide a shorter cut to social improvement than industrial action.

Yet even those who were most sanguine about the prospects of the Labour Party were surprised by the rapidity with which it actually came to form a government. At the end of 1923 Stanley Baldwin, the new Conservative Prime Minister, decided to try to reunite his rather divided party by fighting a general election on the tariff-reform issue. The country was still not prepared to commit itself to tariff reform, and so both the Labour and Liberal Parties won seats – the Labour Party rising to 191, and the Liberals, now reunited, securing 158. The Conservatives were still the largest party, but having lost the election, they could hardly retain office. Asquith, the Liberal leader, declared that his party would support a Labour Government, and so in January 1924 the King asked Ramsay MacDonald to take office.

MacDonald naturally faced considerable difficulties in forming his ministry. His party was a minority party, and in addition it was woefully short of administrative experience and talent. The new Prime Minister had never held Cabinet office before; many of the senior Labour M.P.s – mostly veteran trade-union leaders – appeared to lack the capacity to control government departments, while the more promising junior men seemed to be very left-wing. MacDonald overcame his difficulties by bringing into the Cabinet a number of prominent figures from outside the party – Lord Haldane, Lord Parmoor, and Lord Chelmsford. The Cabinet of twenty members in fact contained only seven men from the trade unions.

In its relations with the trade-union movement as a whole, MacDonald's Government behaved singularly like other governments, in spite of the organic link of the unions with the Labour Party. This was partly, of course, because it was a minority government unable to pass legislation without Liberal support. But it was also partly due to the fact that any government necessarily has to take an independent view of industrial problems, and to place the national interest before sectional loyalties. This was shown within a few days, when a strike of 110,000 dock workers took place. The strike was settled in three days; but the Government had already made arrangements to use troops for the movement of essential supplies, under the control of Colonel Josiah Wedgwood – not a union man – as Chief Civil Commissioner. Ernest Bevin is supposed to have commented on this by saying:

I only wish it had been a Tory government in office. We would not have been frightened by *their* threats. But we were put in the position of having to listen to the appeal of our own people.

A few weeks later, a strike of London tram workers took place. It was agreed that the men had a strong claim to higher wages, but the companies could not afford to pay. The strike caused a good deal of inconvenience to the public, and there was a threat of its spread to the Underground. The Government therefore contemplated action under the Emergency Powers Act, the enactment of which its leaders had strongly opposed less than four years previously. Both the General Council and the Labour Party executive protested against this move, but fortunately for the unity of the labour movement a compromise settlement was quickly worked out which enabled the pay advances to be made on the understanding that the Government would sponsor a Bill to coordinate the London transport system.

There were other less important industrial conflicts which created friction between the Labour Government and the unions before the Government fell in November 1924. The experience of only a few months' rule by the political arm of their own movement was enough to convince union leaders, in the words of W. J. Brown at the 1925 T.U.C., that

Even with a complete Labour majority in the House, and with a Labour government which was stable and secure, there would be a permanent difference in point of view between the government on the one hand and the trade unions on the other. . . . The trade unions had different functions to perform than the functions of government.

In any case the Labour Government had not been able to pass any important domestic legislation, and the unemployment problem remained as serious as ever. The Conservatives won a considerable success in the general election of November 1924, gaining a substantial majority of seats and reducing the Labour Party to a total of 151. The only satisfaction that Labour leaders could derive from the results was that the Liberals suffered much worse than they did, being reduced to only forty M.P.s. But there was no alternative now to several years of Conservative rule; and in the meantime great distress prevailed in many export industries, even employed workers being distinctly worse off than they had been before the war. It is not surprising, therefore, that the defeat suffered by the Labour Party turned the trade unions back to a more exclusive reliance on industrial action, and made their leaders contemplate some sort of effectively coordinated action by the newly organized General Council of the T.U.C.

Since 1921, when the General Council came into existence, a good start had been made in building up its administration. Fred Bramley, a well-known Socialist propagandist who had been appointed assistant secretary in 1918, was largely responsible for this. An energetic man still in his forties, he succeeded Bowerman as secretary when the latter retired in 1923. Walter Citrine, assistant secretary of the Electrical Trades Union, who was aged thirty-six, was then appointed to the post vacated by Bramley; and when Bramley died prematurely in 1925 Citrine became acting secretary of the T.U.C. and was confirmed in the post without opposition at the 1926 Congress. Thus, in the space of three years the precedent was established that the secretary should be appointed from within the Congress staff; and by the accident of Bramley's death the T.U.C. secured its youngest secretary for half a century.

The size of the staff recruited by the secretary rapidly increased. For some years in the early 1920s there were a number of joint departments with the Labour Party, which were supervised by the Joint Council representing the two bodies. These were the Research, the Press and Publicity, and the International Departments. But Bramley soon concluded that the economy secured in joint operation was not worth the clumsiness and friction that resulted. The period of the Labour Government was decisive: he himself never had more than five minutes' conversation with the Prime Minister throughout. Accordingly, early in 1926 the staffs were separated and the T.U.C. henceforth shared with the Labour Party only a library and a telephone operator. By this time Citrine had also established an Organization Department to deal with the organization of trade unions and similar matters. Yet the General Council had no control over individual unions: it could only endeavour to adjudicate demarcation disputes if both parties agreed that it should do so; and if in a sense its staff had now become the 'general staff' of the movement, it was a 'general staff' able to plan if required but unable to secure the execution of plans.

Under the peculiar conditions of 1925 and 1926, however, the General Council was provided with authority which went far beyond its constitutional powers. A new mining crisis was responsible for this. In 1924 the coal owners agreed to an increase in wages, but in 1925, after the Conservative Government's re-adoption of the gold standard, exports fell off again and the owners demanded a return to low wages and a restoration of the eight-hour day. The Miners Federation refused to accept such terms, but its leaders found themselves at a disadvantage in striking owing to the existing stockpiles of coal. They therefore appealed to the General Council for help, and received a sympathetic reception, for most union officials felt a certain collective guilt for the 'Black Friday' episode four years earlier. Besides, the General Council had swung temporarily to the Left, owing to the loss of its leading moderates, especially J. H. Thomas, to the Labour Government. Acting this time at the request of the General Council, the Railwaymen and the Transport Workers agreed in July 1925 to place an embargo upon the movement of coal.

The threat was sufficient to bring about immediate government intervention. Baldwin, who was again Prime Minister, offered a temporary subsidy in order to maintain miners' wages and hours at their existing levels, while a Royal Commission drew up a scheme for the future of the industry. This offer was accepted, and the unions rejoiced in what they regarded as a victory for united action – 'Red Friday'. But the Royal Commission, under the chairmanship of the former Liberal minister Sir Herbert Samuel, bore no similarity to the Commission of 1919. It contained no members or partisans of the Miners Federation, and when it reported early in 1926 it recommended certain reductions in wages as essential to make the industry profitable. The Miners Federation was now led by a group of bitter and obstinate men; its secretary was A. J. Cook, one of the pre-war syndicalists of the South Wales district, who coined the slogan: 'Not a penny off the pay, not a second on the day!' Accordingly, they rejected the Samuel Report and prepared for a lock-out of the miners on 1 May, when the temporary subsidy ran out.

The General Council now had to prepare for its part in the

struggle. It continued to negotiate with the Government for a settlement of the miners' claims, but at its meeting on 27 April it set up a committee to prepare a plan for strike action. A conference of trade-union executives was summoned, and it met on 29 April at the Memorial Hall in Farringdon Street, where the Labour Party had been founded a quarter of a century earlier. There the delegates had to wait while last-minute negotiations went on between the General Council and the Government. They passed the time singing hymns and popular songs; but on 1 May they were called upon to authorize the General Council to undertake 'the conduct of the dispute', which they did with almost complete unanimity. The roll of the unions was called, starting somewhat in-auspiciously with the Union of Asylum Workers, and in turn they pledged their support. A last-minute attempt at nego-tiation was broken off by the Government on 3 May when the compositors working on the *Daily Mail* held up pro-duction of the paper. On 4 May, the so-called General Strike began.

The Government had been making careful preparations for a General Strike since 'Red Friday' in July 1925. A capable civil servant, Sir John Anderson, had been asked to draw up a plan, and this had been completed by November. In addi-tion, an unofficial body called the Organization for the Main-tenance of Supplies had been set up for the recruitment of volunteers to take the place of strikers. The General Council, on the other hand, had only begun to work out the details of its organization a week before the stoppage began. Yet its arrangements were basically sound, and their success cannot be questioned. In addition to a million miners already on strike, some million and a half more men were called out. They consisted of all types of transport workers, printers of both books and newspapers, some building workers, and those in the iron and steel, heavy chemical, and power indus-tries. Those who were allowed to continue at work included the textile trades and post office and distributive workers. Engineering and ship-building workers were only called out after a week had elapsed. It was not, therefore, in the true sense a 'General Strike', and the General Council refused to call it by this name; nevertheless, because it was much more 'general' than any previous or subsequent strike, it has always been so described.

The success of the immediate strike plan may be judged by the solidarity of the response to the General Council's call. On the railways the proportion of engine drivers who reported for work on 4 May was little more than one per cent; of firemen, considerably less; of guards, about the same. In London the first day saw hardly any buses, trams, or underground trains still running; the docks, the furnaces, and the power stations all became as silent as the pits. The newspapers were all closed down, and the Government had to rely at first on the B.B.C. for the dissemination of news: soon an official paper called the *British Gazette* was issued. In the non-industrial parts of the country life went on much as before; but in all the large centres of population it was a strange and even eery experience.

The General Council at first tried to exercise a general supervision of the strike while sitting in full session at the T.U.C. office in Eccleston Square. Within twenty-four hours, however, Ernest Bevin, although a newcomer to the Council, had taken the initiative and persuaded his colleagues to hand over various responsibilities to sub-committees, under the supreme control of a small Strike Organization Committee. He himself, as secretary of the key Transport and General Workers Union, became a member of this supreme body. Meanwhile, in all provincial cities and towns local strike committees came into existence, usually being based on the trades councils. In many cases they assumed the militant title of 'Councils of Action'. Communications between them and Eccleston Square were maintained by dispatch riders and also, from 5 May, by the publication of a special newspaper on behalf of the General Council, under the title of the *British Worker*.

Meanwhile the Government had been using troops, police, and special constables to secure the maintenance of essential supplies, and volunteers were recruited to get the transport services going again. Large numbers of people, especially students, came forward to try their hand at driving trains and buses and at loading and unloading cargoes as well as other jobs; and many of them enjoyed it enormously. But it was easier to get a few buses on the road than to run the complicated organization of the railways, and very few train services could be restored. There were occasional accidents and frequent long delays; and a local strike committee ironically reported: 'We understand that luncheon cars are to be put on trains running between Westminster and Blackfriars.' Here and there, strike pickets clashed with what they regarded as blackleg labour, and windows of buses and railways carriages on the move were often broken. But probably there were more injuries caused by accidents due to inexperience than by the malice of the strikers. Conditions varied locally: at Plymouth things were so quiet that a football match could be arranged between the strikers and the police; at Newcastle there was rioting, baton charges by the police, and arrests of strike leaders.

After the strike had lasted two days Sir John Simon, a former Liberal Attorney-General, made a speech in the Commons in which he declared that the General Council's action was altogether illegal. He said that trade-union leaders who had called out their men were personally liable for damages, and that trade-union funds would not be immune. The speech was evidently designed to intimidate the strikers, but it had little effect. A few days later it was answered by Sir Henry Slesser, who had been Solicitor-General in the Labour Government. Slesser maintained that the strike was only illegal if it could be proved to be a seditious conspiracy against the State, and there was no evidence that this was the case.

Slesser's views were probably nearer the truth than Simon's. Sympathetic strikes for industrial purposes were not illegal, and in spite of the syndicalist views of a small minority of trade unionists, there could be no suggestion that this was a strike for other than industrial ends. Indeed, this was precisely the difficulty under which the members of the General Council laboured: having no revolutionary purpose in mind, they were as much afraid of a state of political chaos as the Government was; and as the days went by and the Government continued to ensure the movement of essential supplies, they could see no solution except through the resumption of negotiations. Several of them, and particularly J. H. Thomas, seemed afraid that they might lose control of their followers and that matters might get entirely out of hand; they were all the more anxious to grasp at any chance to resume talks with the Cabinet.

The opportunity occurred with the return from abroad of Sir Herbert Samuel, the chairman of the 1925 Royal Commission. Samuel got in touch with Thomas and with members of the Cabinet; and soon he was meeting a Negotiating Committee of the General Council and trying to work out a formula that both sides could accept. He drew up a memorandum of points for the settlement of the Miners' strike along the lines of his Commission's report; and this the Negotiating Committee accepted. Unfortunately there was no Miners' leader on the Negotiating Committee: the Miners Federation executive had dispersed from London, and it was only later that they had an opportunity to see the Samuel memorandum, which not unexpectedly they rejected. This did not, however, prevent the Negotiating Committee from continuing along the same lines: on the contrary, having discovered that the attitude of the Miners was completely negative, they felt relieved from the necessity of consulting them further. Indeed, they hastily persuaded the General Council to undertake to call off the strike on the basis of Samuel's points; and without securing any commitment whatsoever from the Government, a deputation was at once sent to announce this decision to the Prime Minister at 10 Downing Street. Bevin, who was on the deputation but had not been on the Negotiating Committee, endeavoured to secure some sort of undertaking about the reinstatement of strikers and the withdrawal of the coal owners' lock-out notices; but Baldwin in reply was studiously vague, and Bevin began to realize that the return to work was taking place in the form of a complete surrender. As he went out he said to his colleagues J. H. Thomas and Arthur Pugh, the General Council chairman: 'There's something wrong here.' But it was too late to draw back: the decision had been made. It was 12 May, the ninth day of the strike.

The sudden order to resume work was puzzling to many of the strikers, but the Negotiating Committee tried to conceal the fact that it was in fact a surrender. The *British Worker* carried the misleading headline: 'The Terms of Peace: Miners Ensured a Square Deal'. Those returning to their jobs soon found that victimization was taking place, and bewilderment turned to anger: they came out on strike once more, and for some days the life of the country was as uncertain as before. Gradually, it dawned on the men that their nine days' solidarity had ended in a humiliating defeat. As for the Miners, they stayed on strike, feeling betrayed as in 1921.

Was the ending of the General Strike in fact a betrayal of the rank and file? To the extreme Left, it has always seemed so. But neither the leaders nor the great body of the strikers really intended that the strike should turn into a revolutionary outbreak; and consequently, in the face of a government determined to resist its pretensions, the General Council had no alternative but to give way sooner or later. The Negotiating Committee, and particularly Thomas, must bear some blame for their failure to secure the slightest concession from the Government, and for their attempt to conceal their failure from their colleagues. At the same time, the complete inflexibility of the Miners, and the absence of their leaders from London, was equally inexcusable. As for the Government, Baldwin was unwilling actively to seek any compromise solution or to override the owners. By failing to offer any terms, he risked the continuance of civil strife in the future. On both sides there were hardly any leaders who came out of the affair with any credit. In the General Council the only obvious exception was Ernest Bevin, who had not been on the Negotiating Committee, but who had shown energy and decision in the work of organization. In the short run, however, he did not escape a share of the blame.

The dozen years 1914–26 had seen some remarkable ups and downs in the development of trade unionism. It was a period which included a phase of intimate cooperation between the union leadership and the Government, and another phase which culminated in the bitterest conflict between them that the country has ever experienced. It saw both the greatest expansion of trade-union membership – from just over four million in 1914 to twice that figure in 1920 – and also the heaviest loss of members that ever occurred in so short a time – over two and a half millions in the immediately succeeding two years. It saw the rise of the unofficial shop stewards' movement in the munition factories, and its almost complete collapse after 1918. But there were some consistent tendencies in the story of these years. In spite of unemployment, union membership in 1926 was still very much larger than in 1914, and the average size of unions had risen from 3,290 members to 4,480. Generally speaking the proportionate influence of the unionism of the old staple industries, coal and cotton, was in decline: in 1914 the Miners and the Textile Workers between them amounted to over thirty per cent of the total membership of the unions; by 1926 their proportion was down to less than twenty-one per cent. By comparison, transport and general labour unions had gained ground. Unskilled workers had benefited enormously during the war, when flat-rate increases in wages had often been awarded to all, thus diminishing the differential advantage formerly enjoyed by the skilled. Thus, although after the war the problems of the mining industry still dominated industrial politics, it was obvious that the new general unions would play an increasing part in the future control of the movement.

Already in the early 1920s it was the Transport Workers who had pressed for an increase in the powers of the T.U.C., and they had got their way. The old conservatism of the Parliamentary Committee had owed much to the attitude of the Miners in the days of their prosperity, when they could afford to go their own way, ignoring the clamour of the weaker unions for common political and industrial action. By the close of the period that we have been considering the Miners had lost their proud self-sufficiency, and had been forced to call for help from a whole range of unions which at one time they had regarded as of little account. Their leaders, chosen for their obstinacy rather than for their negotiating skill, lacked the capacity to take a long view of industrial problems.

But the bitterness that entered the relations between the Government and the trade-union movement as a whole in this period was not primarily the fault of the unions. Politically, it owed not a little to the effect of the war on the party system, breaking up the Liberals and forcing the electors to choose at once between a very inexperienced Labour Party and a Conservative Party in which employers' interests were dominant. Economically, it stemmed from the increasing unprofitability of the country's staple export trades, which weakened the employers' capacity to provide adequate wages without in any way reducing the workers' expectations. The importance attached by the war-time Government to the cooperation of the unions and of the industrial labour force as a whole only heightened the feelings of resentment which union members felt as a result of their treatment in the post-war period.

The idea of joint industrial action by means of a Triple Alliance, and later by a national sympathetic strike under the General Council's control, certainly owed something to the syndicalism which had flourished in the pre-war era of industrial unrest. But it was above all the logical conclusion of a constant broadening of the field of industrial conflict. The preceding period had seen the forging of the weapon of the national strike, first by the Engineers, but soon also by the Railwaymen, the Miners, and, with less success, the Transport Workers. The idea of cooperation between unions with a large degree of national strength emerged quite naturally from this, and in turn the national strike under the control of the General Council emerged from the failure of the Triple Alliance. Only in 1926 did the union leaders appreciate the political implications of their industrial evolution, and realize that the General Strike – as the public insisted on calling it – was nothing but a dead end. The loyalty of the rank and file in the General Strike showed the extraordinary strength and influence of British trade unionism: the abject surrender of its leaders showed how fundamentally devoid of ulterior political purposes it was. As Beatrice Webb wrote rather sadly in her diary for 18 May that year: 'The failure of the General Strike shows what a *sane* people the British are.'

PART THREE

PROBLEMS OF NATIONAL INTEGRATION

THE SETTING

THE period from the end of the General Strike to the present day has seen the gradual integration of the unions into many but by no means all of the processes of government, and the acknowledgement of many of their purposes in the social policy and legislation of the time, even under governments of a Conservative hue. All this has come about in spite of the bitterness aroused by the conflicts and strikes of the preceding period, which had culminated in the General Strike.

More important than anything else in encouraging integration, on the side of the Government, was the unprecedented economic blizzard of the early 1930s. It is true that this led in the first instance to the precipitate fall of the second Labour Government and the installation of a largely Conservative coalition pledged to recovery on comparatively orthodox lines; but in practice the Cabinet contained enough ex-Liberals and ex-Labour men to strengthen the moderate wing of the Conservative Party on domestic questions, and to ensure a more accommodating attitude towards the unions than had been shown by Conservative Governments previously. State assistance to particular industries brought the Government into closer links with both employers and unions – a tendency reinforced at the end of the decade, with the beginnings of rearmament and the preparations for war-time mobilization.

The Second World War, like its predecessor, brought a deep involvement of the unions in government and administration – with, however, a much greater permanent effect than before. The involvement began early in the war; it was even more extensive than before, and it lasted longer, not merely because the war lasted longer, but because it was maintained almost in its entirety for several years after the end of hostilities. The Labour Government of 1945–51 retained much of the wartime apparatus of control, partly on grounds of principle, partly because of the sheer necessity imposed upon it by the difficulties of recovery. It persuaded the unions not only to agree to this but to go further – to accept a measure of voluntary 'wage restraint' for the sake of the stability of the domestic price level and the encouragement of exports. This would not have been possible if the unions had not been satisfied with the general fiscal and social policies being pursued at the time.

The return of Conservative rule in 1951, no longer as previously in the modified form of a coalition, might have been expected to see a reversion to the attitudes of the 1920s. But times had changed, and with them both the Conservative Party and the unions. The new Government was pledged to the continuation of the policy of full employment, adopted by all parties in the war-time coalition at the time of the publication of the 1944 White Paper. Further, it was anxious to reconcile the unions and to disengage them from their constant support of the Labour Party. The unions for their part wished to maintain the advantages which had now long been accruing to them from close association with the administration. Their position in the industries nationalized in the preceding years was in any case secured by law. Social security and regular employment had healed many of the scars of class conflict, and new advances in the standard of living were tending to break down old social barriers. Manual workers did not necessarily give up voting Labour, but they took their politics less seriously than before. And the T.U.C. itself, especially when it moved its headquarters to its new building in Great Russell Street, seemed to make a point of asserting its complete independence from the Labour Party – a matter of some importance if it were to attract the affiliation of the white-collar unions.

Yet there were clear limits to the extent to which the unions were prepared to become integrated into the administrative machine. Throughout the post-war years, and not least under the Labour Governments on either side of the thirteen Conservative years, the union leaders had always shown a marked reluctance to sacrifice their liberty of action in wage-bargaining. The system of industrial relations which had developed in years of mutual distrust between employer and employed, and when the entire legal profession was regarded as hostile, was too well established to be easily transformed. And although the T.U.C. was prepared to co-operate with governments of the day in the search for a voluntary incomes policy, it could not secure the effective collaboration of its constituent unions for any proposal to make such a policy compulsory. The basic problem of how to secure justice for wage-earners without inflationary damage to the economy was never solved.

There were difficulties for the unions, too, which were presented by their very success in institutionalizing themselves and winning a say in government administration. Industrial developments did not correspond to union structure; there was much overlapping of recruitment, particularly in new industries, and the old system of local branch organization outside the factory was widely being rendered obsolete by the growing power of shop stewards. Unofficial strikes, over which the official leaders had little or no control, became more and more frequent and did much damage to the reputation of the unions. The Donovan Commission of 1965–8 pointed the way to a gradual cure of these disorders; but a new Conservative Government, elected in 1970, insisted on the application of more immediate and drastic remedies.

The T.U.C.'s fight against the Industrial Relations Act, 1971, and its eventual success, is dealt with in the penultimate chapter. For a time the Social Contract with the Labour Government elected in 1974 appeared to offer a solution of the problem of wage inflation. With its breakdown in 1978–9, and the consequent election of a new Conservative Government, the unions had again to face legislation designed to weaken their bargaining strength in various ways. How far this legislation's success was due to more successful formulation than in 1970–1, and how far it was simply due to the recurrence of mass unemployment, is something that remains to be determined in the late 1980s.

CHAPTER TEN

SLUMP AND RECOVERY, 1926–39

THE immediate sequel to the General Strike was a considerable loss of prestige to the unions in general and to the General Council in particular. The total union membership affiliated to the T.U.C. declined by almost half a million between 1925 and 1927. Especially strong criticism of the General Council naturally came from the Miners Federation, whose members remained on strike until the end of November. The tiny Communist Party also attacked the trade-union leadership, and began to recruit members rapidly, especially among the miners, so that by the end of the year its membership had doubled to a total of some 12,000. Through the agency of the National Minority Movement, the Communists sought to build up opposition to the existing union leaders, with a view to their eventual replacement. There was also a much more widespread dissatisfaction with the explanations given for the failure of the General Strike, and a demand for a full post mortem. But in response to a request from the Miners Federation, the General Council's formal report to the unions on its conduct of the strike was delayed until after the Miners' struggle was over. It seemed at first that the delay would be especially damaging to the General Council's reputation, for its members could not in the meantime defend themselves against attack.

Yet by January 1927, when the General Council did make its report to a conference of trade-union executives, the tide of opinion was flowing strongly against the Left. A few months' reflection, combined with the failure of the Miners' strike, had had the effect of convincing unionists that the weapon of the General Strike was itself at fault, rather than the leaders who had endeavoured to wield it. The sympathy with syndicalist methods which had existed in some quarters – described by Beatrice Webb as 'a proletarian distemper which had to run its course' – was now clearly in decline. The end of the Miners' struggle was followed rapidly by the exodus from the Communist Party of almost all its new recruits; and the Federation itself was weakened by losses of membership and by the competition of a so-called 'nonpolitical' union formed in Nottinghamshire by George Spencer, a right-wing Labour M.P. Spencer opposed the continuance of the strike in the knowledge that the owners in the more prosperous areas, including his own, were willing to make favourable local agreements.

Meanwhile, the political and industrial sides of the Labour movement had been brought closer together in resistance to the Government's injudicious legislation against unionism. In 1927 a measure was passed, under the title of the Trade Disputes and Trade Union Act, to declare illegal any sympathetic strike action in furtherance of a trade dispute except from 'within the trade or industry in which the strikers are engaged', or any attempt to 'coerce the government either directly or by inflicting hardship on the community'. In addition the Act declared various forms of industrial action illegal as 'intimidation', introduced a 'contracting-in' system for the payment of the political levy to the Labour Party, and forbade established civil servants to join trade unions in affiliation with the T.U.C. The measure was bitterly opposed at all its stages by the Labour Party in Parliament, but it was forced through the Commons by the use of the 'guillotine'.

The immediate effect of the Trade Disputes and Trade Union Act was to reduce the Labour Party's income from trade-union affiliation fees by a third. This was because the party lost the financial support of those who did not bother to contract-in, but who previously had not bothered to contract-out. But the long-term result was to strengthen the trade-union leaders' support for the Labour Party, for they resented the Act as an infringement of their privileges. Although the clauses against sympathetic strikes were never invoked, they stood upon the Statute Book as a constant threat; and the union leaders determined to have them repealed as soon as possible. They were not successful in this for almost twenty years; but in the meantime the somewhat battered relationship between the unions and the Labour Party was strengthened by their resolve.

Nothing could have provided a clearer indication of the change in the temper of the union leaders than their willingness to take part in what became known as the Mond–Turner talks of 1928–9. Sir Alfred Mond was the chairman of Imperial Chemical Industries and Ben Turner was the chairman of the T.U.C. General Council in 1928. It was Mond who suggested that there would be mutual advantage to both employers and union officials in a frank discussion of their points of difference; and the General Council, finding that no subjects were to be ruled out of the discussion, decided to accept the invitation. The remarkable thing was not that the union leaders should want to meet the employers face to face, but that they dared to risk the hostility of the Left and the suspicion of the rank and file in doing so. In fact, not much came out of the talks, except a frank admission by the employers participating that it was 'definitely in the interests of all concerned in industry' for workmen to belong to unions. But a bitter attack on 'Mondism' by the Miners' leader A. J. Cook was easily defeated at the 1928 T.U.C.; and the General Council, at a time when its national prestige was low, gained credit in the eyes of public opinion for its undoctrinaire attitude to Mond's initiative. In addition, personal friendships were formed between business men and union leaders which were to be of great importance when collaboration between them again became possible.

In sponsoring the Mond–Turner talks on the T.U.C. side, perhaps the most important single individual was Ernest Bevin. Bevin's position in the trade-union movement was becoming an increasingly influential one. It was advanced by a merger that he negotiated in 1928 between his union and the Workers Union, which was the third largest of the general unions. Although the Transport and General Workers Union was in severe financial difficulty after the General Strike – as indeed were many of the unions – Bevin pressed ahead with his plans for the construction of a large building in West-

minster, which was to house not only the union's headquarters but also the offices of both the T.U.C. and the
Labour Party. The building, known as Transport House,
was officially opened in May 1928, and Bevin became the
landlord of the Labour movement. Even more important
was his role in the development of the *Daily Herald*, which
was running into financial difficulties in competition with
the big popular papers such as the *Express* and the *Mail*. In
1929 Bevin negotiated an agreement with J. S. Elias, the
managing director of Odhams, whereby that firm agreed to
take over and expand the newspaper, while guaranteeing the
maintenance of its existing political standpoint. The General
Council was to nominate four out of a total of nine directors
of the paper, and these four were to have control in questions
of political and industrial policy. The Labour Party, which
had previously had a share in the control, now dropped out,
but it was laid down that the political policy should be that of
the Labour Party. All the same, it was the four T.U.C.
directors who were to interpret that policy. The first ap-
pointees were Bevin, Citrine, and Arthur Pugh of the Iron
and Steel Trades Confederation, who all saw eye to eye on
most issues, and Ben Tillett, the veteran dockers' leader.
Before the agreement with Odhams the paper had a circulation of only a quarter of a million; afterwards it at once
leapt to a million and soon became a power in the land. In
1933 it was the first daily newspaper to reach a regular circulation of two millions. And Bevin, who had made the
agreement with Odhams, continued to play the major role
in the determination of its editorial policy.

Bevin did not always get on with his colleagues: he was too
forceful a personality for that. But he was honest and loyal to
those he trusted, and his attitude was never narrowly sectional. He worked particularly well with Citrine. The two
men were very different in temperament, Citrine's precise
mind contrasting with Bevin's imaginative but undisciplined
intellect. But Citrine has said that he cannot recall a difference in principle with Bevin, and that 'the close resemblance
of our thinking on occasions was very embarrassing to me'.
The collaboration of the two men, however 'embarrassing' to
the T.U.C. secretary, was to provide the movement with the

strongest leadership that it has ever had, over a vital period of some fourteen years.

In May 1929 a new general election took place, the existing Conservative Government having almost reached its five-year term. The persistence of heavy unemployment was perhaps the decisive factor in causing the electorate to turn against the Government: the Labour Party now for the first time emerged as the largest party in Parliament, with 288 M.P.s as against 261 Conservatives and fifty-seven Liberals. A new Labour Government was formed, again with the support of the Liberals, and again with Ramsay MacDonald as Prime Minister. With the experience of 1924 behind him and with the talents of a substantially enlarged parliamentary party at his disposal, MacDonald could make very nearly all his appointments without the need to bring in ministers from outside the labour movement. All the same, the trade-union representation dropped slightly. There were six trade-union sponsored Ministers in the Cabinet, as against seven in 1924, and the only newcomer among them was Margaret Bondfield of the General and Municipal Workers, who became Minister of Labour. Of the appointments outside the Cabinet, eleven came from the ranks of the trade-union sponsored M.P.s compared with seventeen in 1924. To some extent this reflected a decline in the proportion of trade-union sponsored M.P.s in the parliamentary party, which was now only forty per cent, whereas in 1924 it had been fifty-eight per cent. This decline, in turn, was due partly to the shortage of trade-union funds for political activity after the General Strike and the 1927 Act, and partly to the fact that in any case trade-union sponsored candidatures were rarer among the less completely industrial constituencies which the party was now beginning to win.

As in 1924, the Government found itself forced to take an independent attitude during the strikes which occurred while it was in office; but there were in fact none which endangered essential supplies and thus occasioned dramatic government intervention. In 1930 a strike took place in the Yorkshire woollen industry, in which Miss Bondfield intervened only to bring the two sides together, saying with a due Whitehall correctness: 'It is not for me to express any view upon the merits of the case.' In fact, no settlement was arrived at, and the workers went back to their jobs after a humiliating defeat.

To ease the difficulties of the miners, the Labour Party had promised in its election programme to reduce the working day to seven hours. As a result, in December a Bill was introduced to effect this gradually, and in the first instance to establish a working day of seven and a half hours. After some amendment by the House of Lords, which weakened the effect of the reduction, the Bill was passed into law in 1930. The Miners Federation then began to press for a new minimum wage, bringing up to date the Minimum Wage Act of 1912. But the most that they could obtain was the temporary stabilization of their existing wages. The fact was that in the existing state of the industry there was no solution except by subsidy, and Snowden as Chancellor was just as unwilling to subsidize coal as any of his predecessors had been.

The Government's concern for economy in spending was to prove the main stumbling block in its relations with the trade unions, and especially with the T.U.C. General Council. As the economic depression worsened, so the difficulty of making revenue balance expenditure constantly increased. In November 1930 the Cabinet, worried by the way in which unemployment insurance payments were depleting existing funds, decided to establish a Royal Commission on Unemployment Insurance. It did this without any consultation with members of the General Council as to its nature or composition, and the Council reacted vigorously with a private letter of protest, which stated:

There have been a number of incidents which have occurred during the lifetime of the present Government and which have caused perplexity and uneasiness to the General Council, but the Council, conscious as they have been of some of the difficulties confronting the Government, have refrained from any action which might have had the effect of embarrassing the Government, The Council feel they can remain silent no longer, and the way in which they have been treated in respect of this Royal Commission shows an absence of appreciation on the part of the Government of the responsibilities of the General Council's own position.

The Council was with difficulty persuaded to give evidence before the Commission, but it objected strongly to the Commission's report, which recommended increased contributions and reductions in benefit. MacDonald in this instance took note of the Council's objections and decided not to implement the report except in certain limited respects. The Council was somewhat appeased by the Bill which was passed in July 1931, and which made provision for representation of the T.U.C. on the advisory committee set up to report on any anomalies in the operation of the system.

By this time, however, the general economic difficulties of the Government were becoming acute. Unemployment continued to rise, and with Snowden maintaining a rigidly orthodox policy at the Treasury, there seemed to be no possible way of reversing the trend. Revenue fell, while the expense of unemployment benefits went on increasing. Early in 1931 the Liberals had insisted on the appointment of a Committee on National Expenditure, and this body, under the chairmanship of Sir George May, reported on 1 August in favour of heavy cuts in government spending. A few days later a foreign-exchange crisis developed as investors from abroad, alarmed by the general international economic situation, began to withdraw their deposits in gold from the London money market.

The crisis caused a hasty recall of Ministers in mid-August and a decision in principle by the Cabinet that heavy cuts in expenditure would have to be made. Some Ministers, led by Arthur Henderson, were unhappy about the cuts, but they were not at first determined to oppose them. Henderson insisted that the General Council of the T.U.C. should be consulted in the matter, and Snowden reluctantly agreed. Accordingly, the Cabinet Economy Committee, consisting of MacDonald, Snowden, Henderson, and a few other key Ministers, on 20 August met the General Council and also representatives of the Labour Party outside the Government. The meeting heard Snowden's proposals and then broke up for the bodies represented to consider their attitude.

It was only the General Council that reacted quickly to Snowden's proposals. The same evening a deputation led by Citrine and Bevin met the Cabinet Committee and declared its hostility to any cuts and indeed its opposition to the entire policy of deflation which the Government was following. Beatrice Webb recorded in her diary the annoyance of her husband, who was in the Cabinet at the time: 'The General Council are pigs, they won't agree to any cuts of Unemployment Insurance Benefits or salaries or wages.' But the General Council's opposition at once strengthened the will of Henderson and other Cabinet Ministers who had been doubtful of Snowden's policy; and it became clear to MacDonald that he could not carry his proposals without a serious Cabinet split. He therefore resigned office on 23 August, but was at once invited by the King to form a National Government with Conservative and Liberal support – a commission which he accepted. In this new government MacDonald offered Cabinet posts to three of his former colleagues – to Snowden, who was to remain as Chancellor, to J. H. Thomas, and to Lord Sankey. All of them accepted.

MacDonald no doubt hoped that a substantial section of the parliamentary Labour Party would support him in his new role as a coalition leader. But he had overestimated his own influence with the parliamentary party, and he had underestimated the influence and power of decision possessed by the new T.U.C. leadership. The General Council's reaction to the crisis had already had a marked effect in accentuating the divisions within the Labour Cabinet; and now Bevin in particular threw himself into the work of winning the remainder of the party away from its elected leader. Although he was not an M.P. nor a member of the party's National Executive, he had powerful political weapons at his disposal – his control of the *Daily Herald*, his influence on the twenty-four members of his union who belonged to the parliamentary party, and the potential weight of his union's vote at the next party conference, which would amount to almost ten per cent of the total. Hugh Dalton's diary of that week in August 1931 gives a graphic impression of Bevin's role at the moment of crisis in the party:

The trade union leaders are full of fight. They speak of financial assistance. 'This is like the General Strike,' says Bevin; 'I'm prepared to put everything in.' They send for X of the *Herald*, to settle the line of tomorrow's leader . . . The *Herald* in the days that followed, under Bevin's influence, gave a fine lead.

There follows another entry of equal significance:

August 28th. Historic meeting of the Parliamentary Labour Party, at Transport House . . . Members of the General Council are invited to be present. This is an innovation, suggested by Uncle [sc. Arthur Henderson] to mark unity.

Clearly at this point Bevin, supported by Citrine and the General Council as a whole, had determined to throw Mac-Donald and his colleagues out of the Labour Party and entirely deprive them of support from any part of the labour movement. In this he was successful, although it is impossible to determine exactly how far the result was due to his own considerable efforts. MacDonald carried with him, apart from Snowden, Thomas, and Sankey, only eleven junior Ministers or back-benchers. The great bulk of the party was united in opposition to the new government, and on 28 September MacDonald and his tiny band of supporters within the party were expelled by the National Executive.

This is not the place for a full discussion of the 1931 crisis in all its aspects. But the role of the trade-union leaders aroused much controversy, and there were many charges of attempted 'dictation' by the General Council to the Labour Cabinet – charges that were repeated by Snowden in his memoirs. Yet as Citrine pointed out, it could hardly be dictation for the General Council, at the invitation of the Government, to say whether or not it would support proposed government measures, provided it did not contemplate any unconstitutional action to enforce its views. Undoubtedly the General Council could be criticized for taking a narrowly sectional standpoint, if its opposition to cuts took no account of the national economic situation. But in fact its principal spokesmen had a far clearer grasp of economic realities than had either MacDonald or Snowden, and in retrospect we can see that their attitude was justified. Bevin, who had served on the Macmillan Committee on Finance and Industry in 1930, had learnt a great deal about the need for economic expansion, rather than deflation, from

J. M. Keynes, who was also a member. Through the Economic Committee of the General Council, a body set up in 1929, he had helped to educate other union leaders, and in March 1931 the General Council had published an extremely well-argued statement on economic policy which urged the maintenance of consumer purchasing power.

It was this capacity to master the economic problem from a national point of view that enabled Bevin and his colleagues to act decisively in the crisis and to convince the faltering members of the Labour Party, both in Parliament and outside, that the attitude of the General Council was the correct one. No doubt it was also an advantage to them that MacDonald, absorbed in the details of international diplomacy, which was his principal interest, had totally neglected to cultivate close ties with the back-benchers of his party. But the party's respect for the T.U.C. leadership was no purely temporary phenomenon, as was clearly shown by the fact that its intervention in August 1931 was turned into a form of tutelage which lasted for the remainder of the decade.

Perhaps partly as a result of his formal expulsion from the Labour Party, MacDonald soon gave way to Conservative pressure for a general election, and this took place at the end of October 1931. The position of the Labour Party, deserted by its former leaders, and faced in most constituencies by the combined voting power of the other parties, was naturally a very difficult one. In the outcome, the party's total vote, compared with 1929, fell by a quarter; but the effect upon its representation in Parliament was disastrous. While MacDonald and his supporters won 556 seats, the Labour Party was reduced to forty-six. There were also another five M.P.s belonging to the I.L.P., who had fought the election separately from the Labour Party owing to the conflict between their organization and the National Executive of the Labour Party – a conflict that was to end in the disaffiliation of the I.L.P. from the Labour Party in 1932. Of the Labour Party's remaining leadership, the only former Cabinet Minister to be returned to Parliament was the left-winger George Lansbury: he now became the acting parliamentary leader, although for a short time Henderson remained in the titular position, to which he had been elected in place of MacDonald shortly before the election.

The new parliamentary party was not only smaller than any of its predecessors since 1918, it was also extremely weak in talent. Lansbury himself was a man of great integrity and no little shrewdness, but he was already over seventy and, moreover, he was too much on the Left to be a satisfactory spokesman of party policy. Clement Attlee, who served as his deputy, and Stafford Cripps, the former Solicitor-General, were Lansbury's principal assistants in the leadership; but both were also inclined to be distinctly left-wing, and neither of them as yet had the confidence of the trade-union hierarchy. It is true that most of the rank and file of the party were former union officials, as was naturally the case when the party lost all but its most heavily industrial constituencies; but even the rank and file seemed very unrepresentative of trade unionism as a whole, for no less than half the entire party were nominees of the Miners Federation – men who in many cases assumed a doctrinaire attitude to politics which was hardly typical of the movement as a whole.

It was under these circumstances that the General Council staked its claim to exercise a continuous political influence over the party. Citrine submitted a memorandum to the National Joint Council (which was supposed to coordinate policy between the two organizations), in which he declared that

... the General Council should be regarded as having an integral right to initiate and participate in any political matter which it deems to be of direct concern to its constituents.

So that this could be effected, he urged the reconstruction of the National Joint Council itself, which had only rarely met in the preceding decade. The Labour Party representatives agreed to this, and a new constitution for the National Joint Council was drawn up, giving the T.U.C. General Council as many representatives on it as those of the parliamentary party and the National Executive combined, and stipulating that it should meet at least once a month.

In the immediately following years the National Joint

Council functioned much as Citrine had wished. It met regularly and discussed the main issues facing the labour movement, on which it issued influential pronouncements. In 1933 the Labour Party conference agreed to a proposal that no future Labour leader should take office as Prime Minister after a general election until he had been advised on the matter by the National Joint Council; and it was also laid down that during any future Labour Government a Cabinet Minister should be appointed to attend meetings of the Council 'in a consultative capacity'. There was, of course, no opportunity to put these arrangements into operation in the 1930s, and in the changed circumstances of 1945 there was no attempt to follow the procedure laid down in 1933. But their endorsement by the conference provides a striking indication of the degree to which, immediately after 1931, the party was prepared to accept the supervision of the T.U.C. Lansbury himself accepted it, at least in theory, and described his own role as that of a 'spokesman' of the party rather than that of a 'leader'.

There were two main issues on which the General Council gave an important lead to the party in these years, largely through the agency of the National Joint Council, or the National Council of Labour, as it was renamed in 1934. One of them was the attitude to be adopted towards the Communist Party. In the period 1928–32 the British Communists, following the Moscow 'line', had adopted a policy of extreme sectarianism, denouncing the leaders of both the Labour Party and the T.U.C. as 'social fascists', and even refusing to cooperate with left-wing members of the Labour Party. As a result, their influence in the labour movement as a whole was almost entirely extinguished, and they could reap very little advantage from the crisis of the Labour Party in 1931. During this period attempts were made to found Communist unions in some industries, in rivalry to the existing bodies; and in two cases – the United Mineworkers of Scotland and the United Clothing Workers (which came into existence in the East End of London) – these attempts were successful. But this policy naturally aroused the strongest hostility on the part of the great majority of union leaders.

Gradually in the period 1932–4 the Communist 'line'

changed, and Communist Parties in all countries moved towards the advocacy of a United Front of all working-class parties and unions against the threat of Fascism. In Britain the party abandoned its attempts to maintain the National Minority Movement, which had become very weak in the preceding years, and in 1935 it even allowed both the existing Communist unions to go out of existence. As early as March 1933 it formally proposed to the Labour Party and to the I.L.P. that a United Front should be formed. Within a few days of the receipt of the invitation, however, the National Joint Council issued a manifesto entitled *Democracy and Dictatorship* in which it reaffirmed its belief in constitutional principles and its opposition to Communism and Fascism alike. At a time when many Socialist intellectuals, under the influence of Harold Laski and others, were inclined to toy with the idea of 'proletarian dictatorship', this was an important pronouncement; and it was followed in 1934 by the so-called 'Black Circular' from the General Council, which advised the unions to exclude Communists from posts of responsibility and actually made the exclusion of Communist delegates obligatory on trades councils wishing to retain formal recognition by the T.U.C. Although a succession of Labour Party conferences spent much time in discussing the issue of the United Front, the strong lead given by the General Council, both directly and through the National Joint Council, did much to keep the party independent of Communist influence in a period when the idea of collaboration had much superficial attraction.

The second issue on which the policy of the General Council was of great importance in influencing the party was the related but wider issue of foreign policy in general. In 1934, over a year after Hitler's rise to power, the General Council in full session met with the National Executive and the parliamentary committee of the Labour Party to discuss foreign policy. The result was a statement entitled *War and Peace*, which disavowed any policy of pure pacifism or reliance upon the 'international general strike', and stated clearly 'the duty unflinchingly to support our Government in all the risks and consequences of fulfilling its duty to take part in collective action against a peace-breaker'. As in the

First World War, the pacifist element in the party seemed to be much stronger among the intellectuals than among the trade unionists. Possibly the latter felt that a policy of collective security in the sphere of foreign affairs offered a parallel to their collective bargaining in the sphere of industrial relations.

In the course of 1935, as Mussolini's attack on Ethiopia became imminent, and as a new general election began to loom on the horizon of politics, it became more and more embarrassing to the Labour Party to have as its leader a man who, being a pacifist, was opposed to the party's announced policy on the most important issue of the day. But Lansbury for some time ignored suggestions that he should retire. The turning-point came, however, at the Labour Party conference in the autumn, when he opposed the National Executive's statement of the party's foreign policy. After he had spoken, Bevin followed him to the rostrum and brutally accused him of 'hawking your conscience round from body to body to be told what you ought to do with it'. Bevin went on to detail the meetings of the National Council of Labour, and other conferences, at which the policy was determined which Lansbury now repudiated. The policy statement was overwhelmingly accepted at the end of the debate, and a few days later Lansbury resigned his leadership, to be succeeded by Attlee.

In November there followed a general election, which was largely fought on issues of foreign policy. The Labour Party had much lost ground to make up; and it suffered from the disadvantage that the Government, now under Baldwin's leadership, espoused the cause of collective security through the League of Nations, thus stealing the Labour Party's thunder. The economic recovery that had now begun to develop, although by no means complete, enabled the Government to claim that it had 'saved the country' since 1931. The result was that although the Labour Party made about a hundred gains, its representation in the new House, at a total of 154, was far smaller than it had been in 1929. The National Government was thus confirmed in office; and although it was for a time saddled with the policy of collective security through the League of Nations, the failure of its somewhat half-hearted attempts to coerce Italy by League 'sanctions' in the following months enabled it to abandon the policy in the course of 1936.

The Labour Party remained committed to a policy of collective security, either through the League, or, if that proved ineffectual, through some alliance of states willing to resist aggression. But by 1936, with the rapid rearmament of Germany now taking place, it became necessary for the party to support a vigorous British rearmament programme. At first many Labour supporters showed great unwillingness to accept this change of policy, although it was becoming increasingly urgent. Socialist doctrinaires took the view that the National Government could not be trusted to use the weapons of war in a righteous cause; sentimental pacifists felt that rearmament was morally wrong; and all elements of the party realized that rearmament might well mean the postponement of social reform. On this issue, however, the General Council of the T.U.C. again took the lead in the direction of greater firmness and consistency. The outbreak of the Spanish civil war in the summer of 1936 helped to strengthen its hand. At the Labour Party conference of that year Bevin resolutely declared his support of rearmament, but the issue was not then finally decided, and it was only in the course of the following year, with Bevin serving a term as chairman of the General Council, and Dalton, who agreed with his attitude, occupying the post of chairman of the Labour Party, that the policy of the party was completely brought into line with that of the T.U.C. The 1937 conference of the Labour Party finally committed the party to rearmament, and it also confirmed the National Executive's demand for the dissolution of Sir Stafford Cripps's Socialist League, which had been urging the need for a United Front with the Communists. At the end of his year in office as chairman of the General Council Bevin resigned his membership of the National Council of Labour. His task of educating the Labour Party towards a responsible foreign policy had been successfully accomplished.

It remains to say something about the attitude of the trade-union leadership to the Labour Party's evolving domestic programme. While the General Council had been exerting its influence on the major issues of current policy through various channels, especially that of the National Council of Labour, the Labour Party's National Executive had been busy with plans for nationalization to be undertaken by the next Labour Government. Herbert Morrison, who as Minister of Transport in the 1929 Government had drawn up the arrangements for the take-over of London transport, was largely responsible for the formulation of the new proposals. He envisaged the formation of public corporations, under the general supervision of Ministers of the Crown, but largely managed by persons chosen for their ability as administrators or technicians. This did not satisfy those who had absorbed the teachings of the syndicalists and the Guild Socialists in earlier years; and at the 1932 Labour Party conference Harold Clay, an official of the Transport and General Workers, with Bevin's support, urged that there should be direct trade-union representation on the boards of nationalized industries. Feeling was sufficiently strong for the issue to be remitted for further consideration; and in the course of the following year a compromise on the question was hammered out in discussion between the National Executive and the General Council. A Memorandum on the subject was presented to the 1933 Conference, in which some concessions were made to the idea of trade-union representation, though only at the highest level. Clearly some union leaders were hesitant about the idea of trade-union representation, for fear that the essential function of the unions as negotiators on behalf of the persons employed in the industry should be lost sight of. The Memorandum declared that 'trade union rights, including the right to strike, must be fully maintained'. And then it went on to say bluntly that 'the day-to-day administration' of industrial concerns 'is quickly becoming a profession, and the persons undertaking this work will have to be trained business administrators'.

When this Memorandum was presented to the 1933 Congress of the T.U.C. an amendment demanding a much more generous proportion of workers' control was moved by Charles Dukes, the secretary of the General and Municipal Workers, and defeated by a considerable but not overwhelming margin. It was evident that Bevin at least was prepared to accept the compromise terms embodied in the Memorandum. A month later, however, Dukes renewed his criticism at the Labour Party conference, and this time, in spite of Bevin's opposition, he succeeded in carrying a resolution similar to that which he had moved at the T.U.C. It seemed as if the constituency Labour Parties were keener on the idea of workers' control or trade-union representation at all levels in industry than the unions were themselves. When the next Labour Government had an opportunity to put its principles into practice, however, it was the spirit of the Memorandum, rather than that of Dukes's resolution, which was to prevail.

The T.U.C. leaders would have carried little weight in the political sphere if they had allowed their industrial strength to go on declining as it did after the General Strike. In some industries with a contracting labour force, such as coal mining and the textile trades, a loss of membership was inevitable. The Miners Federation, which had 804,236 members in 1929, had sunk to 588,321 in 1939, but its proportion of the total labour force in the industry had if anything increased. In the intervening period, however, the Federation had suffered from two major challenges to its position, both of which it took several years to overcome. One of them was the emergence of the Communist union in Scotland, which, as we have pointed out, lasted until 1935. The other was the competition provided by the Spencer union, which was still active in that year, and which earlier had spread widely through the various areas of the Federation. The Spencer union had originally obtained much of its funds from the National Union of Seamen, which in the final years of Havelock Wilson's life seemed to have become little more than a 'company union' – that is, a union controlled by the employers. The Spencer union followed the same course, but by 1935 its influence was largely confined to Nottinghamshire, where it had originated. The Nottinghamshire Miners Association, which was the body affiliated to the Ministers Federation, could claim only 8,500 members out of a total work force in the area amounting to 43,600. In 1937, after disturbances and a prolonged strike at Harworth colliery, the Miners Federation threatened a national strike to bring the Nottinghamshire owners to recognize the Nottinghamshire Miners Association. The result was that after intervention by the Government's Mines Department an arrangement was made for the merger of the Spencer union with the Nottinghamshire Miners Association and for the affiliation of the new body to the Federation.

In the cotton trade employment also fell considerably in this period, but the proportion of trade-union membership was roughly maintained. In 1938 it amounted to some 230,000 or 240,000, still divided into about 200 separate unions which were loosely linked in the same so-called 'amalgamations' as before the First World War. The conservatism of trade unionism in the industry was astonishing – and it was also proving increasingly expensive, for costs were naturally high in proportion to membership. In the woollen and worsted trades, which had always been less effectively organized than cotton, the system of collective bargaining broke down, and after complete defeat in a series of strikes in the early 1930s the National Union of Textile Workers, itself an amalgamation formed only in 1922, merged with the Amalgamated Society of Dyers and Finishers and the Bolton Bleachers and Dyers Amalgamation to form a new body called the National Union of Dyers, Bleachers, and Textile Workers. Although a number of small unions of skilled workers continued to exist, this new body took the lead in the re-establishment of collective agreements in the industry in the later 1930s.

A different set of problems faced unions which catered for workers in industries which were expanding rather than contracting. Many of them were caused by the fact that the expansion largely took place in parts of the country where unionism had previously been weak or nonexistent – and especially in southern England, where factories sprang up in what had previously been rural areas or sleepy country towns. Other problems arose from the fact that in comparatively new industries, such as motor manufacture, there were serious demarcation conflicts between different unions, especially skilled unions, and there was little prospect of the emergence of a single bargaining agency for the whole industry. The unions, short of funds as they often were after the depression, were slow to take advantage of the opportunities in the new areas, and often it was a rank-and-file movement, not infrequently led by Communists, which led to the 'capture' of new factories in the London suburbs, at Oxford, and elsewhere. Two of the unions which benefited most markedly from this extension of the frontiers were the Amalgamated Engineering Union and the Electrical Trades Union. The A.E.U. had finally decided in 1926 to open its ranks really generously to less-skilled engineering workers; and as a result its membership doubled in the years 1933-9, reaching a total of 390,873 in the latter year. It had taken the lead in campaigning for holidays with pay for its members, with considerable success in the 1930s. It also gained the right to negotiate for apprentices, and in many firms secured the forty-hour week. The Electrical Trades Union, which with a membership of only 70,000 in 1939 was very much smaller than the A.E.U., had nevertheless more than doubled since 1929.

The general unions had also grown considerably in these years, and it was in 1937 that the Transport and General Workers exceeded the size of the Miners Federation, and with a total membership of 654,510 became not only the largest union in Britain but also the largest in the world. Each of the union's national trade groups – altogether nine in number – was the equivalent of a national union in itself: the largest of them was the Road Passenger Transport Group, which had a membership of over 150,000 in 1938. Within this group, the section which caused the most trouble to Bevin, the general secretary, was that formed by the London busmen. In 1933 his leadership of the union was challenged by the Busmen's Rank-and-File Committee, which was a body largely sponsored by the Communist Party. He was compelled to humour this unofficial organization until 1937, by which time it had won control of the union's Central London Bus Committee and had insisted on fighting a strike for a reduction in hours. Bevin had advised against the strike, which proved a failure and aroused a good deal of public hostility because it took place during the Coronation celebrations. He now turned the weight of union officialdom against the rank-and-file leaders, and secured their expulsion from the union. The second largest general union, the General and Municipal Workers, increased its size from 269,357 in 1934, when Charles Dukes succeeded the veteran Will Thorne as secretary, to 467,318 in 1939. This union had solved the problem of Communist influence by simply banning their election to union office – a drastic measure which may have been facilitated by the strength of Irish Catholicism within the membership.

In 1939 G. D. H. Cole, surveying the British trade-union scene, enumerated five categories of employed workers which were still largely unorganized. These were: domestic servants, clerks and typists, agricultural workers, the distributive trades (except for cooperative workers), and unskilled and general labour. He also added that women workers were in general inadequately organized, but many of them were, of course, included in the five categories. The list indicated that the general unions, in spite of their existing strength, had plenty of opportunity to win further recruits. The National Union of Agricultural Workers, which had been founded in 1906, had a membership of only about 32,000 in 1937, although there were a certain number of agricultural workers in the Transport and General. It is obvious that there were special difficulties in recruiting workers in the categories listed by Cole: the domestic servants and the agricultural workers could not easily be canvassed or induced to act together; the shop assistants, clerks, and typists thought of themselves as of a higher social status than the bulk of those who belonged to unions; and women generally were often engaged in industry for too short a period to concern themselves with the opportunities for betterment that trade unionism offered. But while so many workers remained not merely unorganized but in many cases without even the chance of being invited to join a union, the movement could not be complacent about its progress. The General Council itself realized the need for concerted action to 'spread the gospel'; and it encouraged the trades councils to initiate local campaigns – a form of activity of which some of the more right-wing leaders disapproved because of the persistent radicalism of many trades councils. It also set up special committees to advise the unions on the organization of women, of catering workers, of clerical workers, and of non-manual workers in general.

As the unions grew in strength, so did the number of disputes among their officials about the demarcation of their respective areas of recruitment. The General Council, as we have seen, was empowered at its foundation to find ways and means of easing this problem, and the 1924 Congress approved an inter-union code of conduct which served as the basis for the work of a Disputes Committee set up by the General Council. The Committee naturally took up a somewhat conservative attitude, urging respect for established union interests and endeavouring to prevent the 'poaching' of the members of one union by another; but at first it did not discourage voluntary transfers of unionists who were dissatisfied with their existing union. At the end of the 1920s, however, even this existing loophole for change began to close. This was partly a result of the disruptive tactics of the Communist Party at that time, and partly because of the not entirely dissimilar behaviour of the Spencer union among the miners – a union which seemed to be supported by the coal-owners. The increasing influence of the large general unions, which already had very extensive areas of recruitment, was also exercised on behalf of the strict maintenance of the *status quo*.

When Congress was asked in 1939 to agree to a new and more precise statement of principles to govern inter-union relations – the so-called 'Bridlington Agreement' – it was laid down quite clearly that no union should attempt to organize workers at any industrial establishment where another union already represented and negotiated on behalf of a majority of the workers. The result of this was undoubtedly to limit the individual worker's freedom of choice, and also to make life more difficult for a number of small unions already in competition with large ones, such as the Chemical Workers Union, which tried in vain in the inter-war years to secure membership of the T.U.C. against the opposition of the general unions. On the other hand, it was an advantage to the workers as a whole to prevent the multiplication of bargaining agents on their behalf, which in most cases would have reduced their collective influence.

Finally, there was the grave problem of the unemployed
– less numerous, admittedly, in the later 1930s than at the
height of the depression, but still numbering over a million
at the outbreak of war. The T.U.C. had for many years
held to the idea that the unemployed worker remained the
responsibility of the union to which he had belonged when
he was employed and so did not need special consideration.
But in the face of long-term unemployment – and as a
result of the claims of the National Unemployed Workers
Movement, a body under Communist control, to represent
the unemployed workers as a whole – the General Council
was stirred to take some action. It did not, like the
N.U.W.M., encourage the unemployed to go on 'hunger
marches' in protest against government policy; instead it
called upon the trades councils to establish local unemployed associations, which it then supplied with foot-
balls and chess boards and other facilities for recreation.
The fear of getting involved in left-wing agitation, and of
interfering with the rights of the unions, apparently prevented the T.U.C. from taking a more active role in the
organization of the unemployed.

The decade of the 1930s was not a good time for established
trade-union movements. On the continent of Europe they
were being crushed under the heel of dictatorship, and in the
United States an entirely new national body, the Congress of
Industrial Organizations (C.I.O.), sprang up to challenge the
authority of the American Federation of Labor. Yet in Britain, in spite of a certain amount of criticism of the leadership
for its conservatism and moderation, nothing comparable
happened, and the T.U.C. was able not only to expand its
membership but also to advance its status both with the
Government and with the public. The degree of acceptance
now accorded to British trade unionism as a whole, at least in
the industries where strikes were readily practicable, and the
cautious policies adopted on both sides of the bargaining
table, are clearly indicated in the statistics of industrial
disputes in the period. In the years 1934–9 the number of
working days lost as a result of disputes only once exceeded
two million, whereas between 1919 and 1926 it had never

been less than seven million and had averaged several times that figure.

In securing the respect of the Government, the steady constitutionalism of the leaders of the General Council played a part. Unlike intellectuals such as Harold Laski and Stafford Cripps, Bevin and Citrine were quite undoctrinaire about the possibilities of cooperation with the Government even when Labour was out of office. One of MacDonald's last acts as Prime Minister was to offer knighthoods to Arthur Pugh and to Citrine – honours which they accepted. The incident was significant, for it showed that the Government was once more prepared to accord the T.U.C. leaders a degree of recognition, and it showed also that the T.U.C. leaders were willing to accept that recognition, with the responsibility that went with it. In the later 1930s the T.U.C. was gradually drawn into the machinery of consultation which accompanied State intervention in industry. The textile unions were associated with the task of reorganizing the cotton industry, by Acts of 1936 and 1939; the T.U.C. was consulted in the appointment of representatives to advise the Government on the structure of the fishing industry, by legislation of 1935 and 1938; and it was a natural development in 1938 and 1939 that the Government should ask the General Council for help in preparing its plans for war mobilization and air-raid precautions.

In the last two years of peace, when Chamberlain was still busily pursuing the will-o'-the-wisp of 'appeasement', the T.U.C. policy of firm resistance to aggression was repeated in successive pronouncements of the labour movement. Early in September 1938, when the crisis that culminated in the Munich agreement was already mounting, the General Council and the two Labour Party executives published a joint statement declaring that

whatever the risks involved, Great Britain must make its stand against aggression. There is now no room for doubt or hesitation.

Later in the year the General Council was taken into consultation about plans for mobilization. A Schedule of Reserved Occupations was drawn up, and the movement was committed to an elaborate scheme for voluntary national service. A special conference of trade-union executives met in May 1939 to approve the arrangements, which it did by an overwhelming vote. By this time, however, the Government had decided to introduce conscription, and the conference passed a resolution protesting against this decision, which largely rendered nugatory all the plans that it had been summoned to approve. In the light of subsequent events the protest was unrealistic, but at the time it seemed to be a natural reaction in the circumstances.

In the final crisis of 1 to 3 September, when Poland was invaded, the annual Congress of the T.U.C. was just assembling at Bridlington. A declaration of support for the war, combined with a moving appeal to the German people, was adopted with only two dissentients.

> The defeat of ruthless aggression is essential [it said] if liberty and order are to be re-established in the world. Congress, with a united and resolute nation, enters the struggle with a clear conscience and steadfast purpose.

And then the delegates, curtailing their meetings to two days only, hastily settled down to the discussion of the practical problems that would arise under war conditions.

CHAPTER ELEVEN

POWER WITH RESPONSIBILITY, 1939–51

THE years from 1940 to 1951 saw the trade-union movement undertaking responsibilities greater than ever before – for the first half of the period in the war-time Coalition led by Winston Churchill, and thereafter in the post-war Labour Government of Clement Attlee. But this era of deep involvement in the processes of government was prefaced by the eight months of the 'phoney war', when the National Government under Chamberlain prepared somewhat ineffectively for the necessities of the total struggle which was forced upon the country.

When war was declared in September 1939 the Government was still hoping to manage without positive controls of labour, and even with fewer negative controls than existed at the end of the First World War. Before war broke out the Schedule of Reserved Occupations had already been put into operation, and an agreement had been made between the A.E.U. and the Engineering Employers Federation for the 'relaxation of customs', that is, for the temporary abandonment of practices limiting the most effective deployment of labour for productive purposes. But the Ministry of Labour had no plans for the control of wages, for the direction of labour, or for compulsory arbitration. A National Joint Advisory Committee, consisting of fifteen employers and fifteen trade unionists with a neutral chairman, was set up to assist the Minister in formulating policy, and it was no doubt hoped that the unionists would be more cooperative than in fact they proved to be. But there was a strong legacy of mutual distrust between the Government and the unions, and this could not be cleared away in the somewhat unreal atmosphere of the early months of the war,

which saw no sustained fighting and so failed to provide a
sense of emergency. It was significant that the General
Council of the T.U.C., when asked by the Government for
assurances of support for the war effort, took the opportunity
to request the amendment of the Trade Disputes Act of
1927; and it was equally significant that Chamberlain gave a
reply which could not but annoy the General Council: he
said that it depended on the behaviour of the unions during
the war.

Under these circumstances the Minister of Labour, Mr
Ernest Brown, was reluctant to incur further hostility from
the unions by taking any vigorous steps to organize the supply
of skilled labour for the munitions industry. There was as yet
no difficulty in the supply of unskilled labour – in fact throughout the first year of the war there was a reserve of unemployed
well in excess of half a million. But a shortage of skilled
engineering workers had already developed by the outbreak
of war, and competition for their services began to develop
between different firms working on government contracts.
Men were 'poached' by one employer from another, the result
being a quite unnecessary disturbance to the rhythm of
production. There were two possible long-term remedies for
the shortage of skilled labour – the training of unskilled
workers and the dilution of labour as it had been practised in
the First World War. But in the absence of any real sense of
national emergency, little was done to implement either
course of action; the training centres which existed remained
largely unfilled, and the unions proved unwilling to agree to
any extensive dilution, while there remained, as there did,
considerable reserves of skilled labour either in unessential
industries or in some cases unemployed. The Minister of
Labour was also personally at fault for refusing to regard the
problems of labour supply as pertaining to his department
rather than to the Ministry of Supply and the other
government departments responsible for war contracts.

There was a comparable absence of policy and action in
the Government's attitude to wages. Prices rose considerably
in the early months of the war, but the Chancellor of the
Exchequer, Sir John Simon, seemed to think that all would
be well in the economy provided that the unions undertook

not to press their wage claims. The advocacy of stern financial discipline for all classes of the community was at first left to private initiative: and J. M. Keynes, in letters to *The Times* and in a pamphlet, *How to Pay for the War*, pressed for a system of compulsory savings, steeply graded taxation, family allowances, and subsidies for basic food-stuffs. Of these proposals, the only one that found any place in the existing policy of the Treasury was food subsidies, but as Keynes pointed out, subsidies without other finan-cial measures would only tend to increase inflationary pressure.

The situation was completely transformed in May 1940, when under the impact of the successful German offensive in Scandinavia Chamberlain's Government collapsed, and Churchill was asked to form a Coalition in its place. The parliamentary Labour Party played an important part in securing the change of Prime Minister, not only by moving the decisive motion of censure but also by refusing to serve in any Coalition under Chamberlain. It was natural, there-fore, that the new Prime Minister should find places in his government for an even larger proportion of Labour repre-sentatives than the party's membership in the Commons might seem to justify. Attlee and Arthur Greenwood, re-spectively Leader and Deputy Leader of the Opposition, were invited to join the War Cabinet, which at first consisted of only five members. In addition, there were several other Ministers drawn from the Labour ranks; and Churchill also took the unusual step of asking Ernest Bevin, who had never even been a Member of Parliament before, to take office as Minister of Labour. The Treasury was entrusted to the Conservative Kingsley Wood, but Keynes was brought in as a financial adviser, and his ideas soon began to influence policy. All these sudden and dramatic changes marked an entirely new phase in the conduct of the war.

So far as the unions were concerned, the key figure in their relations with the new government was their former colleague and spokesman Ernest Bevin, now Minister of Labour and National Service. Bevin cheerfully accepted the re-sponsibilities that his predecessor had endeavoured to avoid;

and he at once held a meeting of the rather unwieldy National Joint Advisory Committee, and persuaded it to agree to the appointment of a smaller and more manageable Joint Consultative Committee of seven employers and seven trade-union leaders. He also held a special meeting of trade-union executives, to the number of about two thousand, expounded to them his approach to the problems of his office, and asked for their support, which was expressed with great enthusiasm. Parliament meanwhile passed the Emergency Powers (Defence) Act, which enabled the Government to issue regulations giving it complete control over persons and property; and Defence Regulation 58A, which was immediately issued under this Act, put enormous powers for the control of labour into the hands of the Minister of Labour. It may be that for a time Bevin toyed with the idea of controlling wages: at the first meeting of the new Consultative Committee, on 28 May, he put to them proposals to the effect that, subject to a review every four months, wages should be kept at a constant level. The members of the Committee, and especially the unionists, were hostile to the idea, and it was dropped. But Bevin did secure the Committee's agreement that the existing negotiating machinery should be supplemented, as a final resort, by a National Arbitration Tribunal, the decisions of which should be binding on both parties in industry. This meant that strikes would become illegal. An Order in Council to establish the Tribunal and to declare the prohibition of strikes and lock-outs was accordingly made a few weeks later, under the title of Order 1305.

Bevin also acted quickly to end the 'poaching' of workers by rival employers. By the Restriction on Engagement Order of June 1940 he made it obligatory for employers to engage their labour only through the employment exchanges or through an approved trade union. At the same time the national emergency had created a climate of opinion which favoured more effective arrangements for the dilution of labour. In the summer of 1940 a number of agreements were made between the Engineering Employers Federation and skilled unions in the industry; and Bevin undertook to secure statutory guarantees, as in the First World War, that practices abandoned by the unions would be restored if desired at the end of the war. This was effected by the Restoration of Pre-War Practices Act of 1942.

The new spirit of cooperation in industry which developed in the summer of 1940 was due, of course, to the general sense of involvement in defence against the threat of invasion. It owed little to the legislative or administrative actions of the new government, important though these were. The First World War had already shown that strikes could not be conjured out of existence by legislation alone. Yet the year 1940 is conspicuous in the records of industrial relations for the fact that fewer working days were lost by strikes in its course than in any other year since statistics were first kept half a century earlier. In every munitions works, where immediate increases in output were regarded as essential, the problem was not how to get the workers to work longer hours but how to prevent them from overworking. This was in spite of the dislocation, discomfort, and suffering caused by air raids and the other incidents of war.

As the war continued, however, fresh problems emerged which would have proved intractable without the exercise of governmental powers. Although Bevin had assumed, by the Restriction on Engagement Order, a negative control over the employment of labour, he had been reluctant to use the positive control of direction which was available to him under the Emergency Powers Act. But by the end of 1940 the increasingly critical shortages of skilled labour were forcing his hand. On the advice of Sir William Beveridge, he introduced a system whereby employment in certain factories or other undertakings could be designated as 'essential work'. By the Essential Work (General Provisions) Order of March 1941, skilled workers were required to register themselves, and could be directed to enter employment which fell into the 'essential' category. But the Order contained important provisions which went some way to compensate the workers for the loss of their freedom of engagement. All undertakings classified as 'essential' were to satisfy minimum requirements of wages and conditions, and were to have adequate provision for the welfare of the employees; and while workers were forbidden to leave their employment without the permission of an officer of the Ministry of Labour, a similar restriction was placed upon the employer's right to dismiss any of his employees.

By this time the trade-union leadership was heavily committed to the Government's policy and involved in its administration at every level. Union officials served on innumerable committees for the encouragement of production, for the operation of rationing schemes, and for a wide range of other purposes. The annual reports of the T.U.C. General Council began to read like the records of some special government department responsible for coordinating policy in the social and industrial spheres. As in the First World War, the union leadership was vulnerable in this situation to any rank-and-file movement of discontent which might grow up, especially if it were favoured by the shop stewards, whose power was again rapidly on the increase. But fortunately for union officialdom, the obvious focus of opposition – the Communist Party – was committed to the fullest possible support of the war effort after the invasion of Russia in June 1941. The Engineering and Allied Trades Shop Stewards National Council, which had a strong Communist element in its composition, then became the most enthusiastic supporter of higher productivity and the fiercest opponent of unofficial strikes. The influence of the Communist Party itself must not be over-rated, for the number of unofficial strikes certainly rose considerably in the latter part of the war, as we shall see; but clearly the problem might have been much worse than it was.

The Engineering Shop Stewards National Council held a widely publicized conference in London in October 1941, to discuss ways and means of increasing production; and one demand which received especial emphasis was for the establishment of joint workshop production committees, where an exchange of ideas could take place between the management and employees' representatives. There was already by this time a Central Production Advisory Committee on which the unions were represented, to advise the Government on production problems; but machinery at the regional, local, and factory or shop levels was still lacking. Early in 1942 a Ministry of Production was established and, on the recommendation of a special committee chaired by Walter

Citrine, new national and regional production boards were set up. The following two years saw a remarkable development of consultative machinery at the factory level, starting in the Royal Ordnance Factories and then gradually adopted by industry as a whole, including even the private shipyards, where industrial relations were more difficult than elsewhere. The effectiveness of the committees naturally varied widely; but under favourable circumstances they were able to provide much help for managements which were at a loss to know how further to quicken the tempo of output.

In spite of the extent of governmental control over so many aspects of the country's economy, the remarkable fact remains that the peace-time system of collective bargaining was never superseded. Even Order 1305 was as Bevin said 'virtually a collective agreement, given the clothing of law'. As we have seen, there was no State control of wages in general; the Government went no further than to make occasional calls for restraint, as in the 1941 White Paper on Price Stabilization and Industrial Policy. In some essential industries which before the war had exceptionally low wage rates – notably mining and agriculture – the Government found it desirable to allow wage increases much above the national average: it had been very embarrassing to the Minister of Labour to have to direct men into these industries when it involved a heavy loss of wages. At the same time the trade boards continued to operate as they had done before the war, and Bevin secured Cabinet authorization for two measures to improve and extend the system. One of these, the Catering Wages Act of 1943, made arrangements for the establishment of wage determination in the catering industry, which had always presented great problems for union organizing; the other, the Wages Councils Act of 1945, converted trade boards into wages councils with extended powers and range.

The Government's appeals for restraint in pressing wage demands did not, in general, go unheeded. This is evident from the fact that by the spring of 1944 the level of wage rates had not risen during the war more than eleven per cent above the cost of living. It is true that wage rates do not give a clear indication of the improvement in average earnings: a large proportion of the money in the workers' pay packets was overtime and piece-work payment. But if higher total wages were offset by higher production the Government had no reason to cavil. In early 1944 the chief industrial problem was not so much the wage level as the separate though related issue of unofficial strikes. Things had changed since 1940: for in 1944 the loss of working days was in excess of any year since 1932.

The trouble was at its worst in the coal industry, which was responsible for one-half of the total loss of working days in 1943 and for two-thirds in 1944. As we have seen, wages had been unduly low in this industry before the war; and it was ironical that the trouble reached its peak just after the Greene Award guaranteed workers in the industry the not ungenerous basic rate of £5 a week. Unfortunately, no immediate steps were taken to improve miners' piece rates; consequently, many of them came out on strike. Bevin, who was never fully at home in dealing with the miners, was rattled by this behaviour: he spoke of the miners' action in the Sheffield area as having inflicted more damage on the country's industry than a heavy air raid; and detecting the influence of Trotskyist agitators in this instance, he introduced a new Defence Regulation (1AA) making it an indictable offence to 'instigate or incite' a stoppage of essential work. This Regulation, which aroused a good deal of opposition both in Parliament and among the miners, was allowed to lapse as soon as the war with Germany was over; and no prosecutions were ever initiated under it. As for the miners, their discontent rapidly subsided as soon as the level of their piece rates was attended to.

The public reputation of the trade unions had risen considerably during the war. At the start they shared the mood of the country in their unwillingness to accept the logical consequences of their verbal commitment to the war effort. The victories of the Nazi war machine and the entry of their own leaders into the Government soon jerked them out of this mood, and from May 1940 onwards their officials worked unceasingly to improve industrial relations and to increase output. Many of them assumed heavy additional responsibilities without complaint and with very little compensation. Their leader Ernest Bevin showed himself an able administrator; and he and many of his colleagues won the respect and friendship of businessmen and civil servants.

During the war the unions gained not only in prestige but also in membership, as they had done during the First World War. The total numbers rose from 6,053,000 in 1938 (including 4,669,000 affiliated to the T.U.C.) to 7,803,000 in 1945 (6,671,000 affiliated). Naturally the changes in the structure of industry during the war were reflected in the varying rates of progress of individual unions. The Transport and General rose from less than 700,000 to over a million members, the increase being largely concentrated in its Metal, Engineering, and Chemical Trade Groups. The A.E.U. became for a time the second largest union, more than doubling its size from 334,000 in 1939 to 825,000 in 1943, but later falling back with the contraction of the engineering industry in the last phases of the war. A good deal of the A.E.U. expansion was among semi-skilled workers in the munitions factories, and in 1942 it was decided to admit women to membership, which resulted in the recruitment of no less than 139,000 in the first year. The General and Municipal Workers challenged the A.E.U. for second place: it rose from 467,000 in 1939 to a peak of 726,000 in 1943, its female membership jumping from 56,000 to 124,000. The Miners Federation rose only slightly, from 588,000 to 602,000 in 1944; and thus its position among the other large unions of the country dropped from second to fourth. Meanwhile, many small unions, including the Electrical Trades Union, the National Union of Public Employees, and the National Union of Agricultural Workers, more than doubled their membership.

The growth of trade unionism and the structural changes in industry gave rise to renewed demands for a radical revision of union structure. It was obvious, for instance, that the multiplicity of craft unions in the engineering and shipbuilding industries militated against effective industrial relations, partly owing to the difficulty of collective bargaining where so many unions were concerned, partly owing to the demarcation disputes which tended to arise between the different unions. The worst trouble was as usual in the shipbuilding industry, and at times during the war it seriously interfered with the efficiency of the shipyards. In the summer of 1941, for instance, the reluctance of the Boilermakers Society to allow members of the Constructional Engineering Union to work on ships led to a strike on the Clyde, which was only solved when the C.E.U. members agreed to join both unions. In 1944 there was a strike on Tyneside over the refusal of the Boilermakers to work at all unless a new American flame-planing machine were operated by members of their union. Even when the firm withdrew the machine from service the men remained on strike, and only returned to work after being summoned and fined.

Conscious of difficulties like these, and of the failure of the existing machinery to deal with them, the T.U.C. of 1943 accepted a resolution calling upon the General Council to

examine trade union structure and to report subsequently to Congress with special regard to (*a*) uneconomic overlapping and competition; (*b*) what amalgamations are desirable; (*c*) structural or other changes necessary to ensure maximum trade union efficiency in the future.

From this promising initiative, however, very little emerged. Citrine and his colleagues, aware of the danger of appearing to infringe on trade-union autonomy, produced for the 1944 Congress an able survey of the problems involved and of their history since the last major discussion in 1924; but they offered no more concrete suggestions than that amalgamations of unions should be encouraged and that, in their absence, the most hopeful course would be to develop collaboration between unions by increasing the effectiveness of federations. They also recommended that the T.U.C. system of advisory committees covering particular industries should be extended, and that the T.U.C. headquarters should be provided with additional research and educational facilities. The report was accepted by the 1944 T.U.C., but the only immediate outcome was that Citrine began to plan for the construction of a new T.U.C. building, with increased accommodation for his staff and with rooms for educational activities as well.

All the same, there were a few important developments in trade-union structure during the war, although not as many as in the First World War. Perhaps the most important was the consolidation of the Miners Federation into the National Union of Mineworkers, effected in 1944. Ever since its foundation, the central office of the Federation had been grossly inadequate for its tasks, and the different county unions – sometimes themselves federations – had retained almost complete autonomy. This was what Noah Ablett had called in 1932 'the tribal system in operation, with all the little chieftains'. But the Federation had long fought for the centralization of all wage negotiation, and now, during the war, this battle had been won against the opposition of the mine owners. On 1 January 1945, therefore, the forty-one constituent bodies were replaced by a National Union. The change was not, however, quite as drastic as it sounds, for twenty-one area organizations were brought into existence, and these retained a large degree of the autonomy which the old associations had had. In short, the National Union was no more than a somewhat stronger federation than its predecessor, drawing a substantially larger income from the miners and so able to perform a much more effective service for them.

Amalgamation of unions took place only rarely, partly because, as we have seen in earlier chapters, it was a difficult process to secure the approval of the memberships. The one outstanding case during the war period was the merging of the National Union of Distributive and Allied Workers, which catered largely for cooperative employees, with the National Union of Shop Assistants. The merger, which was only completed in 1947, had been under way for several years: it resulted in the creation of the Union of Shop, Distributive, and Allied Workers, a body with a membership of 374,000, almost half of them being women. This union, with the two big general unions, the A.E.U., the Mineworkers, and the Railwaymen, formed the 'big six' which together contained and still contain more than half the total membership of the T.U.C.

The other major change in war-time was the development of a more effective federation in the engineering industry.

There had been a partial federation in the industry since 1890; and since 1936 it had been called the Confederation of Shipbuilding and Engineering Unions; but it included neither the Foundry Workers nor the most important union of all, the A.E.U. In 1941 the needs of war-time negotiation at a national level led to the formation of a National Engineering Joint Trades Movement representing all three bodies; and this collaboration led to a breakdown of the suspicions which had kept the constituent bodies apart in previous years. The Foundry Workers voted to join the Confederation in 1944; the A.E.U. did likewise in 1946. This was the sort of development which seemed to justify the General Council's hopes for the federal principle – especially at a time when that other, more long-lived federal body, the Miners Federation, had been able to transform itself into the status if not quite the reality of a National Union.

Whatever the limitations of their own reconstruction, the union leaders ended the war feeling that they had earned a right to have a say in the reconstruction of British society and industry. With their increased membership and national prestige, they therefore looked forward to the post-war era with high expectations.

So far as the unions were concerned, the domestic political situation could not have turned out better than it did at the 1945 general election. The Labour Party, whose policy had been carefully coordinated with that of the T.U.C. by the interlocking of membership on drafting committees, won a complete victory at the polls, securing a total of 393 M.P.s in the new House. Of this total the union-sponsored proportion, it is true, was smaller than it had ever been before. But this was in large part due to the fact that the party's candidates had for the first time won a large number of seats in constituencies which were wholly or largely middle-class in social structure. In fact, of 124 union-sponsored candidates, all but four were elected. In the new Cabinet of twenty members Attlee, who became Prime Minister, found posts for six union-sponsored M.P.s – three of them being from the Mineworkers, whose strength in the House had always been proportionately large. Among the three was Aneurin Bevan, who had won his way to leadership by oratorical skill rather than by any particular loyalty to trade unionism: he became Minister of Health. Ellen Wilkinson of the Distributive Workers became Minister of Education; George Isaacs of the Operative Printers and Assistants, who was chairman of the T.U.C. at the time, took Ernest Bevin's former post as Minister of Labour; and Bevin himself, the most influential of all, became Foreign Secretary and in practice the closest confidant of the Prime Minister.

It is not surprising, in view of the T.U.C.'s concern with the matter even during the war, that one of the first measures of the new Parliament was a simple repeal of the Trade Disputes Act of 1927. This restored the position to where it stood after the Liberal Government's Act of 1913. In practice, there were two main results. First, the civil service unions were now free to rejoin the T.U.C., and several of them at once did so, including the Civil Service Clerical Association and the Union of Post Office Workers. Secondly, the Labour Party's trade-union membership at once rose by over half, owing to the substitution of 'contracting-out' for 'contracting-in' in the payment of the political levy. The Labour Party thus received a considerable accretion to its funds from the members of unions with political funds who had not previously taken steps to contract-in, and who now with equal passivity failed to contract-out.

The new Government was committed to a considerable programme of nationalization, laid down in precise form at the 1945 Labour Party conference; but as the Report of the General Council pointed out to the T.U.C. delegates in the following September, there was no suggestion that the role of the unions in nationalized industries should be radically changed. The aim was to be 'public control of industry, rather than workers' control as such', and while the boards of the nationalized industries were to contain persons 'of wide experience and knowledge of workpeople's interests', at the same time 'care should be taken to avoid the creation of dual responsibility'. In other words, if union representatives were appointed to the boards they were to be freed from all their union duties. All this was a restatement of the position agreed between the General Council and the Labour Party Executive after the debates of 1932–4, to which we have already referred.

True to its pledges, the Government rapidly proceeded to measures of nationalization. The Bank of England was taken over in 1946, and although the National Union of Bank Employees claimed the right to be consulted about appointments to its Court, the Chancellor of the Exchequer, Hugh Dalton, felt justified in refusing in this case, where the representation of special interests seemed undesirable and the union in any case was weak. Next to be nationalized was the coal industry, which was vested in the hands of a National Coal Board on 1 January 1947. Emanuel Shinwell, the Minister of Fuel and Power, set a precedent for other industries by consulting the General Council and the Mineworkers about appointments to the board and selecting one person nominated by each. The two men appointed in this case were Sir Walter Citrine, on whom a peerage was conferred, and Ebby Edwards, who had been secretary of the Mineworkers since 1932. Other prominent unionists were later appointed to the regional boards.

In 1947 the British Transport Commission was established to take control of the railways, canals, and road haulage. In 1948 the British Electricity Authority was created, with subordinate Area Electricity Boards, to run the electricity industry; and in 1949 the British Gas Council and Area Gas Boards were set up. Finally, in 1951 the firms in the iron and steel industry were taken over and placed under a public authority. By this time the trade-union movement, although not extravagantly represented in the control of any industry, had nevertheless lost many of its leaders to the public boards. Citrine had been appointed to the chairmanship of the Electricity Authority and had been replaced on the Coal Board by Sir Joseph Hallsworth of the Distributive Workers (who had been knighted in 1946). The general secretaries of the Railwaymen and the Locomotive Engineers left the General Council for posts on the Transport Commission and the Railway Executive respectively; and among others, James Bowman, who became chairman of the Northern Division of the National Coal Board in 1950, was a particularly severe loss to the Mineworkers. On the whole, it was the abler union leaders who were given these government appointments. Vincent Tewson, the former assistant secretary of the T.U.C. who now replaced Citrine as secretary, was not as powerful a man as his predecessor and former chief; and although much of the initiative on the General Council was now taken by Arthur Deakin, who had succeeded Ernest Bevin as secretary of the Transport and General Workers, he, too, was not quite of the same outstanding calibre.

Meanwhile, the trade-union movement was faced by fresh and unexpected problems in its relations with the Government – problems which arose from the difficulties of post-war recovery. American 'lend-lease' assistance was suddenly cut off in the autumn of 1945, and although an immediate dollar loan was negotiated to tide the country over the next few years, it was apparent that a tremendous production effort would be necessary to secure a favourable balance of payments. The Minister of Labour persuaded the General Council to agree to the continuation of Order 1305, which made strikes illegal and enforced on both parties to a dispute the decisions of the National Arbitration Tribunal. The General Council also agreed that the Restoration of Pre-War Practices Act, 1942, should not become operative for the time being. Early in 1946 Ernest Bevin addressed a meeting of trade-union executives, to emphasize the importance of increased production; and the General Council nominated a number of its own members to the National Production Advisory Council on Industry, which met under the chairmanship of Sir Stafford Cripps, the President of the Board of Trade.

In the following year, 1947, the urgency of increased production was brought home to all by the winter fuel crisis and then by the foreign-exchange crisis, which forced the Chancellor of the Exchequer to abandon the convertibility of sterling. The General Council responded readily to the Government's call for cooperation. It agreed to the reintroduction of a Control of Engagement Order; urged the reconstitution of the joint production committees in the factories, which had mostly faded away after the war; and undertook to examine the possibility of itself recommending a measure of 'wage restraint' upon its constituent unions.

The problem of restricting wage increases, at a time of full employment, was crucial for national recovery, for if wage increases were immediately reflected in higher costs, then the export drive would fail. Such, at least, was the argument of the economists at the time, in whose reasoning the members of the Labour Government concurred. In February 1948 Attlee felt the need to draw immediate public attention to the problem, and without consulting the T.U.C. he made a statement calling for a voluntary stabilization of prices, profits, and wages. The General Council, increasingly aware of the urgency of the problem and anxious not to come into conflict with the Government, agreed to endorse the policy; and a new conference of trade-union executives did likewise.

A policy of 'wage restraint' was a dangerous one for the unions to pursue, particularly in peace-time. It threatened to drive a wedge between union officials and their members, just at a time when there was a good deal of rank-and-file suspicion of those of their leaders who took or wanted to take posts on the boards of the nationalized industries. Yet in 1949, when there was a renewed foreign-exchange crisis, occasioning a devaluation of the pound, the General Council was asked by the new Chancellor, Sir Stafford Cripps, to make its advocacy of 'wage restraint' even more rigorous. Fortunately, the way was made easier by Sir Stafford's effective leadership in the 'austerity' campaign, his strong fiscal measures of discipline against all classes, and at the same time the Government's obvious determination to maintain a high level of provision for the social services, which they had already done much to build up. In November 1949 the General Council therefore agreed to recommend that existing wage rates be held stable 'while the Interim Index of Retail Prices remains between upper and lower limits of 118 and 106'.

In the course of 1950 the trading position of the country greatly improved. The assistance of the American Government under the Marshall Plan played an important part in this; so, too, did the export drive, which hardly needed the stimulus of devaluation at a time when there was still very much of a sellers' market for manufactures. In its report to the T.U.C. that year the General Council commented on the difficulties which its policy had already encountered, partly with unions which had sliding-scale agreements with their employers, partly with skilled workers, who resented the decline in their differential advantage over the unskilled – a process which had been going on now for a long time. The Council therefore declared that while the policy of restraint should not be abandoned, 'there must be greater flexibility in the future'. By the time that Congress met, however, the cost of living was rising rapidly, owing to the effects of devaluation and the international impact of the Korean War, which broke out in the summer; and so in spite of a speech by the Prime Minister, a resolution declaring that there was now 'no basis for a restraint on wage applications' was carried against the General Council.

The Government's policy was thus defeated by its own supporters in industry; and in the following two years both wages and profits rose rapidly. But this is not to say that the policy had been a failure. It is difficult, indeed, to say what might have happened if it had not been pursued – whether wages would in the long run have risen more than in fact they did; but at least a definite degree of voluntary discipline was successfully imposed, and this gave industry a breathing space and set an example to other sections of the community. The only alternatives – given the existing economic situation – were either a 'wage freeze' or a national wages policy imposed by the Government. Neither of these alternatives was acceptable to the T.U.C., whose adherence to the voluntary system of collective bargaining was as complete as ever. The Labour Cabinet had no option but to accept this attitude; and as Attlee told the 1950 T.U.C.:

The government has not at any time given directions as to the line which they should take to those who have the duty of arbitrating on claims, whether as members of the Industrial Court, the National Arbitration Tribunal or Wages Councils or as single arbitrators. To have done so would clearly have been to destroy the utility of this machinery.

The difficulties of the General Council in maintaining its support for the Government, and in particular the policy of 'wage restraint', were much increased by the development of a formidable Communist opposition within the union leadership. Considering the weakness of the Communist Party nationally – it had only secured the election of two M.P.s in 1945 – this may seem rather difficult to explain; but the fact was that during the period of the United Front agitation before the war, and again from 1941 to 1947 when the Communist Party was supporting the Government of the time, members of the party by careful collaboration and enthusiasm had won an increasing number of key positions in the union hierarchies.

First of all, there were a few unions which fell completely under Communist control in this period. The largest of these were the Electrical Trades Union, the Foundry Workers, and the Fire Brigades Union. Then there were a few of the largest unions which had significant Communist groups established within their officialdom, which threatened to take over the whole union. This was true of the Mineworkers, whose Welsh and Scottish constituent unions had fallen under Communist control, and which had a Communist secretary from 1946, when Arthur Horner replaced Ebby Edwards. The A.E.U. also had a strong Communist element among its officials, particularly in the London area; and, most serious of all for the established leadership, by 1946 there were nine open members of the party out of thirty-four on the Executive Council of the Transport and General Workers.

The problem of Communist penetration of the trade unions only became acute in 1947, when the international political situation rapidly worsened and the 'cold war' began. The Eastern European countries refused to join in the Marshall Plan, or the European Recovery Programme which developed from it; and the Communist Information Bureau, which was set up to coordinate the policies of international Communism, denounced the Governments of both the United States and Great Britain and spoke of Attlee and Bevin as 'poisoning the outlook' of the working class. The British Communist Party, accepting this lead, threw itself into a campaign of hostility to the Government and in particular to the production drive and the European Recovery Programme. Its members refused to collaborate in the policy of 'wage restraint', and in some cases they seemed anxious to secure industrial stoppages for political purposes only.

The General Council of the T.U.C., which had only one Communist member – Bert Papworth, of the Transport and General Workers – recognized the strength of this challenge, and reacted vigorously against it. In October 1948 it issued a statement denouncing the Communist aim of 'sabotage of the European Recovery Programme', and followed this up with a fuller statement, under the title *Defend Democracy*, which was circulated to the unions. It urged them to act in order to prevent Communists from holding key union posts and from acting as union delegates. The justification for such action was that

it is contrary to the whole conception of our movement, foreign to its traditions and fatal to its prestige, if it permits its democratically determined policy to be deflected at the behest of an outside body.

It was only to be expected that the response of the unions to this circular would vary widely. Some unions, as we have seen, were already under Communist control; others, on the contrary, among them the General and Municipal Workers, already had rules to prevent Communists from occupying key posts. In yet others, such as the Civil Service Clerical Association, the battle was already joined between a pro-Communist and an anti-Communist faction. In the Mineworkers Arthur Horner had embarrassed his executive in October by going to France and pledging his union's support for a French miners' strike, which was apparently political in origin; and Will Lawther, the union's President and a loyal supporter of the policy of the T.U.C. General Council, did not hesitate to disavow him and to insist on disciplinary action by the union's executive. The decisive battle, however, took place in the Transport and General Workers Union. Arthur Deakin, who was, after all, the main protagonist of the General Council's official policy, persuaded the union's Biennial Delegate Conference in July 1949 to carry a resolution to prevent Communists from holding office in the union. The end of the year therefore saw the dismissal of nine full-time officials, including Bert Papworth, who also lost his position on the T.U.C. General Council.

Thus, the Communists suffered a severe setback in their efforts to control the largest of all the unions by penetration of the chain of command; and the battle to inflict damage on the European Recovery Programme was perforce transferred to the local level. The Transport and General Workers, with its enormous membership, was especially vulnerable to agitation directed against its official policies. Among the dockers in particular there had already been a serious revolt, in the form of an unofficial strike in 1945; and a 'National Port Workers' Defence Committee' came into existence at that time to represent the unofficial movement. This body, which had a number of Communist members, was involved in fresh strikes in 1948, 1949, and 1950; and Arthur Deakin was not slow to accuse the Communist Party of having deliberately fomented these disputes. But even if there was some truth in his charges, it is difficult to believe that the men would have been willing to accept the lead of a handful of political agitators if they had not had genuine economic grievances. It was, incidentally, the unsuccessful prosecution by the Government of some unofficial strikers among the dock membership of the Transport and General Workers Union which finally led to the withdrawal of Order 1305, with its prohibition of the right to strike, in August 1951.

The 'cold war' also had its effect upon the international labour movement. In the latter part of the war the T.U.C. had played an important part in the construction of a new body called the World Federation of Trade Unions, which, because it included the Russian trade-union movement and the American C.I.O. as well as the main European labour movements, seemed to be as comprehensive an organization as the United Nations. The only trouble was that the American Federation of Labor, the older focus of trade unionism in the United States, refused to have anything to do with a body which included the Russian unions, which they did not believe to be genuinely independent of the Russian Government. This was certainly embarrassing to the T.U.C., which for so many years had had fraternal relations with the American Federation of Labor. Nevertheless, the World Federation of Trade Unions was formally constituted in Paris in October 1945, and Citrine was elected as its President.

The unity of West and East within the World Federation lasted for little more than two years. In the autumn of 1948 the question of attitude to the Marshall Plan split the organization wide open; and at an Executive meeting in Paris in January 1949 Arthur Deakin, who had succeeded Citrine as President, proposed that its activities should be suspended. The suggestion naturally did not appeal to the Russians and their sympathizers, who controlled the secretariat; and the result was that the T.U.C., the C.I.O., and other Western trade-union organizations withdrew from membership, and later that year, at a conference in London, a new body was set up to include all the seceding groups and the American Federation of Labor as well. It held its foundation conference in London at the end of November 1949; Paul Finet of the Belgian trade unions became President, and Arthur Deakin was among the vice-presidents. The International Confederation of Free Trade Unions, as it was called, at once planned and undertook activities to encourage the progress of the European Recovery Programme and to further the growth of unions in underdeveloped countries. In 1951 Finet had to retire from the Presidency, and Vincent Tewson was elected as President in his place.

In his forthright speech at the 1946 Congress, Citrine declared that during his term as T.U.C. secretary the trade unions had 'passed from the era of propaganda to one of responsibility'. Certainly, responsibility was the keynote of the five years before and after his resignation. The leadership had become closely integrated with the Government at every level; in return for the privilege of being consulted and of taking part in innumerable administrative decisions, it gave up, albeit only temporarily, some of its own most precious rights, including the right to strike. It became deeply committed to many of the processes of management, and at the end of the period its representatives, who under Marshall Plan auspices had the opportunity of examining the best American practice, came back advocating union cooperation in the introduction of 'scientific management' – an idea which would have aroused bitter hostility as recently as the 1930s.

There were, however, two vitally important aspects of the

trade-union way of life which remained fundamentally un-changed in this period. One was the voluntary system of collective bargaining which, in spite of the spread of Wages Councils, still accounted for much the larger part of wage negotiation. Although the existence of Order 1305 and the formal prohibition of strikes had placed restrictions on the operation of this voluntary system, both the Government and the employers knew only too well that the Order could last only as long as the unions wished it to; this in itself encouraged them to show an accommodating spirit in wage negotiation. The statistics of industrial relations compared well even with the comparatively peaceful 1930s: the number of working days lost by strikes did not exceed two and a half millions in any of the years 1946–51.

The other unchanged element in trade-union life was the pattern of union growth and structure. As we have seen, a few amalgamations took place, and nearly all the unions grew considerably during these years. There was no question, however, of the great bulk of the unions redrawing the boundaries of their fields of recruitment to suit the new pattern of industrial development, so as to simplify the prob-lems both of organizing and of bargaining. The most powerful opponents of change were the great general unions, which had spread so widely through the economy of the country. We have already noticed the vigour of their reaction to new industrial challengers, such as the Chemical Workers Union; they used their influence with the Government to deny negotiating rights to such challengers, and at Congress they voted against all proposals for a re-examination of trade-union structure – such as that proposed in 1950 by the indefatigable Bryn Roberts of the Public Employees, who had this to say in support of his resolution:

If the General Council rode up to Congress in a hansom cab, wearing bowlers and beards, it would be quite in keeping with our present-day economic machinery. We send production teams to America, while in our factories and services there are swarms of competing trade union organizers who fall over each other trying to do a job that could be better done by a few.

It was no wonder that the leading cartoonist of the period,

David Low, always portrayed the T.U.C. as a horse – reliable and sturdy, no doubt, but rapidly growing outdated in an age of faster and faster means of transport.

By the end of 1951 trade-union memberships had reached a total of almost nine and a half millions, of whom over eight millions, or 84·5 per cent, were affiliated to the T.U.C. The unions were often in such a strong bargaining position that they could insist on the 'closed shop' – that is, compulsory unionism for all employees. There were several cases of stubborn non-unionists being forced out of employment as a result. Opponents of the unions argued that this was a gross infringement of the liberty of the individual; but union leaders countered with the argument that it was equally an injustice that non-unionists should enjoy the rights and privileges won by union effort and sacrifice.

In this comparatively strike-free era it was not at all clear how fully union members retained a sense of loyalty to their organizations. In general elections, at least, many of them failed to vote as they were expected to. At the election of February 1950 the Labour majority in the Commons was reduced to only nine – a figure so precarious that a further election after only a few months was inevitable. Ernest Bevin died in April 1951, and Stafford Cripps retired from the Government at about the same time, owing to an illness which proved to be fatal. The strain of rearmament occasioned by the outbreak of the Korean War caused a clash within the Cabinet on the question of fiscal policy, and Aneurin Bevan with two supporters retired from the Government. When in October 1951 the new and expected general election took place, the Conservatives secured a majority of seventeen seats. The labour movement was free at last for what it seemed to need – an opportunity to put its own house in order before fully resuming the tasks of government.

CHAPTER TWELVE

ON THE PLATEAU, 1951–62

AFTER the victory of the Conservatives in the 1951 election the General Council of the T.U.C. at once made it clear that it was not going to abandon its close association with the processes of government and administration just because the Labour Party was now in opposition. A statement was issued which declared:

Since the Conservative administrations of pre-war days the range of consultation between Ministers and both sides of industry has considerably increased, and the machinery of joint consultation has enormously improved. We expect of this government that they will maintain to the full this practice of consultation. On our part we shall continue to examine every question solely in the light of its industrial and economic implications.

The new government, in turn, was only too happy to maintain as good relations as it could with the unions. Like its predecessor, it had only a tiny majority in Parliament and could not afford to antagonize the union leaders at a time when their cooperation appeared to be essential to prevent wage increases from outpacing increases in national productivity. The new Chancellor of the Exchequer, R. A. Butler, did not take long to suggest to the union leaders that they might in fact be prepared to accept a method of linking wage increases to productivity increases, so that 'the national wage bill will advance in step with national production, but not outstrip it'. But the General Council's Economic Committee demurred, realizing that there would inevitably be serious disagreements among the unions if such a proposal were put into force, and preferring not to risk novel experiments in peace-time and under the aegis of a Conservative Government.

Butler did not press his proposal when he found the
T.U.C. to be opposed to it. Both he and his colleague at the
Ministry of Labour, Sir Walter Monckton, felt obliged to
move forward only in agreement with the union leaders: to
attempt to do otherwise would be to violate the accepted
conventions of industrial relations, which had developed
throughout the previous generation and which had roots
going back to the nineteenth century. Sir Walter himself was
a significant choice for the post of Minister of Labour: he
had had virtually no experience of party politics, and had
come to notice so far almost exclusively as a barrister and as a
war-time administrator. He was known as an extremely
skilled negotiator – a reputation that he was to enhance in his
new post. There was only one conflict of any note between
him and the T.U.C. leaders, and this was early in his tenure
of office: in the summer of 1952 he referred back a number
of pay awards proposed by Wages Councils for particular
groups of employees. This caused the T.U.C. Economic
Committee to demand a special interview with the Prime
Minister, Winston Churchill, to whom they explained the
concern that they felt at such an inroad into the normal
processes of wage determination. The upshot was that
Monckton was obliged to disavow any intention of

interfering with any of the functions of Wages Councils, including
that of submitting proposals for fixing the remuneration of workers,
or of undermining their authority.

The awards were then confirmed without alteration.

For their part, the T.U.C. leaders, led by Deakin of the
Transport and General, Tom Williamson of the General
and Municipal, and Will Lawther of the Mineworkers, saw
to it that the cautious and moderate policy which they had
pursued under the Labour Government was maintained
under the Conservatives. Among other things, they ensured
that resolutions denouncing all forms of wage restraint –
such as were regularly submitted to Congress by the
Communist-dominated unions – were voted down by adequate majorities. When in 1952 a resolution was carried,
against the General Council, asking for the preparation of a
list of industries for fresh nationalization, their influence at

Transport House had the effect of producing for the succeeding Congress a report that was very conservative in tone, definitely recommending only the nationalization of water supply. And when in 1953 the Government asked for a trade-union nominee for the post of full-time vice-chairman of their Iron and Steel Board, which was to supervise the denationalized iron and steel industry, they put forward the name of Sir Lincoln Evans, the secretary of the main union in the industry, and then ensured that his appointment was approved by Congress in spite of a chorus of ideological protests from the left-wing unions.

The end of the Korean War boom in 1952–3, and the decline of import prices which resulted, temporarily halted the rise in the cost of living, and this in turn took a good deal of pressure out of the demand for wage increases in the years 1953 and 1954. The unions, however, tended to put forward their annual demands, partly because each felt it could make a special case for its own members; partly because the Government's fiscal policy – reducing food subsidies, and giving relief in direct taxation, for instance – seemed to them to impair the living standards of their members; partly, no doubt, because the workers in many trades had by now got used to the annual increase in their wages. Employers, on the other hand, were now emboldened to refuse any increase at all. At the end of 1953 national strikes were threatened on the railways and in engineering and shipbuilding, and it appeared as if the industrial peace of the post-war years was at last coming to an end. But Sir Walter Monckton stepped in to effect a compromise settlement of both disputes – the increases for railwaymen naturally being provided at the expense of the taxpayer, now that the railways were nationalized and failing to pay their way. These increases in turn led to a general increase of wages throughout industry. The Government had thus shown that for the sake of industrial peace it was willing to abandon its original object of curbing the inflation which had manifested itself in the later years of Labour rule.

It was not very surprising that the Government made a further attempt to persuade the union leaders to agree to some form of permanent machinery for the settlement of industrial disputes. In dealing with the engineering and shipbuilding wage claims, the Minister of Labour had appointed courts of inquiry which were presided over by Lord Justice Morris. These courts, in making their reports, suggested that permanent bodies should be established to consider the complicated economic arguments which they had been called upon at short notice to assess. Sir Walter Monckton welcomed this idea, and passed it on to his National Joint Advisory Council for the consideration of the two sides of industry. At about the same time the Permanent Secretary of the Ministry, Sir Godfrey Ince, proposed that all industries should have provision for arbitration as a last resort in their negotiating procedure. The T.U.C. leaders, however, lost little time in rejecting both proposals, for they felt that there were no fresh circumstances to justify a change in their existing attitude. It was perhaps paradoxical, but it was inevitable, that the Conservative hopes of solving one of the most important economic problems with which they were faced should founder on the individualism of the trade-union leaders.

Partly as a result of the Government's Fabian tactics, the early 1950s were strike-free to a degree quite comparable with those of the previous two decades. Neither the number of stoppages nor the total of working days lost increased significantly in the years 1952–4. On the whole, public opinion was not unfriendly to trade unionism, and if there were some cases of unions restricting the rights of the individual through the 'closed shop', there was at least one anachronistic example of a firm insisting on non-unionism among its employees. This was D. C. Thomson's, the Dundee printers, which in April 1952 dismissed a number of its men when they went on strike for union recognition, and resisted all forms of pressure for their reinstatement.

But the election year of 1955 saw a considerable rise in the number of stoppages and a loss of working days which was half as much again as in any other year since the war. It might have been supposed that this would prove more damaging to the Government in power than to the Opposition; but in fact the public blamed the unions for the disputes, and as a result of the organic connexion between the unions and the Labour Party, this benefited the Conservatives at the general election. To understand how this came about, it is necessary to examine the three major strikes which took place either shortly before, during, or immediately after polling day on 26 May.

We may take first the dispute among the dockers, which had its immediate origin in a strike at Hull in August 1954. The Hull dockers objected to the hand-scuttling method of unloading grain, and went on unofficial strike; but their union, the Transport and General Workers, knew that they were in breach of agreement and ordered them back to work. According to the Transport and General Workers, the National Amalgamated Stevedores and Dockers took advantage of their resentment to recruit them to their own ranks, in defiance of the Bridlington Agreement; according to the Stevedores, the Hull dockers insisted on joining them. They were followed by substantial numbers of dockers at Birkenhead, Liverpool, and Manchester; and in October the Stevedores called a strike of London dockers against 'compulsory overtime', which led to a stoppage of large numbers of men belonging to the Transport and General Workers as well as of their own members. The London strike proved to be a failure, and the Stevedores did not make any recruits there; but at the end of the year it was reckoned that some ten thousand provincial dockers who had formerly been in the Transport and General Workers had transferred to the Stevedores.

The Transport and General Workers did not have very much difficulty in persuading the T.U.C. Disputes Committee that the Stevedores were in breach of the Bridlington Agreement, and in securing their suspension from membership of the T.U.C. pending the return of their new members to their old allegiance. But by this time the men concerned were refusing to accept orders as to which union they should belong to. In March 1955 the Merseyside men won a two-day strike against the local Dock Labour Board in order to break the Transport and General's 'closed shop' there, which the Board had accepted; and in May – the election month – a more widespread struggle, which lasted forty days but ended in failure, was fought to secure representation for the Stevedores on the provincial port joint committees. Later in the year, having failed to break the Transport and General Workers' monopoly position on these committees, and being faced by the threat of expulsion from the T.U.C., the Stevedores decided to return the provincial dockers to the Transport and General Workers; but they then found themselves prevented from doing so by a Liverpool docker called Francis Spring, who took out an injunction against them to restrain them from excluding him from membership. This injunction was upheld in the High Court in March 1956. The T.U.C. Disputes Committee then asked the Stevedores to strike off their books all the provincial dockers who had joined their union except for those in the same position as Spring; but the Stevedores refused to accept these terms and were eventually expelled from the T.U.C. in 1959.

It will be seen that this strike, which like most other strikes involved inconvenience and annoyance to many persons not involved in the quarrel, was discreditable to the trade-union movement for two reasons: it was a strike which owed its origin to a demarcation dispute between two rival unions; and it involved the attempt of one union, and that the stronger one, to prevent the workers concerned from belonging to the union of their choice. It did not matter that the Transport and General was the more efficient organization, which had done far more than the Stevedores in the past to improve the pay and condition of the dockers; the fact was that in 1955 it was no longer the union which they cared to have as their own.

Another strike which attracted wide attention, because of its impact on the public, was that precipitated by the maintenance men at the newspaper printing-presses. These men, who belonged either to the A.E.U. or to the Electrical Trades Union, resented the fact that they were not able to negotiate directly with their employers, but had to accept terms negotiated on their behalf by the printing unions. They therefore struck to obtain the necessary direct recognition. This also, therefore, was largely a conflict between unions, although there was no question of the printing unions seeking to incorporate the men concerned within their own ranks. When the strike began on 25 March, the printing of newspapers came to an end, and the printers' unions, whose men were thrown out of work, approached the T.U.C. General Council to intervene on their behalf. The trouble was clearly due in large part to the policy of the E.T.U. and of the London districts of the A.E.U., in which Communist influence was strong and industrial militancy was regarded as a special virtue. The E.T.U. in fact went so far as to declare all strikes as automatically official from the start. In this case, with London newspaper production entirely halted, it was not until 6 April – almost two weeks after the stoppage – that any contact took place between the leaders of the printers' unions and those of the unions to which the maintenance men belonged. The strike was finally settled only on 19 April, after a joint committee of the unions concerned had come to terms with the Newspaper Proprietors Association. Here was another glaring example of industrial stoppage being occasioned primarily by lack of liaison between unions.

As soon as the public had their newspapers returned to them, they read of the threat of a national railway strike. The railway unions had long been demanding a fresh increase of pay, and when early in 1955 the Transport Commission at last found itself in a position to make an offer which the unions could accept it fell foul of the disagreement between the Railwaymen and the Locomotive Engineers on the size of the differential between skilled and unskilled men. The Locomotive Engineers, the footplate men's union, demanded an increase which the Transport Commission, having already come to precise terms with the Railwaymen, was unable to give them. The result was a national strike, originally announced for 1 May, but then postponed to 29 May – three days after polling in the general election, but close enough to throw its shadow over the political campaign. The strike lasted for over a fortnight, and was eventually ended by an agreement to accept the report of an independent referee.

None of the three disputes which we have discussed would have deserved more than passing notice solely on the basis of its size and duration and its effect on the economy. Even a national rail strike was not what it had been in the days before road transport had fully developed. Their significance lay rather in their causes and in the consequent impact on the general reputation of the trade-union movement. A Gallup Poll in the spring of 1955 revealed that a large majority of people felt that the Government had if anything erred on the side of weakness in dealing with the unions, and this was true even of Labour supporters. The effect of the strikes on the actual results of the election is difficult to assess; and speakers on both sides were chary of discussing it in their campaign speeches. But in considering the reasons why the overall majority of the Government was increased from seventeen to sixty, most observers felt that this was an important factor. As we shall see, it also marked a turning-point in the public reputation of the unions themselves.

The incidence of labour disputes in the spring of 1955 caused the correspondence columns of the leading newspapers and journals to be full of proposals for trade-union reform. Some thought that there should be legal provision for a ballot of union members before any strike took place. This, of course, would not prevent unofficial strikes, but there were also those who thought that unofficial strikes should be declared illegal. Presumably they had forgotten, or had never known, what had happened when strikes were illegal during the two world wars. Another not unrelated suggestion was that there should be a system of compulsory arbitration for all disputes. Finally, there were the more cautious critics who urged the appointment of a commission of inquiry into the trade unions – a course of action which in fact formed part of the Liberal Party's election programme.

To the relief of the T.U.C., none of these suggestions won the approval of the Government. Monckton, who continued for a time as Minister of Labour, was apparently satisfied, in the absence of enthusiasm for changes in the law on the part of the T.U.C., to carry on in the traditional way. He made this quite clear, not only in conversations with T.U.C. leaders but also in a debate on industrial relations in the Commons shortly after the new Parliament assembled. As for the leaders of the General Council, they had learnt one thing from their recent experiences, and that was that it was desirable for them to have powers to intervene in a dispute before it had developed into a stoppage, instead of being obliged to wait until the stoppage had already begun. They requested and secured from the 1955 Congress the necessary approval for this addition to T.U.C. powers.

But this change, useful though it no doubt was, could do nothing to grapple with the fundamental causes of such things as demarcation disputes, unofficial strikes of all kinds, and instances of injustice to the individual worker. The question was, could the union leaders themselves, or the T.U.C. General Council on their behalf, institute sufficiently sweeping reforms in their structure and administration to enable them to win back their good name? It did not seem very likely, for the General Council was naturally dominated by the big general unions, and these were precisely the unions which had most to lose by any recasting of union structure on industrial lines. In any case, as it happened, the united leadership of the General Council was broken up in 1955. Arthur Deakin collapsed and died at a May Day meeting, and was succeeded by Arthur Tiffin, the Assistant General Secretary of the union, who himself died before the year was out. In 1956 the succession passed to Frank Cousins, a left-wing militant whose opinions contrasted sharply with those of his predecessors. Tom Williamson carried on as secretary of the General and Municipal Workers, but his personality was by no means as forceful as Deakin's. Vincent Tewson was still the T.U.C. secretary, but he was not the sort of person to take a determined initiative. The one leader of a major union who appeared to favour a substantial re-organization of industrial structure was Jim Campbell of the Railwaymen, but he was killed in a motor accident in Russia in 1957.

Meanwhile, industrial relations continued to be more unsettled than they had been before 1955. In each of the years 1955–8 the annual number of stoppages due to strikes or lock-outs was higher than before 1955, and with one exception the annual number of working days lost as a result was higher than in any year since 1944. It would be very mistaken to suppose that the bulk of these stoppages were due to faults of trade-union structure; but it would be equally mistaken not to acknowledge that this was an important factor in many of them. The point may be illustrated from the experience of the motor industry, which since 1945 had joined coal, engineering, shipbuilding, and the docks as one of the most strike-prone occupations. The other industries in this category had special reasons for their bad industrial relations, such as the discomfort and danger of the work and the prevalence of high unemployment between the wars; but these reasons did not apply in motor manufacturing. Yet by the later 1950s the motor industry was suffering a loss of working days which was seven or eight times the national average. It is difficult not to believe that the trouble was due in part at least to the large number of unions which had bargaining rights in the industry, and to the strength and independence of the shop stewards and their committees.

Such an interpretation gains force from examination of the report of the 1957 Ministry of Labour inquiry into industrial relations at Briggs Motor Bodies factory at Dagenham, where constant friction, culminating in the dismissal of a shop steward, had caused innumerable stoppages of work. The inquiry revealed that the shop stewards' organization at Briggs was a body of exceptional independence, financed by a lottery which in five months had brought in £16,150, of which only £9,339 was spent in prizes. The disbursement of the profit was subject to no control by the unions to which the men belonged; and it could be said that the shop stewards' committee constituted a completely independent focus of power. The court recommended that the unions should at once take steps to restore their authority over the committee and deprive it of its excess power; but it was difficult to see how they could combine to do this, as so many unions with widely divergent policies were represented among the workers of the factory.

In the years 1957 and 1958 there was an uneasy balance within Congress, owing to the disarray of both the left wing and the right wing. The Communist Party was suddenly suffering from numerous defections and unpopularity owing to the Soviet suppression of the Hungarian uprising at the end of 1956; and the right wing was weakened by the fact that the Transport and General Workers under Frank

Cousins was no longer clearly on its side. Frank Cousins himself hovered ambiguously in the middle, using left-wing phraseology but acting cautiously when the interests of his union were directly threatened. The result was a tendency of Congress to pass resolutions denouncing the Government with acclamation, but to do nothing to put its own house in order. At the 1957 Congress there were no card votes whatsoever; and the 1958 Congress was also much less controversial than usual.

To some extent, it is true, the unanimity of Congress arose from the feeling of most trade-union leaders that they were being pushed more and more on the defensive against public opinion, the courts, the Government, and the employers. In 1957 the employers in the engineering and shipbuilding industries had been prepared to risk a strike in an effort to prevent the usual annual increase of wages; and in fact a strike had taken place, lasting for seventeen days in shipbuilding and ten days in engineering. The political weakness of the Government after the failure of the Suez operation, combined with the temporary inflation of prices that followed, no doubt accounted for the readiness of the new Minister of Labour, Mr Iain Macleod, to find an excuse for intervention and a compromise settlement. A year later, however, the Government felt stronger, and buttressed its views on the undesirability of wage increases with the aid of an expert Council on Prices, Productivity, and Incomes, under Lord Cohen. Consequently, the Minister of Labour refused to intervene in a strike of London busmen. Frank Cousins, to whose union the men belonged, attempted to persuade the T.U.C. General Council to intervene on his behalf, but it became apparent that most of his colleagues were afraid of the consequences of such action; and so he was obliged to make terms with the London Transport Executive which were very little different from those which he could have obtained before the strike. The London busmen had been out for six and a half weeks, and not a few of them took the opportunity to leave their jobs once and for all.

It was in accord with this tougher attitude on the part of the Government that the Minister of Labour should announce in October 1958, that he was allowing the National

Arbitration Tribunal to go out of existence. The Tribunal, which had survived the abandonment of the war-time Order 1305 in 1951, had been valued by the unions because it usually led to the award of a pay increase, however small. The Industrial Court, of course, remained in existence as an alternative resort, but it was not compulsory. As the 1950s drew to a close it looked as if the climate of industrial relations was becoming more and more unsettled.

Throughout the 1950s, and to an increasing extent as the decade ended, the unions were in the political limelight because of their role within the Labour Party. In a period which saw considerable dissension within the party on grounds of policy, the power of the union leaders to determine the issues at annual conferences by the weight of their 'block vote' attracted a good deal of notice. Naturally, the minority which was voted down by the 'block vote' – that is to say, the left wing, at least until the end of the decade – was full of protestation at the way in which a small group of union leaders could exercise so much power. Aneurin Bevan, the leader of this minority, went so far as to describe the use of the 'block vote' at the 1951 conference as 'a travesty of the democratic vote'. The right-wing union leaders, for their part, made little attempt to soften the impact of their authority and influence. Arthur Deakin, for instance, when faced with a hostile audience at the 1952 Party conference, said bluntly: 'You know you would listen if you wanted to get money from the trade unions.' And later on at the same conference, he took the opportunity of his position as the T.U.C. fraternal delegate to demand the dissolution of the Bevanite groups and an end to the 'carping criticisms' of their weekly organ, *Tribune*.

The most decisive intervention made by Deakin and his right-wing colleagues was at the 1954 party conference. There were two important issues to be decided on this occasion, namely, whether the party would support the rearmament of Germany, and who should be elected to succeed Arthur Greenwood, who had lately died, as the party treasurer. The party leadership had decided to support the Government's policy of encouraging rearmament by West

Germany, but there was a good deal of popular concern and mistrust of the policy, which could easily be exploited by the left wing. At the Trades Union Congress in September approval for German rearmament was carried by only a very small majority, and it was expected that the Labour Party conference in October would see the majority reversed, because the vote of the constituency parties would be against it and there were also some right-wing unions in the T.U.C. which did not belong to the party. In fact, the leadership's decision was approved at the conference by a small majority – and this was because the 'block vote' of the Amalgamated Society of Woodworkers was transferred from opposition to support. The transfer was contrary to the view expressed by the Woodworkers' delegate conference, which had discussed the question only a few months before. It was alleged at the time that it was the result of a threat that George Brinham, one of the union's leaders, would lose his seat on the Labour Party executive if his union voted against German rearmament. Such a threat could only have been carried into effect by the combined action of those controlling the largest 'block votes' – that is, by Deakin and his colleagues, Tom Williamson of the General and Municipal Workers and Will Lawther of the Mineworkers.

The struggle for the post of party treasurer might seem, by comparison, to be a mere domestic squabble. But at this juncture it was of vital importance as a gesture of support by the conference for one or other of the contenders for the party leadership in succession to Attlee, who was on the point of retirement. Bevan was naturally the candidate of the left wing, and had the support of the left-wing unions. The nominee of Deakin and his right-wing colleagues, on the other hand, was no longer Herbert Morrison, the senior right-wing political leader, who was now felt to be too old, but Hugh Gaitskell, Attlee's last Chancellor of the Exchequer, who had the advantage of being several years younger than Bevan, and was therefore likely to outlast him. Gaitskell was elected by over four million votes to Bevan's two million. After this, it was not surprising that when Attlee retired from the party leadership at the beginning of the new Parliament in November 1955, Gaitskell secured a clear majority in the parliamentary party's election for a new leader, in which he was opposed by both Bevan and Morrison.

We have already seen, however, that the right-wing control of the unions began to break up in 1955; and this soon had its effect on the balance of power within the Labour Party. With the accession of Frank Cousins to power in Deakin's union, it became apparent that the Transport and General Workers could no longer be relied upon for support of right-wing policies. On the other hand, the union was not yet committed to a definite left-wing stand; and the first three years of Gaitskell's leadership saw an increasing reconciliation between left and right wings which in part was due to the realization of weakness on both sides and in part to a determination to present a united front to the electorate at the next general election. Bevan accepted the responsibility for foreign affairs in Gaitskell's 'shadow' Cabinet, and defended the parliamentary party's policy of multilateral rather than unilateral nuclear disarmament; and since the Communist Party accepted the same policy in 1957 and 1958, the opposition to the official resolutions on defence at the party conferences of those years was insignificant.

It was in 1959, the year of another general election, that portents of dissension to come appeared in the decision of the conferences of the two largest unions, the Transport and General Workers and the General and Municipal Workers, to support unilateral nuclear disarmament. The decision of the General and Municipal Workers, normally a consistently right-wing union, was reported to have taken place by accident: the political vote was taken after a lot of exhausting industrial business, and many delegates, thinking the result was a foregone conclusion, had gone out to enjoy the sunshine. This provided the excuse for Tom Williamson to reconvene the conference and to reverse the vote. But the Transport and General Workers' officials had no wish to reverse the decision of their own conference, which in fact was an endorsement of the views of its general secretary. With the addition of this union's million and a quarter votes, there was inevitably a large minority against the official foreign policy resolution at the Trades Union Congress in

September; and the uncertainty about Labour's future policy that this suggested may well have had some influence on the outcome of the general election, which took place in October. Another factor, reminiscent of the 1955 election, was an unofficial strike of 2,000 oxygen workers, which began ten days before polling and lasted over a week: it had the effect of causing lay-offs among large numbers of workers in motor manufacturing and kindred industries.

The Labour Party lost still more ground in the 1959 election, and the overall majority of the Conservative Party in the Commons rose to exactly one hundred. But if there was already some concern about the link between the unions and the Labour Party, and the way in which individual trade-union leaders, or determined minorities, could control the 'block vote' at party conferences, it was as nothing to the shock created by the 1960 party conference, when a resolution in favour of unilateral disarmament was carried against the opposition of Gaitskell and his parliamentary colleagues. The resolution, which was put forward by the Transport and General Workers, attracted the support of the A.E.U., whose small policy conference, known as the National Committee, had a large Communist element; of the Shop, Distributive, and Allied Workers, which had something of a left-wing pacifist tradition among its members; and of the Railwaymen, whose annual general meeting endorsed the resolution by a majority of only one vote. Thus, of the six largest unions affiliated to the party, four were willing to defy Gaitskell's policy – and their vote was decisive.

It was now, of course, the turn of the right wing in the Labour Party to complain of the tyranny of the 'block vote' and of the undemocratic way in which the large unions determined their political attitudes. Gaitskell himself, in declaring the independence of the parliamentary party, had suggested that the large unions did not arrive at their political decisions with sufficient care. This comparatively mild criticism was taken a great deal further by most organs of opinion outside the party itself. It was argued that the unions existed, primarily, for an industrial purpose; it was all very well for their leaders to support a political party, but for them to attempt to formulate foreign and defence policy was really an abuse of their powers. In any case, the democratic process within the unions was often imperfect, and in many cases appeared to be exercised by small minorities of the members. How could the change in policy of the Transport and General Workers be explained, except in terms of the succession of Frank Cousins to the place of Arthur Deakin? Yet this change of individuals meant a transfer of a million votes at the party conference. And then there was the power of the tiny Communist minority in the Electrical Trades Union and in important sections of the A.E.U., as well as in some smaller unions.

In the winter of 1960–1 Gaitskell continued his battle against the conference decision, and succeeded in retaining a considerable majority of the parliamentary party in his support. Gradually the right wing within the unions rallied its forces, and in the spring the union conferences began to change their minds on the unilateral issue. In May the conference of the Shop and Distributive Workers reverted to multilateralism, and the National Committee of the A.E.U. did likewise. In July the Railwaymen followed suit, and this left the Transport and General Workers as the only one of the 'big six' unions supporting unilateralism. The party was now 'in step' once more, at least temporarily; but the by-elections and opinion polls of this period showed only too clearly what damage had been done to the reputation of the party by its bitter and at times squalid internal dissensions.

As early as 1952 an American research student, Joseph Goldstein, had published a study of apathy in a branch of the Transport and General Workers. He showed that with only two or three per cent of the members attending branch meetings, control easily fell into the hands of a small clique, which might well be a group of Communists. The study was criticized at the time as being unduly sensational and perhaps unrepresentative; but four years later B. C. Roberts of London University concluded from a considerably wider survey that the average branch attendance was not much more than about five per cent of total membership.

Since questions of political significance are generally regarded by union members as being of less importance than purely industrial matters, it is clear that a small group of determined and disciplined members such as the Communists can easily make remarkable headway in a union in which their views are shared by only a fraction of the total membership. This explains how it is that many unions can fall under Communist control at a time when Communist parliamentary candidates regularly lose their deposits. And once in control, a Communist group may be exceedingly difficult to dislodge, for its members, not believing in genuine political democracy, will be quite willing to subvert the union's electoral system in their own favour; and British law provides an altogether insufficient remedy to the union members who suffer in consequence.

All this was illustrated in the most remarkable fashion by events within the Electrical Trades Union, the seventh largest of the unions, with a total membership in 1960 of almost a quarter of a million. It was during the Second World War that this union fell completely into Communist hands, and although in the early 1950s there were a few of its members who were prepared to try to break the grip – notably John Byrne, a Glasgow Catholic – they made little impact either on the union members or on the general public. This situation was changed, however, as a result of the Hungarian revolt in 1956, when about a third of all the card-carrying Communists throughout the country resigned or lapsed from membership – among them two leading members of the E.T.U., Les Cannon and Frank Chapple. Cannon, who was the head of the union's unique Education College at Esher, was deprived of his post, and although he had just been elected a delegate to the 1957 T.U.C. Congress, he was prevented from attending – an incident which caused a minor scandal at the time.

With Cannon and Chapple collaborating with Byrne and other opponents of Communism inside the union, the prospects for reform of the union gradually began to improve. The Communist leadership, for its part, had to intensify its struggle to maintain control, and this resulted in increasing evidence of fraud in union elections – forged ballots, arbitrary disqualification of branches voting against official nominees, and direct falsification of returns. Specific accusation of malpractice were made by Woodrow Wyatt, the right-wing Labour M.P., on the basis of this evidence, both on the B.B.C. 'Panorama' programme and in the press, particularly in the *New Statesman*. The General Council was reluctant to intervene in the internal affairs of an affiliated organization, but at the end of 1958 it finally decided to do so, because, as it declared,

it was increasingly difficult . . . to ignore the possible effect . . . on the prestige and public reputation of the trade union movement as a whole.

It therefore asked the E.T.U. for an explanation, and a long correspondence ensued in which it became apparent that the union's leaders had nothing to say in their own defence. The General Council urged that the union should take legal action against its supposed traducers, but they maintained in reply that they had 'little faith in either the competence or the impartiality of the Courts' – a view which, as they pointed out, had been shared by non-Communists such as Citrine. To this the General Council replied agreeing that

. . . it is generally the tradition in the Trade Union Movement to avoid rather than to embark on litigation. The present circumstances are, however, quite exceptional. Some of the statements made about the E.T.U. and its officers are not vague and general insinuations, but quite specific and unequivocal accusations.

A number of months were then taken up while the E.T.U. conducted an inquiry of its own into the accusations – an inquiry which exonerated the union officers, but which the General Council felt to be completely inadequate. In the spring of 1960 the General Council had reached the point of directing the union either to take legal proceedings or to cooperate with the General Council itself in a thorough inquiry.

It was at this juncture, however, that Byrne and Chapple issued writs against the union and its officers for alleged fraud in the 1959 election for general secretary, when Byrne stood against the retiring secretary, Frank Haxell, and was supposed to have been defeated. The General Council thereupon suspended further action until the conclusion of this case. The hearing took place about a year later, before Mr Justice Winn, and judgment was given on 28 June 1961. The judge found that a group of Communist leaders of the union, including Frank Foulkes, its President since 1945, and Frank Haxell

conspired together to prevent by fraudulent and unlawful devices the election of the plaintiff Byrne in place of the defendant Haxell as General Secretary of the defendant's union.

He declared Byrne to be general secretary forthwith.

This was not the end of Communist control of the union. Foulkes was still in office as President, with a largely sympathetic executive; and between them they succeeded in drastically curtailing the powers of the new secretary. The General Council therefore recommended to Congress in September that the union should be expelled from the T.U.C., and this was carried by an overwhelming vote. The Labour Party took similar action in October. But the situation was transformed by the results of the autumn election for the executive, which was conducted under safeguards against fraud and which resulted in the unseating of most of the existing members and their replacement by supporters of Byrne. The new executive took office on 1 January 1962, and at once set about restoring the union to its rightful place in the movement. In the course of 1962 the union was re-admitted both to the T.U.C. and to the Labour Party.

From the first publication of evidence about fraud in the union to the final break-up of the caucus responsible had been a period of altogether six years. It is hardly surprising that in the course of this tortuous affair voices should have been raised to demand legislation to deal specifically with ballot-rigging in the unions, and also more generally with infringements of the rights of individuals. There were several legal decisions in the later 1950s which suggested that the courts were more ready to take cognizance of the need to safeguard the member against his union, especially if the union by means of the 'closed shop' had a stranglehold upon the opportunities of employment in the trade concerned. In 1955 Spring's case, which we have already mentioned, showed that a union member suing for wrongful expulsion could upset the machinery of the T.U.C. for the settlement of inter-union disputes. In 1956, in *Bonsor* v. *Musicians Union*, damages were awarded to a union member for breach of contract by the union in expelling him contrary to rule, and hence depriving him of his occupation. In 1957, in *Huntley* v. *Thornton and Others*, an engineering worker prevented from obtaining employment because of victimization by a number of union branches was awarded £500 damages. Yet many such cases could easily be avoided by the unions if they took care to amend their rules; and as we have seen it took many years for malpractices in the E.T.U. to be brought to book, and even then some of those responsible were left in office in the union. It was widely suggested that the Minister of Labour – from July 1960 this was John Hare – should obtain powers for the Registrar of Friendly Societies to scrutinize the rules of unions seeking registration, and if necessary to withhold approval. Hare decided, however, to follow the practice of his predecessors in not attempting to override the views of the T.U.C.; and he expressed himself as satisfied with the action taken by the General Council in bringing pressure to bear on the E.T.U. officers and in eventually expelling the union from membership.

In March 1958 the official opening took place of the new headquarters of the General Council in Bloomsbury. The building, which was to be known as Congress House, was built in the modern style, with wide expanses of windows, and its appearance was enhanced by two striking pieces of sculpture – one by Sir Jacob Epstein, which was placed in an interior courtyard, and another by Bernard Matthews dominating the main entrance. State trumpeters of the Royal Horse Guards (the Blues) sounded a special fanfare for the occasion, and John Clements, vice-president of Equity, the actors' union, spoke well-known lines from *Cymbeline* in honour of trade unionists who had fallen in the Second World War:

> Fear no more the heat o' the sun,
> Nor the furious winter's rages;
> Thou thy worldly task hast done,
> Home art gone, and ta'en thy wages ...

The handsome new building was not only a memorial to those who had died; it was also a legacy from the able leaders who had guided the T.U.C. in the war years – a legacy of imagination and foresight from a time when the movement, though in the midst of innumerable pressing problems, was at the height of its popular repute.

By the late 1950s the T.U.C. had lost much of that popular repute, and was widely felt to be unable to adapt itself to the changed social conditions of the time. There were some 9,800,000 trade unionists altogether in Britain in 1960, of whom about 8,300,000 were affiliated to the T.U.C. – a gain of half a million in ten years. But the proportion of trade unionists to the total civil employed population, at a little over forty-one per cent, had fallen from a peak of forty-three to forty-four per cent in the late 1940s. This was partly due to the growth in the proportion of white-collar workers in the labour force, for they were distinctly less willing than manual workers to join trade unions. Furthermore, the leading unions in this field, notably the National Association of Local Government Officers and the National Union of Teachers, were not affiliated to the T.U.C. Meanwhile, union dues as a proportion of the worker's basic weekly wage dropped from about one and a half per cent in 1939 to about half that in 1960. In spite of savings in administrative costs, it is hardly surprising that officials were, by and large, inadequately paid and found it impracticable to obtain the skilled professional assistance that they often needed.

There was no reason to question the basic loyalty of most trade unionists to their unions. Strikes in recent years showed much the same degree of solidarity as ever before. But this solidarity no longer extended as fully to the political and social sphere as it once used to do. In the general elections of the 1950s about three in ten unionists must have voted Conservative; and the *Daily Herald*, 'Labour's own national daily', began to lose money heavily towards the end of the decade and in 1960 had to be released from its pledge to support the official policies of the T.U.C. and the Labour Party.

But early in the new decade things began to look up again. At the 1959 Congress the T.U.C. had acquired a new general secretary. Sir Vincent Tewson retired owing to ill-health, and was succeeded by the former assistant general secretary, George Woodcock. Woodcock was a new type of trade-union leader – a man who after several years working as a cotton weaver from the age of thirteen, had won an adult scholarship to Oxford and secured a first-class degree in Philosophy, Politics, and Economics. He was fully aware of the problems posed by the unions' loss of public support, and the need for them to modernize themselves, improve the salaries of their officials, and secure expert professional assistance for their work. In the absence of powerful trade-union leaders of the ability of Ernest Bevin, it was not easy for him to direct the policy of the General Council along consistent lines. But it was probably in large part due to his influence that as the 1960s drew on the trade-union movement began slowly to recover some of the good repute among the wider public that it had lost in the middle years of the 1950s. In 1962, as ten years previously, the Gallup Poll reported that at least two people out of three were prepared to say that 'generally speaking, and thinking of Britain as a whole', the trade unions were 'a good thing'.

CHAPTER THIRTEEN

THE STRUGGLE AGAINST STATE
INTERVENTION, 1962–70

CHANGES of public opinion even at the highest levels do not always coincide with changes of government, and if we are to choose a date for the beginning of widespread concern about the need for a national incomes policy, then 1962 is a better year to choose than 1964, when the Conservative Government was defeated in a general election. In 1962 the strong opposition that the 'pay pause' had encountered suggested that for the future some more flexible and less negative approach to the control of incomes was essential. The government therefore proposed to follow the 'pause', which was due to end in March 1962, with a period of moderate and orderly advance which it hoped to substitute for a 'free-for-all' of rapid increases in wages by the stronger unions, designed to compensate for the period of the standstill. Selwyn Lloyd, the Chancellor of the Exchequer, therefore informed the T.U.C.'s Economic Committee that for the rest of the year wage settlements should conform to a 'guiding light' of a $2\frac{1}{2}$ per cent increase. He invited the T.U.C. to join in sponsoring this policy and to agree to representation on a new body, to be called the National Economic Development Council, which would examine the long-term prospects for growth in the economy and advise on the processes for securing it.

The T.U.C. reaction was one of caution. The members of the General Council, after their unfavourable experience of the 'pay pause', refused to accept any responsibility for the government's policy of restraint in wages. But they were anxious not to be left out of any new planning machinery, if such it was to become, and so they agreed to join the National Economic Development Council. They regarded the sudden

Conservative interest in planning as little more than a death-bed conversion, for it did not seem, from the way the by-elections were going, that the Government would survive for long. At Orpington in March a normally very safe Conservative seat was captured by a Liberal. Further by-election setbacks took place in July, and Harold Macmillan undertook sweeping changes in his Cabinet in order to give the Government a new appearance. Reginald Maudling replaced Selwyn Lloyd at the Treasury and several younger men entered the Cabinet for the first time. The Prime Minister also announced a decision to set up a National Incomes Commission, to inquire into major wage claims and to express an independent opinion about them, from the point of view of the national interest. The T.U.C. was invited to join this body also, but the General Council could see clearly enough that this was only another way of trying to get union support for wage restraint: it naturally refused. In fact, the National Incomes Commission was never very influential and it expired when the Conservatives left office.

The following months were not marked by any notable recovery in the popularity of the Government. An exceptionally severe winter in 1962–3 led to relatively high rates of unemployment, especially in the north; and in January President de Gaulle placed a veto on the British application to join the Common Market. The Labour Party, on the other hand, was closing its ranks in the expectation of an early general election. Gaitskell delighted the left wing of the party by vigorously opposing the Market application; and even when he died suddenly in January 1963 there were no serious re-criminations over the succession between the left and right wings of the parliamentary party. Harold Wilson, who was elected to take Gaitskell's place, had been counted on the left since his resignation from Attlee's Government in 1951. There was no strong right-wing candidate to oppose him, and even if there had been, there was no time for the right-wing union leaders to build him up as Gaitskell had been built up in 1954–5: nor for that matter did the right-wing union leaders have the power which they had had in Deakin's time. In the event, Wilson was accepted readily enough as leader and soon gained the popular standing that Gaitskell had only gradually attained in his years as Leader of the Opposition.

In May the Profumo scandal gave the impression that the Prime Minister was not properly informed about security matters and that he was out of touch with the junior members of his Government. Harold Wilson, on the other hand, was winning ovations for his speeches outlining a programme for a new state-sponsored, science-based industrial growth. Macmillan's illness in the autumn and his consequent resignation of the Premiership did not improve the fortunes of the Conservatives, for Sir Alec Douglas-Home who succeeded him did not give the impression of new and vigorous leadership, and the manner in which he was chosen for the succession led to open quarrelling within his party. Douglas-Home naturally decided to postpone the election as long as possible, and in the end it took place right at the close of the legal term of the 1959 Parliament – in October 1964.

There was no doubt that the trade unions would give the Labour Party fuller support than in 1955 or 1959. Union officials had been thoroughly alienated from the Conservatives by the events of Selwyn Lloyd's Chancellorship, and in addition they now had a particular grievance in the refusal of the Government to grant them any early legislative redress for the adverse effects of the Lords' judgment in the *Rookes* v. *Barnard* case. Douglas Rookes was a draughtsman employed by B.O.A.C. at Heathrow Airport, who in 1955 had decided to resign from his union, the Association of Engineering and Shipbuilding Draughtsmen. The local branch of the union, by threatening a strike which would have been in breach of contract, persuaded the B.O.A.C. management to dismiss Rookes in order to maintain full union membership in the shop. Rookes thereupon brought an action for damages against the leading members of the branch and against the union official who had supported them. Rookes won his case, and at first secured substantial damages; but the decision was reversed in the Court of Appeal. Now, in January 1964, the Lords upheld the original decision. What worried the trade-union leaders was not the question of right and wrong in this particular dispute, but the fact that a way had been found, in spite of the terms of the Trade Disputes Act of 1906, to make union officials liable for damages for threatening strike action in breach of contracts of employment.

The Labour Party was less reluctant than the Conservative Government to commit itself to a quick change in the law on the unions' behalf; and so for this reason also, when Congress met a few weeks before the election, the General Council was anxious to show that it was warmly in favour of a Labour victory. Embarrassing motions were withdrawn under pressure, and Harold Wilson was encouraged to speak at length to the delegates in the capacity of a fraternal delegate from the Labour Party. He spoke of freeing the country from the 'stop–go' of Conservative economics, and although he pointed out that Labour too would have to have an incomes policy, his remarks were sufficiently vague to satisfy the great bulk of the delegates. Even George Woodcock, who did not like taking sides too obviously in the party-political battle, said that the Conservatives, if re-elected, would be 'insufferable'.

In spite of this endorsement by the T.U.C., the general election of 1964 was by no means a decisive victory for Labour. Maudling as Chancellor had pursued a policy of expansion, hoping that a domestic boom would lead to growth and hence to more competitive exports, which in turn would gradually rectify a temporary unfavourable balance of trade. The boom, combined with a good summer, probably accounted for a remarkable recovery by the Conservative Party in the months immediately preceding the election. In the end, Labour secured an overall majority of only five seats. Douglas-Home at once resigned, and Harold Wilson took office, the first Labour Premier for thirteen years. He appointed James Callaghan as Chancellor of the Exchequer, but also set up a new Department of Economic Affairs to plan economic development in the long term. This department was to rival the Treasury in its powers, for it was placed in charge of George Brown, who as deputy leader of the Party already outranked Callaghan. Ray Gunter, a former official of the Transport Salaried Staffs Association, became Minister of Labour, and in order to strengthen the trade-union element in the Cabinet – which in view of the increasingly middle-class character of the parliamentary party, could less easily be supplied from the Labour benches – Wilson brought Frank Cousins straight from the secretaryship of the Transport and General Workers to the new post of Minister of Technology, where he was to undertake the task of encouraging the growth of new science-based industry.

The Labour Government of 1964 was thus closely interlocked with the trade-union leadership, though not as much as that of 1945–51 had been. But it was faced with the same economic problems that had beset its Conservative predecessor, and these had been made more acute by the burden of a large balance of payments deficit which resulted from Maudling's unsuccessful bid for strength through expansion. To prevent this situation from deteriorating, within a few weeks of taking office the new government decided to impose an emergency 15 per cent surcharge on all imports except food and raw materials. Meanwhile George Brown proceeded to work out with both employers and trade-union leaders a statement on the principles of incomes policy. This resulted in a 'Declaration of Intent on Productivity, Prices and Incomes', signed in December: both employers and unions were to do what they could to encourage greater productivity, and were to cooperate in the working of new machinery which the Government was to set up for supervising increases in prices and incomes. This machinery took the form of a National Board for Prices and Incomes, the first chairman of which was Aubrey Jones, a Conservative ex-minister of moderate views. For 1965, the norm for wages increases was to be 3 to $3\frac{1}{2}$ per cent, but larger increases were to be permitted where increases in productivity resulted, where the workers were exceptionally ill-paid or had been treated less well than workers in comparable occupations, or where there was a need in the national interest to stimulate recruitment. This was a formidable catalogue of exceptions. Even so, it was significant that the largest of the unions, the Transport and General Workers, voted against the new policy at a special conference of trade-union executives held to endorse the T.U.C.'s promise of support. Meanwhile George Brown pressed on with the preparation of a National Plan, based on the assumption that the economy would grow by about 4 per cent every year.

In accordance with its promises before taking office, the Government put forward and rapidly carried through Parliament a short bill to close the loophole in the Trade Disputes Act of 1906 which had been opened up by *Rookes* v. *Barnard*. The new measure became known as the Trade Disputes Act, 1965. At the same time, but more or less independently, the General Council of the T.U.C. was persuaded to agree to the appointment of a Royal Commission to look into the problems of industrial relations. The General Council made two conditions, however, for its willingness to cooperate with the Commission: one was that the employers' organization should also be inquired into; the other, that the composition of the Commission should not be unfriendly and that George Woodcock himself should be a member. Lord Donovan, an Appeal Court judge who had formerly been a Labour M.P., became the Commission's chairman.

But the problems of incomes policy would not wait for the outcome of the Royal Commission. In September 1965 George Brown pressed the General Council to agree to a compulsory early-warning system for wage claims and price increases. The element of compulsion was again unwelcome to the General Council, and Woodcock suggested as an alternative that the T.U.C. itself should operate a voluntary scheme. Even this was accepted only very reluctantly by the T.U.C.'s constituent unions. All the same, the Cabinet went ahead with a plan to make compulsory the submission of wage claims and price increases for consideration by the Prices and Incomes Board. Shortly afterwards, in March 1966, there was a dissolution of Parliament, as Wilson judged the moment appropriate to try to increase his precarious majority in the House of Commons.

The 1966 general election gave Wilson the safe majority that he needed for a full term of government. The fact that the T.U.C. and the unions appeared to be responding, however reluctantly, to Labour's initiatives on incomes policy probably played its part in the Government's success. The

Labour Party now had a total of 363 M.P.s, and an overall majority of 97. It was noteworthy, however, that the growing middle-class element in the parliamentary Labour Party was reinforced still further: of the new members elected either at by-elections since 1964 or at the new general election, no less than two-thirds had had a university education. But the election itself did not lead to any significant changes in the composition of the Cabinet.

The new Government quickly ran into trouble on the industrial front, owing to a prolonged seamen's strike, which began in May and was not terminated until early July. There was no doubt that the seamen had a strong case for redress, for partly owing to lack of militancy in the earlier leadership of their union, the National Union of Seamen, their pay and conditions had fallen far behind those of other workers. But because of its incomes policy, the Government was reluctant to see the backlog made up immediately; and the shipping companies, encouraged by this, were prepared to resist. The strike threatened serious damage to the economy, as it prevented the fulfilment of export orders and also the earning of 'invisibles'; it also encouraged speculation against the pound. In late June the Prime Minister, who was clearly getting worried, denounced the militant leaders as 'a tightly knit group of politically motivated men'. It was true that some of them were Communists; and it is possible, though not probable, that the attack had some effect in persuading the union executive shortly thereafter to agree to the terms that they were now offered, which were by no means unfavourable. But the main reason for the strong pressure from the Government for an end to the strike became apparent late in July, when an acute sterling crisis developed. This was surmounted only by a package of deflationary measures, including a six-month 'wage freeze' all too reminiscent of Selwyn Lloyd's 'pay pause' of five years earlier.

As was to be expected, this turn of events intensified the impending conflict between the Government and the unions over compulsory wage restrictions. It had been apparent for some time that Frank Cousins, although a member of the Cabinet, was as hostile as he always had been to the use of compulsory powers: and when George Brown in July finally secured Cabinet approval for his Prices and Incomes Bill, which required prospective price, wage and dividend increases to be notified in advance to the Prices and Incomes Board, Cousins resigned from the Cabinet and went back to his old job as Secretary of the Transport and General Workers Union, where he continued to exert powerful influence in opposition to any element of compulsion in wages policy. But the Cabinet, so far from retreating, was driven by the new sterling crisis to increase the powers proposed in its Bill. Although in the first instance ministers still envisaged voluntary wage restraint by the unions, they added new clauses to the Bill to enable the Government, by Order in Council, to impose the 'freeze' on any employers or workers who sought to defy it. The Bill had a stormy passage at the hands of Labour backbenchers on its way through Parliament, but it received the Royal Assent on 12 August 1966. In September the Association of Supervisory Staffs, Executives and Technicians, led by the vigorous Clive Jenkins who shared Cousins's views on incomes policy, won a test case against an employer who was refusing to pay a wage increase which had been agreed before the Act was passed; and when shortly afterwards the printing unions put pressure on the Newspaper Proprietors Association to make wage increases which were similarly already contracted, the Government invoked the clauses of the Act which imposed the 'freeze' compulsorily.

In August George Brown resigned from the Secretaryship of the Department for Economic Affairs, recognizing that the sterling crisis, which had done such damage to his initiatives in incomes policy, had also defeated his National Plan, based as it was upon the expectation of continuous growth in the economy. He was induced to stay in the Government, and exchanged posts with Michael Stewart, the Foreign Secretary. Stewart was less effective than Brown in resisting Treasury influence, and in any case the priority that now had to be given to the task of strengthening the pound inevitably had the effect of subordinating the Department of Economic Affairs to the Treasury. But it fell to Stewart to announce that the six-month 'freeze' would be followed by an equal period of 'severe restraint'. The T.U.C.

undertook the task of examining and reporting on wage claims, in accordance with the voluntary policy for which it had already secured the unions' approval; and in March of the following year (1967) a conference of trade-union executives agreed by a large majority to continue this system after the compulsory powers had lapsed, as they were due to do, in the summer.

But the economy was not responding as it was supposed to do to the limiting measures that were already in force. The closure of the Suez Canal as a result of the Six-Day War, and the prolonged civil war in Nigeria, both had adverse effects on the British balance of payments. Unofficial dock strikes in London and Liverpool, which ironically were caused by reorganization as a result of the end of the old casual labour system, also weakened confidence in sterling. In November a run on the pound on the foreign exchange led to a decision to devalue; this was followed by the resignation of the Chancellor of the Exchequer, James Callaghan, and by the imposition of further restrictions on the economy by his successor, Roy Jenkins. In March 1968 there followed what Jenkins himself described as 'a stiff Budget', and he indicated that this would be followed by 'two years of hard slog'.

In this situation it was inevitable that the Government should wish to continue to maintain control over wages and prices. Although the standstill clauses of the Prices and Incomes Act lapsed in August 1967, the Government had maintained those clauses of the Act which dealt with the need for early warning of wage and price increases. A new Act provided that when the Prices and Incomes Board reported adversely upon proposed increases they could be delayed for a period of six months from the date of their reference to the Board. In 1968, after devaluation, this period of delay was extended to twelve months. A ceiling of $3\frac{1}{2}$ per cent was imposed on wage increases while the Act was in force, although certain exemptions were again permitted. The Labour back-benchers disliked these measures and there were significant abstentions from voting on each occasion. On 15 May 1968 the Amalgamated Union of Engineering and Foundry Workers (the title of the combination of the Engineers and the Foundry Workers, which had lately merged) held a one-day stoppage against the new powers. The separation between the Government and the trade-union leadership seemed to be accentuated by Harold Wilson's decision in April to replace Ray Gunter at the Ministry of Labour with Mrs Barbara Castle, an intellectual Socialist who had been a successful Minister of Transport but who had no close ties with the trade-union movement such as Gunter had had. Mrs Castle also took over from the Department of Economic Affairs the responsibility for incomes policy, and the Ministry of Labour in this expanded form was now re-named the Department of Employment and Productivity, with Mrs Castle as Secretary of State. She was also given the title of First Secretary: it was obvious that Harold Wilson expected the new Department to be in the forefront of legislative action in the ensuing months, especially as the Donovan Commission was coming to the end of its three years of intensive work.

The Donovan Report was published in June 1968. Unlike its predecessor of a century earlier, it was an agreed report, and only one Commissioner, the economist Andrew Shonfield, had major reservations to offer. In general, the Commission accepted the view urged upon it by George Woodcock and by its academic members, especially Professors Hugh Clegg and Otto Kahn-Freund, that legislative reform of industrial relations was largely impractical. 'Britain', the report stated,

has two systems of industrial relations. The one is the formal system embodied in the official institutions. The other is the informal system created by the actual behaviour of trade unions and employers' associations, of managers, shop stewards and workers.

Since the informal system was increasingly important, and the formal more and more restricted, symptoms of disorder in industry became evident: among them were unofficial strikes and the tendency for actual wage levels to move away from those nationally agreed ('wage drift'). But to restore order, there was little that the State could do. It was for employers and unions to adapt their methods and institutions to the new situation: to encourage collective bargaining in the company and factory, 'confining industry-wide agreements to matters which they are capable of regulating'. This process of adaptation could not be enforced, but it could be encouraged, and for this purpose the Commission proposed the creation of a new permanent body to be called the Commission for Industrial Relations. This body would have an advisory function only. Any attempt to use compulsory powers to secure reform, it was argued,

would undo a great deal of the good we hope to see done through the reform of the collective bargaining system which we recommend.

Legislation might be desirable for certain subsidiary purposes, such as to secure the registration of collective agreements, so that the Commission for Industrial Relations would be able to survey the field and make its recommendations to those directly concerned in collective bargaining. The Donovan Report also proposed that in order to persuade employers to recognize unions, the Government should take powers to impose industrial arbitration where collective bargaining was absent, and where a recommendation to this effect was made by the Commission for Industrial Relations.

The Report rejected suggestions to outlaw unofficial strikes, although it recognized that such strikes had become one of the major problems of industrial relations. It also declared that such devices as the 'conciliation pause' or 'cooling-off period' – the enforced postponement of strike notices while inquiry or negotiation took place – and also the compulsory secret ballot of workers to be called out on strike were not likely to be of much value. In line with the findings of recent research into the motor industry and other areas of major conflict, it stated that:

Unofficial strikes and other types of unofficial action in industry are above all a symptom of a failure to devise institutions in keeping with changing needs.

Similarly, attempts to make collective agreements into legally binding contracts, the Donovan Commission thought, would have undesirable side-effects, hiding the true cause of the trouble and encouraging internal disruption in the unions.

Past experience, in particular the Betteshanger miners' strike of 1941, when the imprisonment of the miners' leaders simply led to a prolongation of the strike, suggested that compulsion could not readily attain its object.

In spite of the unanimity of the Commissioners, the Report at once became a matter of controversy. This was largely because public opinion was now highly critical of the state of disorder in industrial relations, and was disappointed to hear that no drastic action was recommended, but rather a prolonged application of minor remedies. The Conservative Party, reversing its policy of 'live and let live' during the Churchill and Macmillan governments, had already published a policy statement, *Fair Deal at Work*, which proposed that collective bargaining contracts should normally be enforceable at law, that a 'conciliation pause' of sixty days should be enforced before strikes took place which endangered the national interest, and that compulsory ballots should be held among union members asked to strike.

Also among the dissatisfied was the new Secretary for Employment and Productivity. As a more dogmatic Socialist than most of her colleagues, Mrs Castle saw no grave problems in the further extension of State powers in this field, and she decided that it was necessary to go further than the recommendations of the Donovan Commission. In persuading other senior ministers, she could point to such damaging contemporary incidents as the strike at the Girling brake factory in Cheshire in November 1968, when a stoppage by twenty-two operatives engaged in an inter-union dispute led to the lay-off of more than five thousand workers in the motor factories. There were now no senior members of the Cabinet who had had extensive experience as trade-union officials, for Gunter, who had been moved from the Ministry of Labour to the Ministry of Power, had already resigned from the Cabinet altogether, complaining that it was 'over-weighted with intellectuals': this became still more true after he had gone. The result of Mrs Castle's consultations was the White Paper *In Place of Strife*, published in January 1969, which made three proposals that went beyond the recommendations of the Commission. First, a 'conciliation pause', restricted, however, to twenty-eight days, was included; secondly, the Secretary of State was to have power to impose a settlement in an inter-union dispute, if neither the T.U.C. itself nor the Commission for Industrial Relations – which was to be set up as the Donovan Report had recommended – had achieved an agreed solution; thirdly, the Secretary should have power to order a strike ballot if the circumstances justified it.

Mrs Castle was still anxious to try to persuade the T.U.C. to accept her proposals; and indeed the draft White Paper was seen by all members of the General Council before it went to the full Cabinet. There were, to be sure, proposals in it which were acceptable and even attractive to the unions, such as that every employee should be given a legal right to join a union, and that public grants and loans should be made available to the T.U.C. and to individual unions in order to encourage mergers or to finance training and research. But opinion on the General Council quickly hardened against the White Paper as a whole. George Woodcock's initial reaction was not unfavourable; but the power of decision really lay with the big unions, and Frank Cousins, who at once opposed the proposals, found a new ally in Hugh Scanlon, the left-winger who had now replaced the moderate Sir William Carron as President of the Engineers and Foundry Workers. Woodcock had been in poor health for some months and at this point he accepted an invitation to become the first Chairman of the Commission for Industrial Relations, which the Government decided to set up at once. He was succeeded as General Secretary of the T.U.C. by Victor Feather, who had served as Assistant Secretary for many years and shared much of Woodcock's outlook. But Feather could not take much of the initiative himself as he had to wait until the following September in order to be confirmed in office by the annual Congress.

Early in March the White Paper was debated in the Commons, and a major revolt of Labour back-benchers, many of them from the normally loyal Trade Union Group, which still had a considerable membership, at once became apparent. Some 53 Labour M.P.s voted against the Government, and another 40 or so abstained. Furthermore, a few days later the National Executive of the Labour Party, on which the trade unions had substantial direct representation, declared its opposition to the White Paper, and it soon leaked out that among the members of the committee who had taken this view was a senior Cabinet minister – James Callaghan, now Home Secretary. This did not prevent Mrs Castle, with the support of Harold Wilson, from pressing on with the preparation of a Bill, and in mid-April, when Roy Jenkins made his Budget speech, he announced that although the Government was prepared to allow the compulsory powers under the Prices and Incomes Act to lapse at the end of 1969, it was bringing forward at once a short Industrial Relations Bill incorporating the main features of *In Place of Strife*. The Bill in fact included the 'conciliation pause' and the power to settle inter-union disputes, but not the strike ballot.

The parliamentary Labour Party was dismayed at this decision and it soon became apparent that the Government was faced with the most formidable revolt of its experience. Groups of M.P.s began to discuss ways of removing Harold Wilson from the leadership; others decided to oppose the Bill, but still hoped that a compromise between the Government and the T.U.C. would prevent it from being voted on in its existing form. But in fact both Harold Wilson and Barbara Castle were unwilling to compromise. Knowing that public opinion was behind them, they were all for pressing the whole Bill as quickly as possible. Such attempt at compromise as was made came from Victor Feather and the General Council. They drafted a statement entitled *Programme for Action* which indicated the extent of the concessions that the major union leaders found tolerable. They were prepared to have the T.U.C. give its constituent unions 'opinion and advice' in unofficial strikes, which did not seem to amount to very much; but they went much further on inter-union disputes, promising to provide extra powers for the General Council on this issue, even to the point of expelling recalcitrant unions. These terms were overwhelmingly approved at a special Congress which was held on 5 June at Croydon. But Harold Wilson himself at once authorized a statement which said that the T.U.C. plan was inadequate, as it did not propose any effective way of dealing with unofficial strikes. On 12 June talks between ministers and the General Council broke down altogether.

The deadlock was broken by Robert Mellish, the Government Chief Whip, who at a Cabinet meeting on 17 June explained to ministers that if the Bill was pressed, it would result in so massive a revolt of Labour M.P.s that the Government would be defeated. Wilson and Mrs Castle were still prepared to risk it, but they were forced by their colleagues to give way and accept defeat. On the following day, at a fresh meeting with the T.U.C. leaders, they agreed to accept the terms of the *Programme for Action*, provided they were embodied in the form of a 'solemn and binding undertaking' by the whole General Council. This was really a major defeat for the Government, and especially for the Prime Minister and his First Secretary: it took place, appropriately enough, on the anniversary of the Battle of Waterloo. But all the same, there was some truth in Wilson's statement that the T.U.C. had moved in the previous few weeks further and faster than at any time in the previous forty years.

While the T.U.C. was fighting its defensive battles against legislative interference, the trade-union movement was gradually changing its character under the impact of the continuing transformation of British industry and society. It had, for instance, begun to recruit a good many of the coloured immigrants who had come into the country in the late 1950s and early 1960s. Since 1955 the T.U.C. had been firmly committed to a policy of opposition to all forms of racial discrimination. But the immigrants undoubtedly sometimes encountered forms of discrimination in employment as a result of xenophobia among trade unionists – though this xenophobia was often the result of economic fears, rather than of racial feeling. London transport workers, for instance, felt that their employers were deliberately recruiting immigrants in order to avoid the necessity of raising wages in order to attract indigenous labour. On the whole, trade-union officials performed a valuable role in preventing fears of this character from developing into an attempt to keep all qualified immigrants out of union membership. But the immigrants could not avoid having difficulties when they sought entry to unions which had always had strict apprenticeship requirements. Sometimes, too, language difficulties and misunderstandings based on cultural differences interfered with good relations; and union officials who in any case had little time for going out to recruit new members failed to make special efforts to recruit the immigrants. As has fairly been said, these were sins of omission rather than sins of commission; and there were at least no real efforts to set up separate unions for the immigrants, such as existed at one time in the United States, or segregated branches of unions such as still exist there. Frank Cousins and his Assistant General Secretary, Jack Jones, were conspicuous among those who sought to eliminate the tensions that arose; and Cousins, who was appointed as the first Chairman of the Community Relations Commission set up under the Race Relations Act of 1968, devoted the bulk of his attention to this work after his retirement from his union post in 1969.

The 1960s also saw significant changes in the pattern of unionism as a result of the continuing transformation of British industry. The decline of employment in the coal industry and on the railways was reflected in the shrinking size of the principal unions concerned, the Mineworkers and the Railwaymen: by 1968 the former had declined to only 54 per cent of its membership nine years earlier, and the latter was down to 60 per cent, and their positions in the size order of British trade unions were now sixth and eleventh respectively. The unions that grew most markedly were those catering wholly for white-collar workers. The National and Local Government Officers Association, for instance, rose by a third in the same period, and the National Union of Teachers by little less: both of these were now among the eight largest unions in the country. In some respects they came to resemble the manual workers a little more closely: their militancy grew, and they both joined the T.U.C. in the 1960s, recognizing that the T.U.C. was increasingly becoming the bargaining agent for all employees in negotiations with the Government.

Both the rapid growth and the increasing militancy of the white-collar unions were important factors in shaping the future of British trade unionism, for the time was not far distant when white-collar workers would outnumber manual workers in the total labour force. Traditionally, white-collar workers had been slow to join unions, and the degree of organization that they had so far achieved was very far below that of many major manual unions, including those such as the Mineworkers and the Railwaymen which are now in steady decline. The growth of white-collar employment, and the increase in the proportion of women in the labour force, were the factors mainly responsible for a slight decline in the proportion of trade-union membership to the total labour force since the late 1940s. It was all the more significant, therefore, that the white-collar unions were now recruiting members at a faster pace – albeit only slightly faster – than that at which the white-collar occupations themselves were expanding; and also that the later 1960s witnessed, in instances of militant action by unions varying in character from the British Air Line Pilots Association to the N.U.T., the use of many of the most traditional methods of bargaining used in the past by the manual unions. On the other hand, it was not unreasonable to suppose that the influence of this type of union upon the T.U.C. would be to encourage greater recognition of the importance of good office-work, training and research in the work of the movement.

These changes in the composition of the labour force did not take place without involving structural difficulties for the older unions. Quite apart from the problems of industrial unions in declining industries, there are the conflicts that arise when the white-collar unions, actively seeking new membership, encounter bodies of white-collar workers perhaps only partially organized by existing, predominantly manual unions. The Iron and Steel Trades Association, for instance, fought back vigorously and successfully when challenged by the Association of Scientific, Technical and Managerial Staffs for the representation of white-collar workers in the re-nationalized steel industry. Some white-collar unions also found difficulty in obtaining an adequate say for themselves inside the T.U.C., for the older unions were reluctant to lose their representation on the General Council, and although changes were made now and again, it was a traditional courtesy that members once elected to the General Council should not be obliged to retire, if they had the confidence of their unions, for any other reason than old age.

In 1962 – the year when the enthusiasm for reform in all national institutions first emerged in strength – the General Council adopted a resolution calling for a new inquiry into union structure. The old demand for the reorganization of the movement along industrial lines was heard again, but the T.U.C. inquiry soon came to the conclusion that the tendencies of the time were against it. It was precisely the industrial unions – the Mineworkers and the Railwaymen – that were in decline. The only significant result of the inquiry was to lead the General Council to ask the Government to pass a measure to make trade-union amalgamations easier than they had been in the past. This was done by the Trade Union (Amalgamations) Act, 1964: according to its terms, a simple majority in a special ballot in each union concerned is sufficient to sanction a merger. The Act encouraged the tendency, which had long been in operation, for the gradual elimination of the smaller, narrower, and more localized unions. Among the major amalgamations of the 1960s were that of the Engineers and the Foundry Workers; the formation of the National Graphical Association out of the London Typographical Society (formerly the London Society of Compositors) and the (provincial) Typographical Association; the merging of three powerful craft unions into the Amalgamated Society of Boilermakers, Shipwrights, Blacksmiths and Structural Workers; the merging of the Electricians and the Plumbers; and the creation of the Association of Scientific, Technical and Managerial Staffs. Total trade-union membership grew in the eight years from 1962 to 1970 from about 9·9 millions to over 11 millions; but the number of trade unions fell in the same period from 626 to 538.

The beginning of the 1970s found the trade-union movement in more defensive mood than for over a century. The T.U.C.'s victory over the Labour Government in 1969 turned out to be a Pyrrhic victory, for it contributed to Labour's defeat in the general election of the following year, and to the formation of a Conservative Government pledged to even more far-reaching legislation. Now, a relatively new group of leaders – Victor Feather, the new T.U.C. Secretary, flanked by the two militants Jack Jones and High Scanlon, at the head of the two largest unions, the Transport and General Workers and the Engineers and Foundry Workers – faced the new Conservative Secretary of Employment, Mr Robert Carr, who had an election mandate to bring the law into industrial relations along the lines of the 1968 policy statement, *Fair Deal at Work*. A fierce conflict lay ahead.

CHAPTER FOURTEEN

THE INDUSTRIAL RELATIONS
ACT AND THE SOCIAL CONTRACT,
1971–9

IT was on 18 June 1970 – one year to the day after Harold Wilson's capitulation to the T.U.C. over Mrs Castle's Industrial Relations Bill – that polling took place in a new general election. On this occasion the Conservatives, under Edward Heath, won a completely unexpected victory with an overall majority of thirty seats. Turnout was the lowest since the 1930s, and it seemed that the Labour Party suffered from abstentions by its regular supporters, perhaps occasioned by the ill-feeling generated by the conflict over union reform. If this was so, the result was to put the unions in an even worse situation. The Conservatives had changed their policy since they were last in office: they now proposed to introduce an Industrial Relations Bill of their own, with the intention of bringing legal restrictions into trade-union affairs far more completely than had been envisaged by Mrs Castle.

The outline of the new bill was published in a consultative document in October 1970 and the bill itself appeared in December. It passed through Parliament in the early months of 1971 in spite of bitter opposition from Labour, although the latter's spokesmen were slightly embarrassed by the fact that some at least of the new bill's provisions resembled those of the Labour bill of 1969. The parliamentary guillotine was used to ensure that the bill reached the Statute Book in the 1970–1 session. It established a new court to have jurisdiction in most industrial disputes, the National Industrial Relations Court. The Court had the authority, on the advice of the Secretary for Employment, to impose a conciliation pause or 'cooling-off' period in industrial disputes, and also to require a strike ballot in cases of major importance. It could also impose fines on unions if they undertook 'unfair industrial practices'. The pre-entry closed shop became illegal, and the right of the individual worker either to belong or not to belong to a union was asserted. The post-entry closed shop was replaced by the American concept of the 'agency shop', whereby a union could acquire sole bargaining rights if it secured the agreement of the employer, or won the support of the majority of the employees in a secret ballot. Collective agreements, unless specifically declared not so, were henceforth to be legally binding, as in the United States; and unions were expected to prevent the breach of the agreements or to face prosecution through the N.I.R.C. Unions were also expected to register with a new Registrar of Trade Unions and Employees' Associations; they would obtain some financial advantages thereby, but the Registrar would have the power to demand changes in union rule books in order to guarantee the rights of the individual worker. Finally, workers sacked unfairly could claim compensation, and unions could force employers to recognize them, through the medium of the Court.

The General Council of the T.U.C. reacted vigorously against the bill, holding regional conferences early in 1971 to explain its details and the Council's objections. Two special rallies were held in London. The first, on 12 January, took place at the Albert Hall and was addressed by Harold Wilson, Victor Feather and the leading labour lawyer, Professor K. W. Wedderburn: all made warmly applauded speeches pointing out the dangers of the bill. Then, on 21 February, there was a march through London from Hyde Park to Trafalgar Square, in which Feather reckoned that some 140,000 had taken part. There were certainly twenty-three brass and pipe bands. There was also a national petition which, in spite of a national postal strike at the same time, collected over half a million signatures before being presented to the Commons in March. Finally, the General Council decided to hold a Special Congress, which took place at Croydon on 18 March. Resolutions were carried urging the repeal of the Act and 'strongly advising' unions not to become registered. Unionists were advised to boycott the National Industrial Relations Court and the already existing Commission on Industrial Relations. This led to the resignation of the first Chairman of the Commission, the former T.U.C. Secretary, George Woodcock.

The bill became law in August 1971; but the Labour Party, which had formed a powerful liaison committee with leading representatives of the T.U.C. in order to fight its passage through Parliament, pledged itself to repeal. In September the annual Congress in defiance of the platform stepped up its instructions to its member unions by 'instructing' them to de-register, instead of merely 'strongly advising' them to do so. This posed real problems for some unions, sometimes because of rules made in earlier days obliging them to register, sometimes because of the tax-relief advantages involved in registration, sometimes because de-registration might expose them to fierce competition from staff associations or might cause difficulty in the retention of recognition rights or even existing closed-shop agreements. But the Congress decision once taken was strictly adhered to, and the upshot of this was that the 1972 Congress suspended thirty-two unions with a total membership of just under half a million, which had not obeyed. This meant, as Victor Feather pointed out, that they lost the T.U.C.'s 'facilities and services', and it exposed them to 'poaching' by other unions which would have been forbidden under the terms of the Bridlington Agreement of 1939. The following year the recalcitrant unions, now numbering only twenty and containing less than 4 per cent of the T.U.C.'s total membership, were actually expelled. They included the British Air Line Pilots Association, the Confederation of Health Service Employees, the National Union of Bank Employees and also Equity, the actors' union.

The National Industrial Relations Court, presided over by Sir John Donaldson, endeavoured to introduce 'the rule of law' into union behaviour, but many of the unions, including the largest of all, declined to put their case to the Court. In spite of its informal appearance – Sir John and his two colleagues wore lounge suits – the Court soon showed that it had teeth. The Transport Workers were the nominal defendant in a case brought by a Liverpool haulier, Samuel Heaton, who complained that the union was 'blacking' his container lorries. The union ignored the Court and also an injunction, and a fine of £5,000 was imposed. After the union refused to pay, a further £50,000 fine was imposed for contempt. The union proved to be willing to take the case to the Appeal Court, and there the decision was reversed. But then it went to the House of Lords which confirmed Sir John Donaldson's decision.

Meanwhile the railway unions, which in April had engaged in a 'work-to-rule' to persuade the Railways Board to increase its pay offer, had suffered the impact of the Court in a different way. The new Secretary for Employment, Maurice Macmillan, who had succeeded Robert Carr, had asked the Court to impose a twenty-one-day 'cooling-off' period, and in default of any attempt by the unions to defend their action, the Court agreed to the proposal, to the extent of fourteen days. Then, as further industrial action was threatened, the Secretary asked the Court to impose a secret ballot on the members of the union to see if they would agree. The Court agreed to this proposal, and the ballot took place; but the outcome was disappointing for the Government, as there was a majority of more than six to one in favour of the union leadership. As the *Sunday Times* put it: 'It would seem that the ballot which was intended to cool off the crisis has only served to do the opposite.' After this fiasco the union leaders were in a stronger position to press their claims, which were eventually conceded almost in full. The 'cooling-off' period and the secret ballot were not again invoked by the Secretary for Employment or by the Court.

Meanwhile there was further trouble at or near the docks, where, in spite of the 'decasualization' of the dockers following the Devlin Report of 1966, the problems of modernization had by no means been solved. In July 1972 the Court ordered dockers to stop 'blacking' vehicles using the Midland Cold Storage Company's depot at Stratford in East London. As the order was not obeyed, the Court gave instructions for five dockers to be gaoled for contempt. The incarceration of the 'Pentonville Five', as they were called, at once led to a national strike by some 170,000 dockers. After a few days the Official Solicitor – an officer of the law previously little known – intervened on their behalf, and secured their release. But industrial peace did not as yet return to the docks. The report drawn up by Jack Jones, of the Transport Workers, and Lord Aldington, the Chairman of the Port of London Authority, had been devised so as to allay fears about redundancy as a result of the growth of container traffic. It had to be further revised in the dockers' favour before they would return to work.

Late in 1972, and also in 1973, there were two cases before the National Industrial Relations Court involving another of the largest unions, the Engineering Workers. In the first, a Mr James Goad appealed against exclusion from a branch of the union in East Anglia. The union refused to plead or to pay an initial fine of £5,000: as in the case of the Transport Workers, an additional fine of £50,000 for contempt was then imposed. As the union still refused to pay, some of its assets were seized but its response was to call a series of nationwide one-day strikes. Then late in 1973 the union was ordered to cease 'blacking' the Woking firm of Con Mech, which would not permit unionism among its workers. Later on, when the union did not obey the Court, it had more assets sequestered, and was a fined a sum of £75,000.

The Act was not in its intention one-sided, and it gave the unions the opportunity to gain recognition from hostile employers. But owing to the union boycott of the Court the positive aspect remained largely inoperative. In his report to the 1973 Congress, Victor Feather reported that the Act 'had not affected the level of membership' and that 'attempts by non-T.U.C. unions and staff associations to secure recognition by employers had failed'. He concluded that 'apart from some isolated and damaging cases, the . . . Act had not had as adverse an effect on unions as was first feared'. He attributed this to the unions' solidarity in refusing to register or to cooperate with the Court. Impartial observers might, however, conclude that if the unions had cooperated they would have actually increased their membership. Meanwhile the principal purpose of the Act, which was to reduce the incidence of strikes, had obviously not been achieved. From an average of less than four millions days a year lost under the Labour Government of 1964–70, the total reached a peak of about 24 million in 1972 alone – the highest figure since 1926.

*

Of course, external factors played some part in this poor record of industrial relations. Inflation was already in 1970 running at a historically fast rate – 11 or 12 per cent a year – and the initial Conservative policy of not helping 'lame ducks' obliged employers and especially those in the nationalized industries to stand firm against wage claims. Early in 1971 the Post Office Workers went on strike and held out for seven weeks, to the considerable inconvenience of the public, but they had no strike fund and their members had to rely upon their own resources. They were therefore defeated, though the terms of the settlement were not entirely dishonourable: they were forced to accept an increase of only 9 per cent. In January and February 1972, however, the government faced a more formidable enemy, for there then took place the first national miners' strike since 1926. Although coal stocks were high, the miners picketed the power stations to prevent any type of fuel being admitted. The action was led by Arthur Scargill, the driving force of an unofficial strike committee at Barnsley, who galvanized both the miners and the members of other unions into vigorous action which culminated in the closure of the Saltley power station at Birmingham. This led to a state of emergency and to three-day working; and Lord Wilberforce was appointed to head a Court of Inquiry into the miners' claim. In fact, although Wilberforce conceded the claim virtually in full, the Mineworkers' Union secured even more in direct negotiation with the Prime Minister at Downing Street before calling off the strike. This was a heavy personal setback for Edward Heath, who had hoped to be able to reduce inflation by leaning upon wage claims. As for Scargill, though still only in his thirties he was, in May 1973, elected President of the Yorkshire Miners Association.

In the general election of 1970 the Conservatives had declared their opposition to a compulsory incomes policy. One of the first casualties of the change of government was the Prices and Incomes Board. Nevertheless, faced by increasing inflation in 1972, the Cabinet reversed its policy and late in the year imposed a ninety-day standstill on prices, dividends and rents. In January 1973 the Prime Minister announced a 'Stage II' of his new incomes policy, to start in

April, and to involve the enforcement of strict controls with a Price Commission and a Pay Board. The proposals were put into statutory form in a Counter-Inflation Act. In October of the same year 'Stage III' was announced: this was to be marked by the limitation of wage increases to 7 per cent, except in the case of 'unsocial hours', and by threshold agreements to permit cost-of-living allowances as the index of prices went up. The new Stage III was to run until November 1974. Unfortunately, even as it was beginning to operate, the whole scheme was gravely damaged by a fourfold increase in the price of oil, which was suddenly occasioned by the action of the Arab oil producers at the time of the Yom Kippur War between Egypt and Israel. For a time it seemed doubtful whether the country would survive the 1973-4 winter without severe privation.

Just at this time the Mineworkers were again in dispute with the government over a pay claim. The Government declared the claim to be beyond the limits of Stage III, whereupon the union imposed an overtime ban. Early in December the Government launched a propaganda campaign called 'S.O.S.', or 'Switch Off Something', in the interests of fuel economy, and enforced a speed limit for vehicles of 50 m.p.h. and a heat limit of 63° F. in offices. What was even worse for popular morale was a ban on television after 10.30 p.m. The dispute continued, however, and partly owing to the reduction in the oil supply and partly because of the overtime ban by the miners and also by the electricity power workers, who were also in dispute, the Government felt obliged to introduce a three-day working week for industry from 31 December. At the end of January 1974 the miners held a ballot on a proposal for a national strike, in accordance with the normal practice of the union and not as a result of any provision of the Industrial Relations Act. The ballot gave the executive powers to call a strike, by an 81 per cent majority of those who voted. It was arranged that the strike would begin on 10 February.

Before that date Edward Heath, who had already been defeated once by the Mineworkers and could not afford another defeat, had decided to call a snap general election. The announcement was made on 7 February, and polling was fixed for 28 February, which left just three weeks for the campaign – the minimum time permissible. Heath meant the election to focus on the issue of the Mineworkers' strike and on the fact that some of their leaders were Communists – as indeed they had been since the 1920s. His slogan was 'Firm Action for a Fair Britain', by which he meant to appeal to a national sense of unity as against any sectional interest, such as that of the Mineworkers or of the trade unions in general.

The Labour Party in opposition had become committed to a wide range of nationalization: development land, shipbuilding, aircraft manufacture, the ports and the newly developing North Sea and Celtic Sea oil and gas. Nationalization is rarely popular in the country, but the issue of the Mineworkers' strike enabled Harold Wilson to reassert the pragmatic lines of his earlier election contests. The Labour manifesto was entitled *Get Britain Back to Work*: it criticized the Government for introducing the three-day week, and, pointing out the special nature of the energy shortage, it urged generous treatment of the miners' claim. An air of moderation was also suggested by Labour leaders speaking of a 'Social Contract' which they had worked out with the unions. Challenged on the details, they could not be very specific; but it was true that since January 1972 there had been several meetings of a new T.U.C.–Labour Party Liaison Committee, which included the most influential men on both sides, and which had come to an agreement on the most immediate measures required of a new Government in order to re-establish industrial peace. There would be a repeal of the Industrial Relations Act, action to limit prices and rents and to transform the taxation system in favour of the poorly paid, and an increase in pensions, and the unions for their part would undertake a degree of voluntary restraint. During the election campaign, the Conservatives could reasonably suggest that this was a shaky basis for industrial peace. Nevertheless, there seemed to be a chance that it might work; and even Campbell Adamson, the Director-General of the Confederation of British Industry, the employers' organization, was prepared to say in public that the Industrial Relations Act must go.

The result of the election was more of a setback for Heath than a victory for Wilson. The Labour Party was the largest party in the new House, with 301 members, but this was less than an overall majority. The Conservatives actually polled more votes, but returned only 297 strong. For a few days Heath stayed on in Downing Street endeavouring to persuade Jeremy Thorpe, the Liberal leader, to join him in a Coalition. Two features of the election were the very large vote secured by the Liberals – six million, although it brought them only 14 seats – and the success of different types of nationalists in Scotland, Wales and Northern Ireland. The electorate, taken somewhat by surprise, had reacted almost as if it was engaged in a vast by-election. But Thorpe felt obliged to refuse Heath's offer; Heath then resigned; and Wilson took office as the leader of a minority government.

When Wilson formed his new Cabinet in March 1974 he could not do what Attlee had done in 1945 – namely, balance the working-class and middle-class ministers roughly on an equal basis. The most senior of the trade-union M.P.s to be given office – in fact, the chairman of the miners' group – was Roy Mason, who became Secretary for Defence. The new Secretary for Employment was Michael Foot, the distinguished left-wing journalist; James Callaghan became Foreign Secretary and Denis Healey Chancellor of the Exchequer. Two of the early acts of the new Government were to settle the miners' strike, more or less on their terms, and to end the three-day week in industry. Stage III of the Conservative Government's incomes policy, with its threshold arrangements, was maintained. Mrs Shirley Williams, who had been appointed to the new post of Secretary for Consumer Affairs, introduced subsidies for basic foods and also made agreements with retailers to keep down the price of other items of the family budget. Rent increases were frozen and mortgage interest rates held down.

Legislation was required to repeal the Industrial Relations Act. The Trade Union and Labour Relations Bill, designed to perform this task, went through both Houses of Parliament in the summer, but as the Labour Party did not have a majority it did not reach the Statute Book without some amendments about the closed shop that displeased both Government and T.U.C. Meanwhile the National Industrial Relations Court, although doomed to die – and indeed described in May by the Prime Minister as 'the putrefying corpse of Tory legislation' – showed that it still had a sting: it sequestered £280,000 in cash and securities belonging to the Engineering Workers. The union promptly called a protest strike, but an anonymous group of industrialists settled the debt of £65,000 which was owing to the Court. This demonstrated that employers preferred a quiet time rather than penal action against the unions. The Court was formally abolished in July, and so was the Pay Board. In September union law reverted, broadly speaking, to its condition before the passing of the Industrial Relations Act. As for the unions' side of the Social Contract, the General Council of the T.U.C. resolved, and the Congress in September agreed, that unions should seek pay rises only to keep up with the cost of living after tax, and should take heed of the threshold payments of the Counter-Inflation Act.

On the whole, owing to budgetary changes the pressure of inflation eased somewhat during the summer, and this made it possible for Wilson to call a general election in the early autumn with some confidence as to its outcome. This second round of polling within the same year (1974) took place on 10 October – only a little over seven months after the previous contest. This time the Labour Party secured a majority in the House, albeit wafer-thin: it was three. There were 319 Labour M.P.s, 277 Conservatives and 13 Liberals, with no less than 26 Nationalists or Independents of some sort. The Liberal tide had ebbed somewhat since February, but the strength of Nationalism, especially Scottish Nationalism, had increased. The vote for the Labour Party was now the largest for any one party, but it was still less than 40 per cent of the national total. All the same, Harold Wilson had no hesitation in regarding it as a mandate for his Government. It was certainly true that the Conservatives were in disarray – so much so that in February 1975 a new election was held for the leadership and Edward Heath was defeated by a former Cabinet colleague, Mrs Margaret Thatcher.

It was fortunate for Wilson that the main opposition party

was disorganized after the election. It was apparent that the whole Western world was moving into an economic depression, and in Britain unemployment was rising and was expected to reach the million mark before the end of 1975 – a forecast that proved optimistic. So far as policy was concerned, the Labour Party was deeply divided over whether Britain should continue to adhere to the European Common Market, to which the Heath Government had secured affiliation, against the wishes of the trade unions, from 1 January 1973. The T.U.C. had voted against the principle of membership at its 1972 Congress; and the Labour Party Conference had followed this lead. But the Party's National Executive had decided to seek a renegotiation of the terms of membership and then to submit the question to a national referendum. It gradually became apparent that Wilson and James Callaghan, his Foreign Secretary, were in favour of staying in the Market, if a few improvements could be made in the terms of membership. They did, in fact, secure some changes, particularly in respect of the British contribution to the Community budget and the degree of access to the Market to be provided for New Zealand dairy produce. After winning these concessions, Wilson converted a majority of the Cabinet to the view that Britain should stay in, and it was agreed that this view should be put as the Government's attitude when the referendum was held. But he acknowledged the right of individual ministers and M.P.s to oppose this policy until the referendum had taken place. This was a unique test of public opinion – unique for Britain, that is, for referenda had accompanied the entry of both Ireland and Denmark, and the decision against entry on the part of Norway, all of which took place at the same time as Britain's entry. The voting took place on 5 June 1975. It was preceded by a brief but vigorous campaign, both sides being granted a subsidy from the Treasury for their activities. Of the unions, a few, notably the General and Municipal Workers, favoured staying in the Market; but the bulk of them were hostile, and the Transport Workers gave a substantial sum of money to the anti-market campaign. The upshot, however, was a decisive victory for staying in the Market, by a majority of more than two thirds of those who voted.

With this issue out of the way, the Labour Government had to turn at once to deal with the mounting problem of inflation. In his budget speech in April the Chancellor, Denis Healey, had said 'pay has been moving about 8 or 9 per cent ahead of prices' and 'I do not believe that anyone would claim that the T.U.C. guidelines were intended to permit this result'. Obviously the Social Contract needed strengthening. On 17 May, Jack Jones, the Secretary of the Transport Workers, suggested in a speech that agreement on a flat-rate increase might prove a solution. It was certainly a proposal that had everything to commend itself to poorly paid workers; but it was naturally less acceptable to the highly paid and to those on salaries. All the same, the idea was accepted by the T.U.C. General Council in June and grasped eagerly by the Cabinet. A T.U.C. policy statement in July argued that:

A flat-rate approach has the advantages of focusing increases on the low-paid and preventing unduly large cash increases being obtained by the high-paid. It is clear and simple, most emphasises the General Council's view about the gravity of the economic and industrial situation, and cuts through the complication of separate provisions for particular groups, which . . . had helped to weaken the previous policy. The General Council therefore conclude that there should be a universal application of the figure of £6 per week.

The Government accepted the proposed figure, and modified the proposal only to amend the upper limit of its extension from £7,000 per annum – above which the General Council urged that there should be no increase at all – to £8,500. The scheme was approved by the Trades Union Congress, meeting in September 1975, by seven million votes to less than three and a half million – though the minority included several important unions, notably the Engineering Workers. In the succeeding year, the voluntary restraint which was involved was largely achieved, and by July 1976 the rise in the rate of earnings had been reduced to about 14 per cent per annum, with prices increasing at about 13 per cent. Denis Healey was naturally anxious to secure a 'Stage II' of his pay policy, and he offered the General Council tax reductions in return for their agreement to an increase of only 3 per cent in the next pay round. The General Council felt, however, that a more realistic figure was 5 per cent, with a £4 ceiling and a £2.50 lower limit, and this was agreed. Although Healey was criticized for in effect allowing the unions to determine the level of tax, the following year (1976–7) saw a distinct cut in real wages, for prices increased by nearly 18 per cent, while wages only rose by 6 per cent.

In the spring of 1976 Harold Wilson retired voluntarily from the premiership and was succeeded by James Callaghan after a contested election. Callaghan was the first former trade union official to become Prime Minister; he had at one time held junior office in the Inland Revenue Staffs Federation. Late that summer he was faced by a sterling crisis – fortunately the last before the arrival of North Sea oil put an end to such troubles for at least a decade. In September Healey had to obtain substantial assistance from the International Monetary Fund and, as a condition, this involved cuts in public expenditure and higher taxation, which in turn caused a further rise in unemployment, to the level of 1,636,000 in August 1977. In the summer of that year Healey had set a target of 10 per cent for wage increases and, although the General Council was now no longer willing to support him, he managed largely to secure its observance in the public sector. Earnings as a whole rose by 14 per cent in the course of 1977, but by July 1978 inflation had fallen to about 8 per cent. The result of the two pay rounds in 1976 and 1977 had thus left the workers – except for those in the public service – very much where they had been two years earlier. Furthermore, stoppages of work were at a low level, although at Grunwick, a film processing plant at Brent, North London, mass picketing took place to support a body of workers, mostly Asian, who had been dismissed for attempting to join a union, the Association of Professional, Executive, Clerical and Computer Staff (APEX). The union was moderate in its leadership, and the object of the strike justifiable, but the scenes of picketing appeared very disorderly on the television, for all sorts of people, including even Yorkshire miners, joined in. A Court of Inquiry chaired by Lord Scarman recommended the reinstatement of the strikers, but it was ignored by the firm, and a conciliation report also recommending recognition of the union was declared null and void by the House of Lords because the decision had been come to without consulting the views of those who continued to work at Grunwick. The episode showed that despite the Government's support of the unions both administratively and by legislation, determined employers could still defy entry into their establishments.

By 1978 a new leadership had emerged in the major unions. Jack Jones of the Transport Workers and Hugh Scanlon of the Engineers both retired, their successors being respectively Moss Evans and Terry Duffy. They both, particularly Moss Evans, seemed less capable of maintaining the Social Contract. On the other hand, the new General Secretary of the T.U.C., Len Murray, had now had five years in which to play himself in. His principal weakness, so far as the manual workers were concerned, was that he was not one of them. He had had a grammar school and university education and had spent his whole career inside Congress House. At the same time the Government was much weakened by having lost its overall majority in Parliament; it had to rely, for 1977–8, on a temporary agreement with the Liberals. No more positive labour legislation of the type wanted by the unions was now possible, though a new Trade Union and Labour Relations (Amendment) Act had been passed in 1976 to strengthen the unions' power to enforce the closed shop. At least the Liberals could agree with Labour about the importance of reducing inflation, and in January 1978 Callaghan called for a 5 per cent limit to wage settlements in the next wage round. This figure was repeated in a White Paper published in July, but it was rejected by the T.U.C. at its September Congress by a large majority.

Callaghan had been expected to call an election that autumn, and as he was still more popular in the country than the new and rather abrasive Opposition leader, Mrs Margaret Thatcher, he would have been well advised to do so. Instead, he decided to wait until the spring of 1979 at least. This was an error, for a series of strikes against the recommended pay norm resulted in a 'winter of discontent'. The Ford Motor Company, after a nine-week strike in the autumn, was forced to settle for a 15 per cent pay increase; but the Government was defeated in the Commons when it tried to enforce sanctions against the company for agreeing to the deal. On the other hand, the Government stood firm on the 5 per cent basis in negotiations with local government, Health Service and civil service workers. This led to strikes in the new year (1979) which affected essential services, such as hospitals, schools, water supply, refuse collection and the gritting of roads in icy weather. The settlements eventually made were at the level of 9 or 10 per cent. There was much popular resentment about the inconvenience to the public that the strikes and picketing occasioned, and the Transport Workers' leadership was induced to issue a 'code of practice' to their local officers and members, intended to ensure the maintenance of essential services. On 14 February a 'Concordat' was agreed between the T.U.C. and the Government whereby the T.U.C. drew up a voluntary code to cover the desirability of strike ballots, the limits of picketing and the closed shop, and the need for securing essential services.

Meanwhile in Parliament the Liberal Party had withdrawn its support from the Government in the summer of 1978 and it was surviving only with the backing of the Scottish and Welsh Nationalists, for whom local referenda about the extension of devolution were to take place on 1 March 1979. Neither referendum, however, showed the population sufficiently enthusiastic to empower the government to inaugurate a local assembly. The Scottish Nationalists thereupon withdrew their support from the Government; and on 28 March Mrs Thatcher won a motion of No Confidence by one vote. Callaghan was forced to ask for a dissolution of Parliament, and polling was fixed for 3 May.

In November 1975 the Employment Protection Bill, the second main section of the Labour Government's trade-union legislation, was placed on the Statute Book. It appointed a new Certification Officer to register trade unions and to verify their independence, and it gave statutory authority to the Advisory, Conciliation and Arbitration Service, which had been set up on an administrative basis in the previous year. It considerably extended the rights of employees in respect of notice of dismissal and compensation for unfair dismissal, and it provided women workers with an entitlement to six weeks' maternity pay. Employers were also required to disclose to trade unions information required for collective bargaining purposes. This measure reflected the thinking of the mid-seventies on the need for an extension of the rights of the individual worker, on the unions' increased responsibility in the bargaining process and, not least, on the need for women to be treated with justice and even with generosity in their capacity as a major element in the work force.

The end of 1975 marked a new stage in women's participation in trade-union membership. The proportion in women in all trade unions had already grown in the years 1968–74 from 23·2 to 27·0 per cent, and the proportion of unions affiliated to the T.U.C. had risen from 20·8 to 26·8 per cent. A further impetus was given by the operation of two other statutes which came into force at this time. One was Mrs Castle's Equal Pay Act of 1970, which had allowed a considerable transition period before employers were obliged to pay women as much as men for the same jobs. The other was the Sex Discrimination Act, 1975, which required employers to offer most jobs to both men and women on equal terms, and which established an Equal Opportunities Commission to deal with any cases of complaint. But this legislation could not remove some of the main reasons for difference in earnings between men and women, such as the large amount of overtime worked by men and the fact that many women were part-time workers. The disparity also applied to full-time trade-union officials, of whom in 1975 only 71 were women, as compared to 2,259 men.

During the 1970s membership of the T.U.C. had risen steadily, and reached a peak of over 12 million in 1979. As the number of separate unions declined, the average membership per union rose from 19,000 in 1969 to 30,000 in 1979. The largest single union, the Transport Workers, passed the 2 million mark and the Engineering Workers, with almost 1 million, were not so far behind. Next came the General and Municipal Workers with less than a million members and then, the relatively recent T.U.C. recruit, the

National and Local Government Officers, with 753,000. As in the 1960s, the fastest-growing unions were those catering for white-collar staff. All the same, the membership of the General Council remained biased towards the old manual unions and at the 1979 Congress Roy Grantham, secretary of APEX, moved a resolution in favour of automatic representation on the Council of all unions with over 100,000 members each. He also called for greater representation of women on the Council. He was not to get his way at once, but his time would come.

Before then, in May, the General Election had transformed the political scene. There is little doubt that industrial relations had an important impact on the outcome; the Gallup Poll in March had found that 81 per cent of respondents disapproved of the Labour Government's handling of the subject. No less than six paragraphs of Mrs Thatcher's manifesto were devoted to proposals for reform in this sphere. She promised to reform the picketing law so that disputes took place peacefully; to restrict the closed shop to firms where 'an overwhelming majority of the workers involved vote for it by secret ballot'; and to 'provide public funds for postal ballots for union elections and other important issues'. She also indicated that unions should 'bear their fair share of the cost of supporting those of their members who are on strike'. Pay bargaining in the private sector would be 'left to the companies and workers concerned'; in the public sector, the criterion would be what 'the taxpayer and ratepayer can afford'. This was immediately followed by a promise to cut income tax. Although Labour's national executive had been proposing promises of a markedly left-wing character – abolition of the House of Lords, compulsory planning powers, bank nationalization and the abandonment of nuclear weapons – all these items were vetoed by Callaghan and the result was a manifesto which, as the *Economist* said, was 'as moderate as any on which the party has campaigned'. But the public was reminded of the link with the trade unions by the creation of a body called the Trade Union Committee for a Labour Victory, which was designed to channel union political funds to the party's candidates and to mobilize union activists in the party's support.

All the same, the country voted for a change. There was a

national swing from Labour to the Conservatives, amounting on average to 5·2 per cent. The Conservatives won 339 seats, giving them an overall majority of 43. Labour was reduced to 269, and there were 11 Liberals and 16 others. In view of the announced Conservative industrial policies, it was clear the trade unions were in for a difficult time.

CHAPTER FIFTEEN

ON THE DEFENSIVE: THE 1980s

ON taking office in May 1979 Mrs Thatcher appointed James Prior as her Secretary for Employment. Prior had previously been the Opposition spokesman on the subject, and he was inclined to favour a live-and-let-live policy. On the other hand, the events of 1978–9 had convinced him and the whole Tory leadership that something had to be done about secondary picketing – that is to say, the picketing of firms not directly involved in a dispute – and also about the closed shop. In July 1979, therefore, he issued a consultative document which called for the limitation of picketing to the employees involved in a dispute and to their place of work, for expansion of exemptions from the closed shop and for the provision of public funds for secret ballots before strikes and in the election of full-time trade-union officers. A bill along these lines (later the Employment Act, 1980) was introduced to the Commons in December 1979 and obtained the royal assent in the summer of the following year. Although Prior began discussions on the bill with the T.U.C., the latter broke them off on 4 March 1980 and called for a 'Day of Action' on 14 May – a one-day strike against the government's policies. But the response of trade unionists to the 'Day of Action' was very patchy, which was not surprising as so few trade-union members actually opposed the policies. On 13 November the Commons also approved a code of conduct to govern picketing and the closed shop. The unions were in any case weakened by the business recession, which led to an increase of unemployment to over two million by the end of the year.

Meanwhile the strict policies of the new Government towards the nationalized industries had led to the British Steel

Corporation offering its employees a rise of only 2 per cent. In January 1980 this precipitated a prolonged strike in the industry, which had previously had a long record of good industrial relations. A three-month stoppage ended early in April. Although the steelmen gained an increase of 16 per cent, they had each lost an average of about £1,000 and the Corporation had lost 10 per cent of its markets. The other nationalized industries evidently faced closures and re-dundancies, and in January 1981, in an attempt to stave this off, a new Triple Alliance was formed between the Iron and Steel Trades Confederation, the Railwaymen and the Mineworkers. In the harsh economic climate of the time it proved more of a gesture than a reality. Other smaller unions sought refuge in merger: the Dyers and Bleachers and the Agricultural Workers decided to join the Transport Workers and the Boilermakers united with the General and Municipal Workers (to give it the new title of General, Municipal, Boilermakers and Allied Trades Union). In the printing indus-try two pairs of unions merged – the Society of Graphical and Allied Trades with the Printers' Assistants to form SOGAT 82 and the National Graphical Association with the Lithographic Artists for form NGA 82.

In the summer of 1981 three railway employees, who had lost their jobs for failing to join the Railwaymen, won their case before the European Court of Human Rights and secured compensation from British Rail. It was not long after this that Mrs Thatcher moved James Prior from the post of Secretary for Employment and replaced him with Norman Tebbit, who at once planned further legislative reform, particularly concerned with the closed shop. The pre-entry closed shop was to be banned altogether, and closed shops were only to exist if a ballot showed overwhelming support for them, to the extent of 85 per cent of those voting. These changes were enacted as the Employment Act, 1982. Further-more, a Green Paper entitled *Democracy in Trade Unions* suggested compulsory secret ballots for the election of union leaders and before strikes were authorized, and a change in the system of political levy from contracting-out to contract-ing-in, as after the General Strike.

At the same time the leadership of one key union was

swinging to the Left. In December 1981 Arthur Scargill, the vigorous and militant Yorkshire Miners' President, won a landslide victory in the contest to become national President in the new year and the union voted to reject a Coal Board offer of an 8 per cent increase in wages. But in January Joe Gormley, the retiring President and a moderate, wrote an article in the *Daily Express* urging his members to 'think hard' before voting for a strike and the result of a strike ballot showed a small majority against. Something similar happened on the railways, where the National Union of Railwaymen's annual conference accepted a 5 per cent increase, although unofficial action continued over the drivers' reluctance to accept 'flexible rostering', which meant the abandonment of the strict eight-hour day. It was not until March 1983 that the Locomotive Engineers agreed to one-man operation of the trains on the Bedford–St Pancras line, in return for an extra £6 a week for the drivers.

In 1981 the Trades Union Congress had expanded the membership of the General Council by three, to increase the number of women elected as such from two to five. In 1982 years of argument over structure ended when it was agreed to accept automatic representation on the General Council for all unions with more than 100,000 members, together with eleven seats for smaller unions, to be elected from their number. At the same time, to keep the proportion, the number of women was increased from five to six. This was a victory for the newer white-collar unions such as APEX which had strongly backed the change and a defeat for the Mineworkers, who were bound to lose one of their two seats. It was also a victory for the opponents of what one speaker in the debate called 'the entrenched patronage of the very large unions'.

This patronage remained, however, in the Labour Party and became even more conspicuous. After the 1979 election the party's internal divisions became very marked, with the entire Left blaming Callaghan for the defeat. In the autumn of 1980 he retired from the leadership, being replaced by his former left-wing colleague, Michael Foot, who defeated Denis Healey in a vote of the parliamentary party. But the 1980 Conference had already decided to choose the party leadership by means of an electoral college, the details of which were to be thrashed out at a special Conference early in the new year. This Conference, which met at Wembley in January, gave the trade unions 40 per cent of the votes and the constituency parties and parliamentary party 30 per cent each. The decision was followed by an immediate split in the parliamentary party, with its more right-wing members led by David Owen and William Rodgers seceding and forming, with Roy Jenkins and Shirley Williams, a new group called the Social Democratic Party. Denis Healey stayed in the Labour Party, and fought a prolonged and bitter campaign against Tony Benn for the deputy leadership which was finally decided narrowly in his favour on the eve of the Conference of 1981. In the meantime the Trades Union Congress had been turned into something like an American nominating convention and the whole struggle threw a lurid light on the union leaders' methods, or rather lack of method, in deciding how to vote.

The Trades Union Congress also held a special Wembley Conference, but this was in the following year, in early April 1982, when union executives were invited to associate themselves with a campaign against both the Employment Act of 1980 and the bill of 1982. It was agreed that unions would not 'seek or accept public funds for union ballots under the Employment Act 1980 ballots scheme'; and a Campaign and Defence Fund was raised by a levy of 10p per member on all affiliated unions. Only Equity, the actors' union, whose council favoured the use of State money for its ballots, sounded a dissentient note.

Almost simultaneously, however, the prospects of a Labour victory in the following general election were dissipated by the Falklands War (April to June 1982). Even though unemployment had reached three million, the Conservatives were able to capitalize on the success of the Task Force in repossessing the islands, and to go to the country with the expectation of an increased majority. In the election, which took place in June 1983, the Conservative manifesto promised, along the lines of the Green Paper already published, further trade-union legislation to enforce ballots for the election of union governing bodies and before strikes, and to force unions to ballot periodically on whether to maintain the political levy. Their agent of industrial democracy was not to be worker directors, as the official Bullock Report had recommended in 1977, but share ownership by employees. The Alliance manifesto also favoured share ownership and compulsory postal ballots for union elections, but it also favoured an independent Assessment Board for public-service pay and a Pay and Prices Commission to 'monitor' pay increases in large companies. Labour promised a 'national economic assessment' – a new title for the Social Contract – but was ambiguous about other important issues on which its leaders could not agree, such as unilateral disarmament and withdrawal from the E.E.C.

In the event the Conservatives gained 65 seats, totalling 397 in the new House. Labour was reduced to 209 M.P.s and there were 23 representatives of the Liberal–S.D.P. Alliance. The Alliance could console itself with the fact that its candidates had come second in 309 contests; but in the existing first-past-the-post system of voting it was at a disadvantage, although it had polled well. It was reckoned that only 39 per cent of trade unionists had voted Labour – the lowest proportion since 1935.

Inevitably the more militant unions came into conflict with the new trade-union laws. In November 1983 the National Graphical Association tried to enforce a closed shop at the Warrington printing works of the *Stockport Messenger* by means of mass picketing, but the employer, Eddie Shah, stood firm and obtained an injunction against the union and, when it was defied, secured a £50,000 fine for contempt. When this too was ignored, a further £100,000 fine was imposed, together with sequestration of the union's assets. After a further two weeks' defiance of the injunction and mass picketing with violence, the union was fined two further sums – £150,000 and £375,000. The union called a national newspaper strike for 24 December and this was backed in the first instance by the T.U.C.'s Employment Committee; but it was declared unlawful by the High Court, and Len Murray, the T.U.C. secretary, repudiated it and secured its suspension by the General Council. In January the Graphical Association accepted defeat and purged its contempt of court, so as to unfreeze its assets. It still had to face substantial claims for damages.

If Murray thought that this episode would be followed by a more peaceful period of industrial relations, he was very soon disillusioned. For on 25 January Sir Geoffrey Howe, the Foreign Secretary, announced that trade unions would be banned at Government Communications Headquarters at Cheltenham. GCHQ had for years been a 'hush-hush' centre for intelligence gathering by radio, in close contact with the American Central Intelligence Agency. Sir Geoffrey's decision followed an objection by the civil-service unions to the introduction of the American lie-detector test. It was in vain that the unions now offered a no-strike agreement: the decision was that all employees should be asked to pledge themselves to leave their unions or be transferred to other departments; in return for the loss of their rights, they were each to receive the sum of £1,000. A few refused to accept the bait and retained their union membership, defying the authorities to remove them; a few others took the money and then rejoined their unions. The General Council of the T.U.C. reacted with unanimous hostility to the decision, ordered a 'Day of Action' for 28 February, and withdrew their representatives from the National Economic Development Council – their one major remaining point of contact with the Government. The Council of Civil Service Unions applied to the High Court for a judicial review of the case, and secured a judgment in their favour; but this was overturned by the Court of Appeal on the grounds of 'national security', and the House of Lords re-echoed the Appeal verdict. Len Murray promised that the case would go to the European Court of Human Rights, and informed the Congress in September 1984 that half a million pounds had been raised to indemnify any union members who were victimized by the Government's action.

But by far the most important conflict of the era was that between the National Coal Board and the National Union of Mineworkers. In September 1983 the veteran Scottish-American industrialist Ian MacGregor, who had just completed a three-year assignment to reduce the losses of British Steel, became the chairman of the Coal Board. In October he offered the miners a wage increase of 5·2 per cent, but this was promptly turned down by the Mineworkers' executive, who imposed an overtime ban from 30 October. On 5 March 1984 MacGregor met the miners' leaders and told them that he was proposing to cut output by 4 million tons, with a loss of 20,000 jobs; the jobs would go as a result of natural wastage or compensation, and no miner would be dismissed. On 9 March the Mineworkers' executive gave official sanction to strikes beginning in Yorkshire and Scotland, where pits had been notified of closure, and authorized areas elsewhere to join in. No instructions were given, however, for a national ballot, which would normally have preceded a strike. Scargill and his colleagues were apparently afraid that a ballot would prove negative, and his vice-president, Mick McGahey, put his policy into words: 'We shall not be constitutionalized out of a defence of our jobs. Area by area will decide, and in my opinion it will have a domino effect.' The strategy was thus for flying pickets to go from areas where the strike was solid, such as Yorkshire, Scotland and Kent, to persuade working miners elsewhere to join in. This soon led to mass picketing with violence, notably at Ollerton in Nottinghamshire, where the miners wished to carry on working. A Yorkshire striker on picket duty was crushed to death in the mêlée outside the pit. On 14 March the High Court gave the Coal Board an injunction against the Yorkshire Miners to stop them organizing flying pickets; but picketing continued and the Board withdrew its injunction, apparently as a matter of policy. The various country police forces were very overstrained in their efforts to control the situation; and to ensure that reinforcements could go where they were most needed, a National Reporting Centre was set up at Scotland Yard.

The Mineworkers had started their strike at the wrong time of year, just when the demand for coal was declining, and since they could not secure a full turnout of their own members, it is not surprising that the support that they received from other unions, such as the Transport Workers and the Locomotive Engineers, was also patchy. The secretary of the Iron and Steel Trades Confederation, who had had little help from the Mineworkers in his three-month

strike of 1980, pointed out that if any of the steelworks were
closed down they would probably not reopen. His members
cooperated with management in securing supplies of coal
and iron ore, if necessary by road. The electricity stations
had plentiful supplies of coal, and the electricians had no
desire to join the strike. In July the Mineworkers had their
hopes raised by a national dock strike, prompted by the use
of contractors to unload iron ore at Immingham docks, but
after two weeks the strike was broken, largely by the action
of angry truckers held up at Dover. It was not until late
September that the striking miners could again hope for
assistance from other workers, for then the Colliery Over-
seers balloted in favour of action; they were vexed by the
Coal Board's insistence that they should cross miners' picket
lines or forfeit their pay. As soon as the Coal Board withdrew
this requirement, however, they withdrew their threat of
action.

Neither side wished to appear to be intransigent, and there
were various meetings of the principals to discuss terms of a
settlement. But they always foundered on the definition of
'uneconomic' pits. As time went on, court actions against
area miners' unions began to take effect. On 31 July the
South Wales Mineworkers were fined £50,000 for contempt
over picketing, and when this sum was not paid, sequestrators
seized £707,000 from their funds. On 10 October the national
union was fined £200,000 for breaking an order declaring
their strike unofficial; and after the union's failure to pay, the
High Court ordered the seizure of all their assets. But the
union had foreseen this and had dispatched its funds abroad,
to Luxembourg, Dublin and elsewhere.

Scargill had cut himself off from the bureaucracy of the
T.U.C. almost entirely. One of his first acts on becoming
President had been to order the removal of the national
headquarters from London to Sheffield; and when it became
necessary to reduce the Mineworkers' representation on the
T.U.C. General Council from two to one, he had left it
himself. But when he appeared at the Congress at Brighton
in September, he was given a standing ovation; and he was
also warmly received at the Labour Party Conference in
October. These propaganda gains were, however, quickly

offset by the discovery late in October that he had been in contact with the Libyan regime, evidently in the hope of obtaining financial assistance.

In November the Board felt that it was time for a back-to-work drive, and it offered a Christmas bonus pay packet to any miner who worked for four full weeks before then. This led to some 15,000 men returning to work; but it also occasioned more violence on the picket lines. The worst incident took place when a concrete block was dropped from a motorway bridge on to a taxi conveying a miner to work in South Wales, killing the driver. Two strikers were found guilty of murder and sentenced to twenty years' imprisonment.

Early in 1985 it became apparent that the country could survive the winter without undergoing any power cuts. But the difficulties of the strikers and their families were acute. A T.U.C. liaison group met first Mrs Thatcher and then Peter Walker, the Minister for Energy, and extracted a few concessions; but they were promptly rejected by the Mineworkers' executive. By late February the idea was being suggested in South Wales of returning to work without any agreement. On 3 March a special delegate conference of the Mineworkers met at Congress House in London and decided, against Scargill's recommendation, to take this course. So the miners returned to work, somewhat raggedly as it turned out, after a strike of fifty-one weeks. They had gained nothing, not even a pay increase, and each miner had lost something like £9,000. The cost to the country could not be precisely reckoned, but it must have run into billions.

A legacy of the strike was the bitterness that remained between striker and non-striker, sometimes within the same family. In Nottinghamshire, where the great majority of miners had worked throughout the strike, area control was taken over by the non-striking miners. They held a poll to break away from the national union and set up their own organization, the Union of Democratic Mineworkers. As the name implies, they originally hoped that it might spread to other areas, but, except for South Derbyshire, this hope was not realized. They did however secure an early pay increase from the Coal Board; on the other hand, they were recognized neither by the T.U.C. nor by the Labour Party.

The year 1984 also saw the early retirement of Len Murray. He had not been in good health, but his departure was almost certainly hastened by the events of his last year, including the G.C.H.Q. affair and the miners' strike. One of his last successes was to persuade Tom King, the new Secretary for Employment, not to include contracting-in to the political levy as one item of his Employment Bill of 1984, on the understanding that the unions gave full publicity to the system of contracting-out. Murray's successor was elected once more from inside the office – it was his deputy secretary, Norman Willis – but as Willis had spent most of his career at Transport House and had the support of the Transport Workers, it could also be seen as a belated victory of the old-fashioned patronage of the larger unions. The fact that Willis's wife was the secretary of Neil Kinnock, the new Labour Party leader, augured well for ties with the party.

Willis soon proved that he was capable of securing a compromise on one issue which threatened to split the movement. The Engineers had accepted State payment for their ballots over the previous three years, in spite of the Congress ban on this agreed in 1982; and the Electricians appeared likely to do likewise. An agreement on the issue was patched up actually during the 1985 Congress, with the Engineers promising to re-ballot their members on this particular issue, explaining the T.U.C.'s attitude on the ballot form. The ballot turned out once again to be in favour of accepting the State money, and the General Council held a special Conference early in 1986 to reverse its stand.

Ballots among trade unionists were becoming more and more frequent, partly owing to the 1982 Act's introduction of them for the closed shop – although the Confederation of British Industry showed itself reluctant to use the mechanism, owing to its unwillingness to disturb good industrial relations – but more especially because of the 1984 Act's requirement of ballots to precede strikes and also its requirement of secret ballots for the election of union executives. Another series of ballots is incumbent upon unions which have political funds every ten years to determine whether or not to continue them. A careful campaign, masterminded by Bill Keys of the Graphical and Allied Trades, ensured that all the unions already affiliated to the Labour Party carried their ballots, and that several more also created political funds.

The economic recovery of the mid-eighties led to a levelling-off of the decline in trade-union membership, but not to an increase. The fact was that the old 'smoke-stack' industries were in permanent decline, and the new development took place in service industries where the great majority of workers were women. There was a distinct increase in national productivity, but this was due to the elimination of inefficient plants in the depression.

In June 1987 Mrs Thatcher secured a renewal of the Conservative Party mandate, with almost exactly the same proportion of the vote as in 1983, and 375 M.P.s. Labour fought a good campaign with its new leader, Neil Kinnock, but its recovery was only partial, and the Alliance actually suffered a slight setback: Labour won 229 M.P.s, an increase of twenty, and the Alliance total was 23. Mrs Thatcher's manifesto pledged her to extend postal ballots for industrial action and for all elections to trade-union office, and to limit the enforcement of the closed shop. It was also proposed to establish an officer to enforce the rights of trade-union members.

Norman Fowler, as Secretary of State Employment, ensured the enactment of the first Employment Bill of the new Parliament in 1988. It removed legal protection from strikes in defence of the closed shop. Workers were given authority to apply for court orders instructing unions to abandon industrial action which was initiated without a secret ballot. Unions were banned from disciplining members who refused to take part in industrial action, even if legitimate; and all union officials, and not just executive committees, were to be elected by secret ballot. Complaints by union members were to be taken up by a new Commissioner for the Rights of Trade Union Members. The first Commissioner was a Mrs Gill Rowlands.

Fowler also prepared a second Employment Bill, but this was carried through Parliament by his successor at the Department, Michael Howard, in 1990. After a 'wild cat' strike on the London Underground, unions were made legally liable for such action by their members if no ballot had been conducted. Furthermore, the closed shop was now deprived of all legal protection, so that job applicants could not be rejected for not belonging to a trade union.

It was against this background of anti-union legislation that leaders of the business world took the opportunity to transform their position. For many years the Fleet Street newspapers had been at the mercy of the printers' chapels. As William Rees-Mogg, the editor of *The Times*, said during the newspaper's long closure in 1978–9: 'We are confronted with a set of seven rusty and ancient fruit machines. To reach agreement we have to line up three strawberries on each of the fruit machines at the same time.' But in 1985 Eddie Shah, fresh from success at Warrington, launched a national newspaper based in London, *Today*, after making a single-union deal with the Electricians. Thereupon the Australian media tycoon, Rupert Murdoch, who now owned *The Times*, the *Sun*, the *News of the World* and the *Sunday Times*, built a fortress at Wapping in which he trained a team of electricians bussed in daily from as far afield as Southampton. When his Bouverie Street and Grays Inn Road staff went on strike early in 1986, he dismissed 5,500 of them and distributed his newspaper from Wapping, not by rail as in the past, but by lorries owned by a nominally separated distribution agency. The mass picketing that followed subjected the unions to legal attack under the new restrictions on secondary picketing. SOGAT 82, which bore the brunt, was heavily fined and had its assets sequestrated. In December of that year, as the strike dragged on, it was reported that the cost of policing the dispute was already £4,700,000. In February 1987, after just over a year, SOGAT accepted defeat.

Something similar happened at Dover, where the P & O management, who owned the cross-Channel ferries, was anxious to cut its costs in advance of the opening of the Channel Tunnel. It reduced the manning levels of the ferry crews and cut wages. In February 1988 the National Union of Seamen went on strike and sought to extend the dispute to other operators, including Sealink. But a High Court ruling at the end of March 1988 maintained that even to hold a ballot of the Sealink members would be illegal. After three heavy fines, heavy legal costs and the sequestration of its assets the union was forced to sell some of its regional offices.

In April 1989 the Government stepped directly into the fray by terminating the National Dock Labour Scheme, which had been set up in 1947 to decasualize the dockers in the more important ports. This was a direct challenge to the Transport Workers, who responded as soon as they could – after ensuring that they would not be liable for prosecution – with a strike beginning in July. But the strike was only effective in London and Liverpool: elsewhere there was a lack of response, and by August the union acknowledged defeat. For many years the ports which were outside the scheme had been making gains at the expense of those covered by it.

There was a growing tendency for firms, notably foreign firms, making new investments in this country, to insist on single-union deals. This was particularly the case when they were building on 'green-field' sites, that is to say, establishing completely new factories. In October 1987 the Ford Electrical and Electronics Division made such a deal for a components factory at Dundee, their chosen union being the Engineers. But other unions with members in the existing Ford factories objected vigorously, and so in March 1988 the parent company at Detroit decided to transfer the plant to Spain – even though Norman Willis went personally to Detroit to plead for reconsideration. A Special Review Body set up by the 1987 Congress decided that, while 'pendulum' or 'final-offer' arbitration – arbitration in which the arbiter has to choose either the union's or the company's final offer – was acceptable, 'no-strike' deals were not: 'the basic lawful rights of a trade union to take industrial action' must remain. Single-union deals were recognized as often inevitable, but where several unions had bargaining rights, they were so far as possible to seek 'single-table' negotiations, so as to simplify the bargaining process.

On the Defensive: The 1980s

The General Council was anxious to uphold the Bridlington Agreement of 1939, which was designed to prevent the
'poaching' of members between unions. In September 1988
the Electricians, who had been severely censured for their
part in the Wapping dispute, were expelled from the
Congress for refusing to accept the decision of the T.U.C.
Disputes Committee in two cases where the decision went
against them. They paid their dues for the year, so that Eric
Hammond, their secretary, could make a blistering speech
in their defence at the Bournemouth Congress.

Not surprisingly, with the development of a hostile legal
environment and, in some cases, a heavy loss of members,
this was a period of frequent union mergers. In 1988 the
Association of Scientific, Technical and Managerial Staffs
(Clive Jenkins's union) and the Technical, Administrative
and Supervisory Section (known as TASS and previously
part of the Engineers) united to form a body with the name
of Manufacturing, Science and Finance. The Society of
Civil and Public Servants joined the Civil Service Union to
form the National Union of Civil and Public Servants; and
the General, Municipal and Boilermakers absorbed APEX.
In 1989 the battered National Union of Seamen found a
haven with the Railwaymen to form the National Union of
Rail, Maritime and Transport Workers; the Broadcasting
and Entertainment Trades Alliance combined with the
Association of Cinematograph, Television and Allied
Technicians to form the Broadcasting and Cinematograph
Technicians Union; and the two printers' unions, the National Graphical Association and SOGAT 82, were preparing to form a new Graphical, Paper and Media Union – a
merger completed in 1991. In the teaching world the Assistant Masters and Mistresses Association was preparing to
unite with the Professional Association of Teachers to form
a body almost equalling in size the more militant National
Union of Teachers but these differences proved insuperable;
the National Communications Union (formerly Post Office
Engineers) and the Union of Communication Workers (formerly Post Office Workers) were also contemplating a merger; and the National and Local Government Officers, with

the Health Service Employees and the Public Employees, thought of forming the largest union of all, with a prospect of 1,400,000 members.

That future recruitment was likely to be more among women workers than among men, and not so much blue-collar as 'white-blouse', concentrated the minds of the General Council on the need to transform their own structure. They persuaded the Congress in 1989 to expand the membership of the General Council to 53, including a minimum of twelve seats for women. This was against a background of continued gender differentials at work, with women manual workers receiving only 72% of the average hourly pay of men, and women non-manual workers only 61%. The Equal Opportunities Commission, which produced these figures, spoke of 'an overwhelming picture of inequality in Britain'. There was also little change in discrimination against black workers, although the General Council did what it could by holding a conference on the topic in 1985 and publishing a pamphlet entitled *Trade Unions and the Black Worker*. For the first time in 1991 a Jamaican-born officer, Bill Morris, was elected to the general secretaryship of a major union – in fact what was still the largest union, the Transport and General Workers.

There was a revival of inflation in 1989–90, and in 1991 a strict monetary policy led to renewed economic depression. The businesses that were hit this time were nation-wide, and both manual and non-manual workers were made redundant. Unemployment in mid-1991 crept up towards 2·5 million. Of the manual unions, only the Engineers had made notable headway for their members in a carefully targeted campaign to reduce the working week from 39 hours to 35. By November 1990 some half a million workers had had their hours reduced to 37 hours or less. Attempts by the T.U.C. itself in 1990 to organize recruitment in specific districts, first of all in Manchester and the London Docklands, proved unsuccessful. One area of activity in which the unions evoked public sympathy was that of safety: a series of railway and maritime accidents pointed up the dangers of employers' cost-cutting. The T.U.C. also embraced the proposals of the Social Charter which were elaborated by

Jacques Delors, the President of the European Commission. Delors was invited to speak at the 1988 Congress and received a standing ovation. Later the European Commissioner for Social Affairs, Vasso Papandreou, spoke at the T.U.C. Women's Conference in March 1989.The T.U.C. was, in effect, calling in Europe to redress the balance of their political adversity at home – an unusual reversal of roles pending a change of political climate in Britain.

It was partly the issue of closer European unity, which she opposed, that caused the downfall of Mrs Thatcher in November 1990, by a most unusual coup inside the Conservative Parliamentary Party. Her successor, John Major, nevertheless pursued most of her policies, albeit with a less abrasive style. He abandoned the Community Charge, or Poll Tax, which she had initiated to raise local government revenue, but he kept Michael Howard at the Department of Employment and authorized a Green Paper published in July 1991 proposing a further series of restrictions on trade-union power: this went so far as to suggest outlawing the Bridlington Agreement, a sure recipe for conflict. But these plans were to await the outcome of a further general election, and they did not as yet recommend themselves to the public. Opinion polls showed that people were now more concerned with unemployment and training than with trade-union reform. The Labour Party policy of introducing a minimum wage won a good deal of support.

At the end of 1990 it looked as if the future of British trade unionism lay with a small number of large conglomerates. If the Transport and General was still the largest, with 1,200,000 members, the General Municipal and Boilermakers under its vigorous leader John Edmonds was not far behind – in 1990 it had snapped up the Tailors and Garment Workers. Next came the Engineers, which with the departure of TASS had reverted to its old title of Amalgamated Engineering Union. With Manufacturing, Science and Finance and with the Public Employees, they formed a group of five unions, each with over half a million members. Next came the Electricians with 366,650: they had balanced any losses in the preceding year by gains at the expense of the Union of Construction, Allied Trades and Technicians, which lost one-fifth of its members owing to financial and political difficulties. The Shop and Distributive Workers numbered 362,000, and next came the Royal College of Nursing, with a membership of 285,000: it had never joined the T.U.C. and was opposed to strike action. These were now the ten largest unions in a movement which had declined by about a third in the years of Conservative rule since 1979.

CONCLUSION

THE British trade-union movement, both in its history and in its present-day characteristics, reflects many of the special features of society and politics in this country. The early growth and strength of the movement were due to the priority of Britain in the process of industrialization; its comparative homogeneity, and in particular the absence of rival national centres such as exist or have existed in America and in countries on the Continent, derive from the national tradition of religious toleration and the fact that immigration has never exceeded the capacity of the country to absorb the newcomer. The continuity of particular unions, in some cases from the beginning of the nineteenth century, or earlier, up to the present, may be attributed to the evolutionary character of our political history. Not all these things, perhaps, have been to the advantage of our trade unions: to have begun late, like many of the American industrial unions in the 1930s, or to have been obliged to start afresh, like the German movement in 1945, may make for greater efficiency in operation.

But we must not forget the benefits which British society has derived from the slow but steady growth of trade unionism. In a country which believes, in theory at least, in the omnipotence of 'the Queen in Parliament', the influence of voluntary associations provides a valuable safeguard against the dangers of centralization. Dicey, the great constitutional lawer of the late nineteenth century, may perhaps be forgiven for seeing the unions solely as the instruments of state collectivism; that the Webbs should come to the same conclusion is a greater tribute to the depth of their socialist enthusiasm than to their powers of observation. In fact, there was never any real likelihood of the unions seeking to identify themselves with the State; on the contrary, as Professor Kahn-Freund has pointed out, their implied philosophy, if it is to be regarded as collectivist at all, is in reality 'collectivist *laissez faire*', which seeks to impose definite limits on the power of the State, at least in the spheres in which the unions themselves operate.

The Webbs believed that in their own time trade unionism was moving from policies of 'Mutual Insurance' to policies of 'Legal Enactment'. In the 1880s and 1890s, when Socialist ideas were influencing more and more of the younger union leaders, there appeared to be some truth in this analysis. But as early as 1894 one of the ablest union leaders of the period, Frederick Rogers of the Bookbinders, had discerned the difference between the objectives of unionism and those of Socialism:

> We shall enlarge the frontiers of the State, and control, so far as Government can control, the power of the capitalist over the labourer more and more. But there must be an independent life within the state to prevent Government becoming tyranny, and the Trade Unions will be chief among those who shall call that independent life into being.

Rogers himself was to be the first chairman of the Labour Representation Committee, out of which grew the Labour Party: he could see the confirmation of his own views in the fact that this party owed its success when he was chairman and long afterwards not to any widespread enthusiasm for State intervention but to the desire of the union officials to escape that encroachment of State authority which they detected in the Taff Vale judgment.

For a long time, indeed until the 1960s, the Labour Party justified the hopes of its founders in acting as the unions' pressure group in Parliament, and in maintaining for them the legal immunity which they have always desired. This is not to say, of course, that the unions could not have maintained that immunity even without the existence of the Labour Party: after all, they had managed to gain it in the first place without such assistance. But at least the Labour Party, in spite of its Socialist constitution, respected the individualism of the unions. In all important aspects, unions in

Conclusion

Britain remained far freer from State intervention than they were in the supposed stronghold of *laissez faire*, the United States; and it was almost true to say, as Aneurin Bevan did in 1944 – echoing a theme of Bernard Shaw's *The Apple Cart* – that

the person in this country who is in the most strongly entrenched position, next to the King, is the trade union official.

Until 1971, the only legislation against trade unions passed in the present century was the Trade Disputes Act of 1927, and this was repealed by the Labour Government in 1946. In 1951 the Conservative Party, which had at first threatened to re-enact the measure, accepted the repeal with the observation from Winston Churchill that

... a wider spirit of tolerance has grown up, and the question may well be left to common sense and the British way of doing things.

After the brief experiment of the Industrial Relations Act the Conservative Party under Mrs Thatcher originally reverted to the Churchillian view. But the 'winter of discontent' converted both her and her colleagues to the view that the solution lay in strengthening the rights of the individual workers vis-à-vis his/her trade union. The approach was made in a series of measures enacted by a succession of Secretaries for Employment. By 1990, with the aid of this legislation and also as a result of the decline of the older industries, the closed shop was becoming a rarity and secondary picketing was heavily discouraged by the unions themselves for fear of sequestration of assets. At that point it seemed likely that the Employment Acts of the period would remain on the statute book long after the Thatcher Government had ended; for, sensing their popularity, the other political parties, even Labour, had come round to accepting them.

Statistical Table

Notes

Columns (1) and (2). Figures refer to trade unions with headquarters in Great Britain and Northern Ireland. Sources: Committee on Industry and Trade, *Survey of Industrial Relations* (H.M.S.O., 1926); *Ministry of Labour Gazette*; *Employment and Productivity Gazette*; *Department of Employment Gazette*.

Columns (3) and (4). Figures for 1893 and 1894 are slightly inflated owing to inclusion of affiliated trades councils. Figures for 1913 are not available owing to the cancellation of the 1914 Congress. Source: T.U.C. *Annual Reports*.

Columns (5) and (6). Figures refer to Great Britain and Northern Ireland. Sources: As for Columns (1) and (2).

Year	(1) Total no. of trade unions	(2) Total no. of trade-union members	(3) Total no. of trade unions affiliated to T.U.C.	(4) Total no. of trade-union members affiliated to T.U.C.	(5) No. of stoppages beginning in year	(6) Aggregate duration in working days of stoppages in progress in year
1893	1,279	1,559,000	179	1,100,000	599	30,440,000
1894	1,314	1,530,000	170	1,000,000	903	9,510,000
1895	1,340	1,504,000	178	1,076,000	728	5,700,000
1896	1,358	1,608,000	180	1,093,191	906	3,560,000
1897	1,353	1,731,000	188	1,184,241	848	10,330,000
1898	1,326	1,752,000	181	1,200,000	695	15,260,000
1899	1,325	1,911,000	184	1,250,000	710	2,500,000
1900	1,323	2,022,000	191	1,200,000	633	3,090,000
1901	1,322	2,025,000	198	1,400,000	631	4,130,000
1902	1,297	2,013,000	204	1,500,000	432	3,440,000
1903	1,285	1,994,000	212	1,422,518	380	2,320,000
1904	1,256	1,967,000	205	1,541,000	346	1,460,000
1905	1,244	1,997,000	226	1,555,000	349	2,370,000
1906	1,282	2,210,000	236	1,700,000	479	3,020,000
1907	1,283	2,513,000	214	1,777,000	585	2,150,000
1908	1,268	2,485,000	219	1,705,000	389	10,790,000

Year	(1) Total no. of trade unions	(2) Total no. of trade-union members	(3) Total no. of trade unions affiliated to T.U.C.	(4) Total no. of trade-union members affiliated to T.U.C.	(5) No. of stoppages beginning in year	(6) Aggregate duration in working days of stoppages in progress in year
1909	1,260	2,477,000	212	1,647,715	422	2,690,000
1910	1,269	2,565,000	202	1,662,133	521	9,870,000
1911	1,290	3,139,000	201	2,001,633	872	10,160,000
1912	1,252	3,416,000	207	2,232,446	834	40,890,000
1913	1,269	4,135,000	—		1,459	9,800,000
1914	1,260	4,145,000	215	2,682,357	972	9,880,000
1915	1,229	4,359,000	227	2,850,547	672	2,950,000
1916	1,225	4,644,000	235	3,082,352	532	2,450,000
1917	1,241	5,499,000	262	4,532,085	730	5,650,000
1918	1,264	6,533,000	266	5,283,676	1,165	5,880,000
1919	1,360	7,926,000	215	6,505,482	1,352	34,970,000
1920	1,384	8,348,000	213	6,417,910	1,607	26,570,000
1921	1,275	6,633,000	206	5,128,648	763	85,870,000
1922	1,232	5,625,000	194	4,369,268	576	19,850,000
1923	1,192	5,429,000	203	4,328,235	628	10,670,000
1924	1,194	5,544,000	205	4,350,982	710	8,420,000
1925	1,176	5,506,000	207	4,365,619	603	7,950,000
1926	1,164	5,219,000	204	4,163,994	323	162,230,000
1927	1,159	4,919,000	196	3,874,842	308	1,170,000
1928	1,142	4,806,000	202	3,673,144	302	1,390,000
1929	1,133	4,858,000	210	3,744,320	431	8,290,000
1930	1,121	4,842,000	210	3,719,401	422	4,400,000
1931	1,108	4,624,000	209	3,613,273	420	6,980,000
1932	1,081	4,444,000	208	3,367,911	389	6,490,000

1933	1,081	4,392,000	210	3,294,581	357	1,070,000
1934	1,063	4,590,000	211	3,388,810	471	960,000
1935	1,049	4,867,000	214	3,614,551	553	1,960,000
1936	1,036	5,295,000	214	4,008,647	818	1,830,000
1937	1,032	5,842,000	216	4,460,617	1,129	3,410,000
1938	1,024	6,053,000	217	4,669,186	875	1,330,000
1939	1,019	6,298,000	223	4,866,711	940	1,360,000
1940	1,004	6,613,000	223	5,079,094	922	940,000
1941	996	7,165,000	232	5,432,644	1,251	1,080,000
1942	991	7,867,000	230	6,024,411	1,303	1,527,000
1943	987	8,174,000	190	6,642,317	1,785	1,808,000
1944	963	8,087,000	191	6,575,654	2,194	3,714,000
1945	781	7,875,000	192	6,671,120	2,293	2,835,000
1946	757	8,803,000	187	7,540,397	2,205	2,158,000
1947	734	9,145,000	188	7,791,470	1,721	2,433,000
1948	735	9,319,000	187	7,937,091	1,759	1,944,000
1949	726	9,274,000	186	7,883,355	1,426	1,807,000
1950	732	9,289,000	186	7,827,945	1,339	1,389,000
1951	735	9,535,000	183	8,020,079	1,719	1,694,000
1952	719	9,583,000	183	8,088,450	1,714	1,792,000
1953	717	9,523,000	184	8,093,837	1,746	2,184,000
1954	703	9,556,000	183	8,106,958	1,989	2,457,000
1955	704	9,741,000	186	8,263,741	2,419	3,781,000
1956	685	9,778,000	185	8,304,709	2,648	2,083,000
1957	685	9,829,000	185	8,337,325	2,859	8,412,000
1958	675	9,639,000	186	8,176,252	2,629	3,461,000
1959	668	9,623,000	184	8,128,251	2,093	5,270,000
1960	664	9,835,000	183	8,299,393	2,832	3,024,000
1961	646	9,897,000	182	8,312,875	2,686	3,046,000

Year	(1) Total no. of trade unions	(2) Total no. of trade-union members	of trade unions affiliated to T.U.C.	trade-union members affiliated to T.U.C.	(5) No. of stoppages beginning in year	(6) Aggregate duration in working days of stoppages in progress in year
1962	626	9,887,000	176	8,315,332	2,449	5,798,000
1963	607	9,934,000	175	8,325,790	2,068	1,755,000
1964	641	10,218,000	172	8,771,012	2,524	2,277,000
1965	629	10,325,000	170	8,867,522	2,354	2,925,000
1966	621	10,262,000	169	8,787,282	1,937	2,398,000
1967	602	10,190,000	160	8,725,604	2,116	2,787,000
1968	582	10,193,000	155	8,875,381	2,378	4,690,000
1969	561	10,472,000	150	9,402,170	3,116	6,846,000
1970	538	11,179,000	142	10,002,204	3,906	10,980,000
1971	520	11,127,000	132	9,894,881	2,228	13,551,000
1972	499	11,349,000	126	10,001,419	2,497	23,909,000
1973	519	11,456,000	109	10,022,224	2,873	7,197,000
1974	507	11,764,000	111	10,363,724	2,922	14,750,000
1975	501	12,193,000	113	11,036,326	2,282	6,012,000
1976	473	12,386,000	115	11,515,020	2,016	3,284,000
1977	481	12,846,000	115	11,865,390	2,703	10,142,000
1978	462	13,112,000	112	12,128,078	2,471	9,405,000
1979	453	13,289,000	109	12,172,508	2,080	29,474,000
1980	438	12,947,000	108	11,601,413	1,330	11,964,000
1981	414	12,106,000	105	11,005,984	1,338	4,266,000
1982	408	11,593,000	102	10,510,157	1,528	5,313,000
1983	394	11,236,000	98	10,082,144	1,352	3,754,000
1984	375	10,994,000	91	9,855,204	1,221	27,135,000
1985	370	10,821,000	88	9,585,729	887	6,402,000
1986	335	10,539,000	87	9,243,297	1,053	1,920,000
1987	330	10,076,000	83	9,127,278	1,004	3,546,000
1988	315	10,387,238	78	8,652,318	770	3,702,000
1989	309	10,158,000		8,150,000	693	4,128,000
1990					620	1,903,000

FURTHER READING

General

The most useful single-volume history of British trade unionism to a fairly recent date is G. D. H. Cole's *Short History of the British Working-class Movement* (1927; revised ed., 1948). But the classic work by Sidney and Beatrice Webb, *History of Trade Unionism* (1894; revised ed., 1920), remains indispensable for any detailed study of the subject. Also of great value is the Webbs' *Industrial Democracy* (1898), an analytical survey of the changing character of trade unionism. H. A. Clegg, A. Fox and A. F. Thompson, *History of British Trade Unions from 1889*, i (Oxford, 1964) covers the period up to 1910; ii (Oxford, 1985) by H. A. Clegg only, covers 1911–33. Both volumes contain new material.

There are a few works devoted to the publication of trade-union documents, of which the most valuable for historical purposes is G. D. H. Cole and A. W. Filson, *British Working Class Movements: Select Documents, 1789–1875* (1951). I. MacDougall (ed.), *Minutes of Edinburgh Trades Council, 1859–1873* (Edinburgh, 1968) has been skilfully edited and is of considerable interest. E. Frow and M. Katanka (ed.), *1868, Year of the Unions* (1968) contains a contemporary account of the first T.U.C. There is a series of small books covering the nineteenth century from a Marxist standpoint: these are Max Morris, *From Cobbett to the Chartists* (1948), J. B. Jefferys, *Labour's Formative Years* (1948), and E. J. Hobsbawm, *Labour's Turning Point* (1948). On the growth of combinations before the nineteenth century, see A. E. Bland, P. A. Brown, and R. H. Tawney, *English Economic History: Select Documents* (1915), and also a valuable collection of extracts from the Home Office papers in the period 1790–1825, A. Aspinall, *Early English Trade Unions* (1949). W. Milne-Bailey, *Trade Union Documents* (1929), gives an impression of the structure and functions of trade unionism at the date of publication. For a more recent series of readings, see W. E. J. McCarthy, *Trade Unions* (new ed., 1985).

The reports and evidence of Royal Commissions and Commons Select Committees form a large body of source material about unions. The most important are those of the Select Committee on Artisans and Machinery (1824), the Select Committee on the Combination Laws (1825), the Select Committee on Combinations (1838), the Royal Commission on Trade Unions (1867–9), the Royal Commission on Labour (1891–4), and the Royal Commission on Trade Unions and Employers' Associations (1965–8). With these may be ranked the report prepared for the National Association for the Promotion of Social Science, *Trade Unions and Strikes* (1860).

The legal history of trade unionism is dealt with by R. Y. Hedges and A. Winterbottom, *Legal History of Trade Unionism* (1930). N. A. Citrine, *Trade Union Law* (2nd ed., 1960), C. Grunfeld, *Modern Trade Union Law* (1966), and K. W. Wedderburn, *The Worker and the Law* (1965) are also useful for historical purposes. For the growth of conciliation and arbitration see Lord Amulree, *Industrial Arbitration in Great Britain* (1929), and I. G. Sharp, *Industrial Conciliation and Arbitration in Great Britain* (1950). Wages councils are dealt with in F. J. Bayliss, *British Wages Councils* (Oxford, 1962). On industrial relations in general, G. S. Bain (ed.), *Industrial Relations in Britain* (1983) is valuable. On strikes, see K. G. J. C. Knowles, *Strikes* (Oxford, 1952), and J. W. Duncan, W. E. J. McCarthy and G. P. Redman, *Strikes in Post-War Britain* (1983). On the closed shop, see W. E. J. McCarthy, *The Closed Shop in Britain* (1964) and J. Gennard, *The Closed Shop in British Industry* (1984).

On the history of the relationship between the trade unions and the State, the following works are of value: W. Milne-Bailey, *Trade Unions and the State* (1934); D. F. Macdonald, *The State and the Trade Unions* (2nd ed., 1976); V. L. Allen, *Trade Unions and the Government* (1960); E. Wigham, *Strikes and the Government, 1893–1981* (1982); and S. Tolliday and J. Zeitlin (eds.), *Shopfloor Bargaining and the State* (Cambridge, 1985).

B. C. Roberts, *The Trades Union Congress, 1868–1921* (1958), is an authoritative study. J. Lovell and B. C. Roberts, *Short History of the T.U.C.* (1968) is a slighter work covering the whole century. See also R. M. Martin, *T.U.C.: The Growth of a Pressure Group, 1868–1976* (Oxford, 1980). For the role of the unions in parliamentary politics see A. W. Humphrey, *History of Labour Representation* (1912), and two books by G. D. H. Cole, *British Working Class Politics, 1832–1914* (1941) and *History of the Labour Party from 1914* (1948). H. Pelling, *Short History of the Labour Party* (new ed., 1991), concentrates on the relationship between the union leaders and the party leaders. Martin Harrison, *Trade Unions and the Labour Party since 1945* (1960), gives a fascinating account of the manifold links, financial and otherwise, between the two sides of the labour movement. This has been supplemented by L. Minkin, *The Labour Party Conference* (1978) and by B. Pimlott and C . Cook (ed.), *Trade Unions in British Politics* (new ed., 1991). On the Trade Union Group of M.P.s, see W. D. Muller, *The Kept Men?* (Hassocks, 1977). On the operation of the political levy, see K. D. Ewing, *Trade Unions, The Labour Party and the Law* (Edinburgh, 1982).

For women's trade unionism see: S. Lewenhak, *Women and Trade Unions* (1977); N. C. Soldon, *Women in British Trade Unions 1874–1976* (Dublin, 1978) and S. Boston, *Women Workers and the Trade Union Movement* (1980).

Trade-union emblems are the subject of R. A. Leeson, *United We Stand* (Bath, 1971), and J. Gorman, *Banner Bright* (1973). R. A. Leeson's *Travelling Brothers* (1979) deals with the tramping system. A useful work of reference is J. Eaton and C. Gill, *The Trade Union Directory* (new ed. 1983).

Histories of Individual Unions

Many important unions have not had their history written, and many have been commemorated only by souvenir volumes of an uncritical character. The following list is of books which deserve mention because of their general interest.

Further Reading

Those which are of particular value to the student are marked with an asterisk (*).

Agricultural Workers. R. Danziger, *Political Powerlessness: Agricultural Workers in Post-War England* (Manchester, 1988). R. Groves, *Sharpen the Sickle!* (1949), E. Selley, *Village Trade Unions in Two Centuries* (1919).

Bank Employees. *R. M. Blackburn, *Union Character and Social Class* (1967).

Blacksmiths. A. Tuckett, *The Blacksmith's History* (1974).

Boilermakers. J. E. Mortimer, *History of the Boilermakers' Society, 1834–1939* (2 vols., 1973 and 1982).

Bookbinders and Paper Workers. E. Howe and J. Child, *Society of London Bookbinders* (1952). C. J. Bundock, *National Union of Printing, Bookbinding and Paper Workers* (Oxford, 1969).

Boot and Shoe Workers. *Alan Fox, *History of the N.U. of Boot and Shoe Operatives, 1874–1957* (Oxford, 1958).

Brushmakers. *W. Kiddier, *The Old Trade Unions* (1930).

Builders. *R. Postgate, *The Builders' History* (1923). W. S. Hilton, *Foes to Tyranny* (1963). R. Price, *Masters, Unions and Men* (Cambridge, 1980).

Civil Servants. B. V. Humphreys, *Clerical Unions in the Civil Service* (Oxford, 1958). H. Parris, *Staff Relations in the Civil Service* (1973). J. E. Mortimer and V. A. Ellis, *A Professional Union: The Evolution of the Institution of Professional Civil Servants* (1980). E. Wigham, *From Humble Petition to Militant Action: A History of the C.P.S.A.* (1980).

Clerical and Administrative Workers. F. Hughes, *By Hand and Brain* (1953). G. Anderson, *Victorian Clerks* (Manchester, 1976).

Cotton Workers. *H. A. Turner, *Trade Union Growth, Structure, and Policy* (1962). E. Hopwood, *History of the Lancashire Cotton Industry and the Amalgamated Weavers' Association* (Manchester, 1969).

Dockers. *J. Lovell, *Stevedores and Dockers* (1969). *D. F. Wilson, *Dockers* (1972). E. Taplin, *The Dockers' Union, 1889–1922* (Liverpool, 1985).

Electricians. J. Lloyd, *Light and Liberty: the History of the*

EEPTU (1990). J. Slinn, *Engineers in Power* (1989).

Engineering Draughtsmen. J. E. Mortimer, *History of the Engineering and Shipbuilding Draughtsmen* (1960).

Engineers. *J. B. Jefferys, *Story of the Engineers* (1945).

Flint Glass Workers. T. Matsumura, *The Labour Aristocracy Revisited* (Manchester, 1983).

Foundry Workers. H. J. Fyrth and H. Collins, *Foundry Workers* (Manchester, 1959).

Furniture Workers. H. Reid, *The Furniture Makers* (Oxford, 1986).

General Workers. *H. A. Clegg, *General Union* (Oxford, 1954). *R. Hyman, *The Workers' Union* (Oxford, 1971).

Iron and Steel Workers. Arthur Pugh, *Men of Steel* (1951). *C. Docherty, *Steel and Steelworkers* (1983).

Journalists. C. J. Bundock, *National Union of Journalists* (1957).

Lace Makers. N. H. Cuthbert, *Lace Makers' Society* (Nottingham, 1960).

Local Government Officers. *A. Spoor, *White-Collar Union* (1967).

Locksmiths. B. Stenner, *The Lockmakers* (Oxford, 1989).

Miners. R. P. Arnot, *The Miners, 1889–1945* (4 vols., 1949–79). *J. E. Williams, *The Derbyshire Miners* (1962). W. R. Garside, *The Durham Miners, 1919–60* (1971). R. Challinor, *The Lancashire and Cheshire Miners* (Newcastle, 1972). R. Fynes, *History of the Northumberland and Durham Miners* (Sunderland, 1923). E. Welbourne, *Miners' Union of Northumberland and Durham* (Cambridge, 1923). A. R. Griffin, *Miners of Nottinghamshire* (2 vols., Nottingham, 1956? and *London, 1962). R. P. Arnot, *The Scottish Miners* (1955) and *The South Wales Miners* (2 vols., London, 1967, and Cardiff, 1975). *E. W. Evans, *Miners of South Wales* (Cardiff, 1961). H. Francis and D. Smith, *The Fed* (1980). F. Machin, *The Yorkshire Miners* (vol. 1, Barnsley, 1958). R. Harrison (ed.), *Independent Collier* (1978).

Plumbers. J. O. French, *Plumbers in Unity* (1965).

Policemen. A. Judge, *The First Fifty Years* (1968).

Postal Workers. H. G. Swift, *History of Postal Agitation* (1929). M. Moran, *The Union of Post Office Workers: a*

Study in Political Sociology (1974). A. Clinton, *Post Office Workers* (1984). F. W. Bealey, *The Post Office Engineering Union* (1976).

Potters. W. H. Warburton, *History of Trade Union Organization in the North Staffs. Potteries* (1931).

Printers. *Ė. Howe and H. E. Waite, *London Society of Compositors* (1948). E. Howe, *The London Compositor: Documents* (1947). *A. E. Musson, *Typographical Association* (Oxford, 1954). S. C. Gillespie, *Hundred Years of Progress* (Glasgow, 1953). *J. Child, *Industrial Relations in the British Printing Industry* (1967). J. Moran, *NATSOPA: Seventy-Five Years* (1964). *R. Martin, *New Technology and Industrial Relations in Fleet Street* (Oxford, 1981).

Quarrymen. R. M. Jones, *The North Wales Quarrymen, 1874–1922* (Cardiff, 1981). J. Lindsay, *The Great Strike: A History of the Penrhyn Colliery Dispute of 1901–1903* (Newton Abbot, 1987).

Railwaymen. G. W. Alcock, *Fifty Years of Railway Trade Unionism* (1922). J. R. Raynes, *Engines and Men* (Leeds, 1921). *P. S. Bagwell, *The Railwaymen* (2 vols., 1963 and 1982).

Seamen. A Marsh and V. Ryan, *The Seamen* (Oxford, 1989).

Shop Assistants. P. C. Hoffman, *They Also Served* (1949). W. B. Whitaker, *Victorian and Edwardian Shopworkers* (Newton Abbot, 1973). W. Richardson, *A Union of Many Trades: The History of U.S.D.A.W.* (Manchester, 1980).

Tailors and Garment Workers. F. W. Galton, *Select Docs. Illustrating the History of T.U.ism: The Tailoring Trade* (1896). M. Stewart and L. Hunter, *The Needle is Threaded* (1964).

Teachers. A. Tropp, *The School Teachers* (1957). W. Roy, *The Teachers' Union* (1968). *R. A. Manzer, *Teachers in Politics* (Manchester, 1970). H. Perkin, *Key Profession: the History of the A.U.T.* (1969). S. M. Turner, *Social Class, Status and Teacher Trade Unionism* (Beckenham, 1985) (Further Education).

Technical Workers. * B. C. Roberts et al., *Reluctant Militants* (1972).

Tin Plate Workers. A. T. Kidd, *History of the Tin Plate &c Societies* (1949).

Further Reading

Transport Workers. *K. Coates and T. Topham, *The History of the Transport and General Workers' Union*, vol. 1 (2 books) (to 1922 only). A. Tuckett, *The Scottish Carter* (1967).
Woodworkers. T. J. Connelly, *The Woodworkers* (1960).

Good histories of trades councils are rare: K. D. Buckley, *Trade Unionism in Aberdeen, 1878–1900* (Edinburgh, 1955), and J. Corbett, *Birmingham Trades Council, 1866–1966* (1966) are the best. There is some useful information, however, in George Tate, *London Trades Council 1860–1950* (1950); and S. Pollard, in his comprehensive *History of Labour in Sheffield* (Liverpool, 1959), deals fully with local trade unionism. A. Clinton, *The Trade Union Rank and File* (Manchester, 1977) is a study of trades councils in the period 1900–40.

Much of value about the lives of individual unionists will be found in J. Saville and J. M. Bellamy (ed.), *Dictionary of Labour Biography* (7 vols. so far, 1972–1984).

Additional Sources for Particular Periods and Topics

CHAPTER 2: THE ORIGINS TO 1825

Eighteenth-century unions in general are dealt with in C. R. Dobson, *Masters and Journeymen* (1980) and J. Rule, *The Experience of Labour in the Eighteenth Century* (1981). For a study of a strike-prone occupation, see J. M. Fowster, 'The Keelmen of Tyneside in the Eighteenth Century', *Durham University Journal*, n.s. xix (1957–8). On the passing of the Combination Laws, there is a useful narrative in J. L. and Barbara Hammond, *The Town Labourer, 1760–1832* (1918), but their significance is more carefully assessed in M. D. George, 'The Combination Laws Reconsidered', *Economic History*, i (1927), and also in J. V. Orth, 'The English Combination Laws Reconsidered' in F. Snyder and D. Hay, *Labour, Law and Crime* (1987). See also J. L. Gray, 'The Law of Combination in Scotland', *Economica*, vii (1928). D. C. Coleman, 'Combinations of Capital and Labour in the English Paper Industry, 1789–1825', *Economica*, xxi (1954) is of relevant interest. N. McCord and D. E. Brewster, 'Some Labour Troubles in the 1790s in N.E. England',

Further Reading

International Review of Social History, xiii (1968) and N. McCord, 'The Seamen's Strike of 1815 in N.E. England', *Economic History Review*, 2 ser., xxi (1968) present new material. On the Luddites, see J. L. and Barbara Hammond, *The Skilled Labourer, 1760–1832* (1919); F. O. Darvall, *Popular Disturbances and Public Order in Regency England* (1934); E. J. Hobsbawm, *Labouring Men* (1964), ch. 2; and R. A. Church and S. D. Chapman, 'Gravener Henson and the Making of the English Working Class', in E. L. Jones and G. E. Mingay (ed.), *Land, Labour and Population in the Industrial Revolution* (1967). On friendly societies in this period, see P. H. J. H. Gosden, *Friendly Societies in England, 1815–71* (Manchester, 1961). For Francis Place, see W. E. S. Thomas, 'Francis Place and Working-Class History', *Historical Journal*, v. (1962). There is much of interest for this period in E. P. Thompson, *Making of the English Working Class* (1963), but its thesis is controversial. A. E. Musson, *British Trade Unions, 1800–1875* (1972) is a useful summary in the Economic History Society series.

CHAPTER 3: HIGH HOPES AND SMALL BEGINNINGS, 1825–60

The struggles of early unionists before the Chartist period may best be explored through two biographical works, I. J. Prothero, *Artisans and Politics in Nineteenth-Century London: John Gast and his Times* (Folkestone, 1979) and R. G. Kirby and A. E. Musson, *The Voice of the People: John Doherty* (Manchester, 1975). For the methods and philosophy of the old trade clubs, see E. J. Hobsbawm, 'The Tramping Artisan', *Labouring Men*, ch. 4; R. V. Clements, 'Trade Unions and Emigration 1840–80', *Population Studies*, ix (1955); and R. V. Clements, 'British Trade Unions and Popular Political Economy 1850–75', *Economic History Review*, 2 ser., xiv (1961). On emigration, see also H. Owen, *The Staffordshire Potter* (1901). On the Grand National Consolidated Trades Union, W. H. Oliver, 'The Consolidated Trades Union of '34', *Economic History Review*, 2 ser., xvii (1964) is of importance; and see also W. H. Chaloner (ed.), 'Reminiscences of Thomas Dunning', *Trans. Lancs. and Ches. Antiquarian Society*, lix (1947). The Tolpuddle case is fully documented in the T.U.C. publication, *The Martyrs of Tolpuddle* (1934). For union links with Chartism, see F. C. Mather, *Public Order in the Age of the Chartists* (1959), and A. Briggs (ed.), *Chartist Studies* (1959). For the miners, see R. Challinor and B. Ripley, *The Miners' Association* (1968) and A. J. Taylor, 'The Miners' Association of Great Britain and Ireland, 1842–48', *Economica*, xxii (1955). K. Burgess, 'Technological Change and the 1852 Lock-out in the British Engineering Industry', *International Review of Social History*, xiv (1969) throws fresh light on the beginnings of the A.S.E. The Preston strike of 1853–4 is described in H. I. Dutton and J. E. King, *Ten Per Cent and No Surrender* (Cambridge, 1981). Links with Methodism are explored in several works by R. F. Wearmouth, of which the most relevant for this period is *Some Working Class Movements of the Nineteenth Century* (1948). An important reassessment of the role of the 'New Model' is to be found in G. D. H. Cole, 'Some Notes on British Trade Unionism in the Third Quarter of the Nineteenth Century', in E. M. Carus-Wilson (ed.), *Essays in Economic History*, iii (1962). J. Benson, 'English Coal-Miners' Trade-Union Accident Funds, 1850–1900', *Economic History Review*, 2 ser., xxviii (1975), draws attention to a neglected topic, as does P. Brantlinger, 'The Case against Trade Unions in Early Victorian Fiction', *Victorian Studies*, xiii (1969). W. H. Fraser, *Trade Unions and Society: The Struggle for Acceptance, 1850–1880* (1974), is a general survey; so is R. Q. Gray, *The Aristocracy of Labour in Nineteenth-Century Britain 1850–1914* (1981).

CHAPTER 4: THE FORMATION OF A PRESSURE GROUP, 1860–80

For the trade-union leaders' entry into politics generally see F. E. Gillespie, *Labour and Politics in England, 1850–67* (Durham, N.C., 1927). On various aspects of the subject see Daphne Simon, 'Master and Servant', in J. Saville (ed.), *Democracy and the Labour Movement* (1954); V. L. Allen,

Further Reading

'The Origins of Industrial Conciliation and Arbitration', *International Review of Social History*, ix (1964); S. Coltham, 'The *Bee-Hive* Newspaper', in A. Briggs and J. Saville (ed.), *Essays in Labour History* (1960); and two articles by H. W. McCready, 'British Labour and the Royal Commission on Trade Unions 1867-9', *University of Toronto Quarterly*, xxiv (1955) and 'British Labour's Lobby, 1867-75', *Canadian Journal of Economics and Political Science*, xxii (1956). A different view of the evidence before the Royal Commission (see p. 56) is provided by C. G. Hanson, 'Craft Unions, Welfare Benefits and the Case for Trade Union Law Reform', *Economic History Review*, 2 ser., xviii (1975). R. Harrison, *Before the Socialists* (1965), contains a useful account of the role of the Positivists in the Labour movement. Also of interest is H. Collins and C. Abramsky, *Karl Marx and the British Labour Movement* (1965). The most useful biographies are W. H. G. Armytage, *A. J. Mundella* (1951); F. M. Leventhal, *Respectable Radical: George Howell and Victorian Working Class Politics* (1971); and G. M. Wilson, *Alexander McDonald* (Aberdeen, 1982). On the foundation and early history of the T.U.C. see A. E. Musson, *The Congress of 1868* (1955); W. J. Davis, *British T.U.C.: History and Recollections* (vol. 1, 1910); and *Henry Broadhurst M.P.: the Story of His Life Told by Himself* (1901). On the beginnings of railway trade unionism see P. W. Kingsford, 'Labour Relations on the Railways, 1835-75', *Journal of Transport History*, i (1953). On unionism in agriculture, see A. Clayden, *Revolt of the Field* (1874); R. C. Russell, *Revolt of the Field in Lincolnshire* (Lincoln, 1956); Frances, Countess of Warwick (ed.), *Joseph Arch* (1898); and J. P. D. Dunbabin, *Rural Discontent in Nineteenth-Century Britain* (1974). J. R. Ravensdale, 'The China Clay Labourers' Union', *History Studies*, i (1968) tells the story of a short-lived union of the 1870s.

Essays on groups of actual or would-be 'Labour aristocrats' will be found in R. Harrison and J. Zeitlin (eds.) *Divisions of Labour* (Brighton, 1985). E. F. Biagini and A. J. Reid (ed.), *Currents of Radicalism* (Cambridge, 1991) also contains useful essays on the 'old unionists'.

Further Reading

For the Knights of Labour, see H. Pelling 'The Knights of
Labour in Britain, 1880–1901', *Economic History Review*,
2 ser., ix (1956). The early stages of New Unionism may
be traced in C. Tsuzuki, *Tom Mann 1856–1941* (Oxford, 1991);
in Will Thorne, *My Life's Battles* (1925); in Ben Tillett,
Memories and Reflexions (1931); in J. Havelock Wilson, *My
Stormy Voyage through Life* (1925); and in *Sir James Sexton,
Agitator: An Autobiography* (1936). There is a valuable
contemporary account of the Dock Strike of 1889 by H. L.
Smith and V. Nash, *The Story of the Dockers' Strike* (1890).
G. Pattison, 'Nineteenth-century Dock Labour in the Port
of London', *Mariner's Mirror*, lii (1966) considers the problems of dock labour from the evidence of the company papers.
On the gasworkers and seamen and on New Unionism generally, E. J. Hobsbawm, *Labouring Men*, chs. 9, 10 and 11 is
valuable. The railwaymen's response to New Unionism is
discussed by P. S. Gupta, 'Railway Trade Unionism in
Britain, c. 1880–1900', *Economic History Review*, 2 ser., xix
(1966). L. J. Williams, 'The New Unionism in South Wales,
1889–92', *Welsh History Review*, i (1963) is a brief survey of
an important subject. For the growth of Socialism and of
the demand for independent labour representation, see H.
Pelling, *Origins of the Labour Party* (new ed., Oxford, 1965).
For legal and industrial developments in the 1890s, see J.
Saville, 'Trade Unions and Free Labour', in Briggs and
Saville (ed.), *Essays in Labour History*; but this should be
balanced by reading A. Fox, 'Industrial Relations in 19th
Century Birmingham', *Oxford Economic Papers*, vii (1955).
On the Eight-hour Day movement, see A. E. P. Duffy, 'The
Eight Hours Day Movement in Britain, 1886–1893', *Man-
chester School*, xxxvi (1968), and B. McCormick and J. E.
Williams, 'The Miners and the Eight-Hour Day, 1863–1910',
Economic History Review, 2 ser., xii '1959). G. Alderman,
'The Railway Companies and the Growth of Trade Union-
ism', *Historical Journal*, xiv (1971), is an important article.
There are useful essays in C. Wrigley (ed.), *A History of
British Industrial Relations, 1875–1914* (Brighton, 1982).

Further Reading

CHAPTER 7: FROM TAFF VALE TO TRIPLE ALLIANCE, 1900–14

For Taff Vale and its political consequences, see F. Bealey and H. Pelling, *Labour and Politics, 1900–06* (1958) and H. Pelling, *Popular Politics and Society in Late Victorian Britain* (1968), ch. 4. General developments of 1906–14 are recounted in E. H. Phelps Brown, *Growth of British Industrial Relations* (1959). R. Gregory, *Miners and British Politics, 1906–1914* (Oxford, 1968) and K. D. Brown, *Labour and Unemployment, 1900–1914* (Newton Abbot, 1971), are useful monographs. For the Osborne case, see W. B. Gwyn, *Democracy and the Cost of Politics* (1962), ch. vii, H. Pelling, 'The Politics of the Osborne Judgement', *Historical Journal*, xxv (1982) and M. Klarman, 'A Judgment Gone Too Far?' *English Historical Review*, ciii (1988). The labour unrest of 1911–14 is discussed in G. R. Askwith, *Industrial Problems and Disputes* (1920); David Evans, *Labour Strife in the S. Wales Coalfield* (1911); Ben Tillett, *History of the Transport Strike* (1911); and A. Wright, *Disturbed Dublin* (1914). More recent treatments will be found in R. V. Sires, 'Labour Unrest in England, 1910–1914', *Journal of Economic History*, xv (1955), in H. Pelling, *Popular Politics and Society*, ch. 9, in S. Meacham, 'The Sense of an Impending Clash', *American Historical Review*, lxxvii (1972), and in G. A. Phillips, 'The Triple Industrial Alliance in 1914', *Economic History Review*, 2 ser., xxiv (1971). J. L. White, *The Limits of Trade Union Militancy* (Westport, Conn., 1978) discusses Lancashire textile workers' strikes in 1910–1914. For syndicalism, see B. Pribicevic, *Shop Stewards' Movement and Workers' Control, 1910–22* (1959). For Guild Socialism see G. D. H. Cole, *Self-Government in Industry* (1917), S. G. Hobson, *National Guilds* (1919), and, more recently, S. T. Glass, *The Responsible Society* (1966). An important autobiography is H. Gosling, *Up and Down Stream* (1927).

CHAPTER 8: WAR AND THE GENERAL STRIKE, 1914–26

An introductory general account of developments during the war may be obtained from W. A. Orton, *Labour in Transition*

(1921). The works by G. R. Askwith and B. Pribicevic, mentioned above, are again of value for this period. Manifestations of revolt are dealt with contrastingly in J. Hinton, *The First Shop Stewards Movement* (1973), and I. McLean, *The Legend of Red Clydeside* (Edinburgh, 1983). For the engineering industry see G. D. H. Cole, *Trade Unionism and Munitions* (1923), and *Workshop Organisation* (1923); for the coal industry, see the same author's *Labour in the Coalmining Industry* (1923). G. Rubin, *War, Law and Labour* (Oxford, 1987) discusses the Munitions Act and their impact up to 1921. The police strike of 1918 is dealt with in G. W. Reynolds and A. Judge, *The Night the Police Went on Strike* (1968). Arthur Gleason, *What the Workers Want* (New York, 1920), is interesting for the quoted views of industrial unionists. On the origins of the General Council of the T.U.C., see V. L. Allen, 'The Reorganization of the T.U.C., 1918–27', *British Journal of Sociology*, xi (1960). For Labour in politics, see R. McKibbin, *The Evolution of the Labour Party, 1910–1924* (Oxford, 1974), J. M. Winter, *Socialism and the Challenge of War* (1974), R. Harrison, 'The War Emergency Workers' National Committee', in A. Briggs and J. Saville (ed.), *Essays in Labour History, 1886–1923* (1971), and R. W. Lyman, *First Labour Government, 1924* (1957). On Anglo-Soviet relations see D. F. Calhoun, *The United Front: The T.U.C. and the Russians 1923–1928* (Cambridge, 1976). The most interesting short account of the General Strike is Christopher Farman, *The General Strike* (1972); for more documentation see W. H. Crook, *The General Strike* (Chapel Hill, N.C., 1931). The fiftieth anniversary produced some further important work, notably G. A. Phillips, *The General Strike* (1976) and M. Morris, *The General Strike* (1976). For seamen's unionism in this period see B. Mogridge, 'Militancy and Inter-Union Rivalries in British Shipping, 1911–29', *International Review of Social History*, vi (1961). A. Bullock, *Life and Times of Ernest Bevin* (vol. 1, 1960) and Lord Citrine, *Men and Work* (1964) are of importance for the whole of the inter-war period; also of value are F. M. Leventhal, *Arthur Henderson* (Manchester, 1989) and B. Webb, *Diaries, 1912–24* (1952) and *Diaries 1924–32* (1956). For T.U.C. attitudes to foreign affairs see H. Pelling, 'British Labour and

Further Reading

Peace without Victory', *America and the British Left* (1956), and S. Graubard, *British Labour and the Russian Revolution* (Cambridge, Mass., 1956).

CHAPTER 10: SLUMP AND RECOVERY, 1926–39

Relations between the Second Labour Government and the trade unions are described in V. L. Allen's *Trade Unions and the Government*, mentioned above. S. Pollard, 'Trade Reactions to the Economic Crisis', *Journal of Contemporary History*, iv (1969) is an interesting discussion. The best account of the T.U.C. role in the crisis at its close is in R. Bassett, *1931: Political Crisis* (1958). For the trade unions in this period, see G. D. H. Cole, *British Trade Unionism Today* (1939); and for industrial relations in general, see H. A. Clegg, *Some Consequences of the General Strike* (Manchester, 1954). Problems of inter-union relations are dealt with in S. W. Lerner, *Breakaway Unions and the Small Trade Union* (1961). For the role of the Minority Movement and the Communist Party, see H. Pelling, *British Communist Party* (1958), and R. Martin, *Communism and the British Trade Unions, 1924–1933* (Oxford, 1969). The evolution of Labour Party and T.U.C. policy on nationalization is dealt with in E. Eldon Barry, *Nationalization in British Politics* (1965) and in G. N. Ostergaard, 'Labour and the Development of the Public Corporation', *Manchester School*, xxii (1954). For the *Daily Herald*, see R. J. Minney, *Viscount Southwood* (1954). For the National Unemployed Workers Movement, W. Hannington, *Unemployed Struggles, 1919–36* (1936), may be used with caution; see also J. Stevenson, 'The Politics of Violence', in G. Peele and C. Cook, *The Politics of Re-Appraisal* (1975). For the last months of peace, see R. A. C. Parker, 'British Rearmament, 1936–9: Treasury, Trade Unions and Skilled Labour', *English Historical Review*, xcvi (1981).

CHAPTER: 11 POWER WITH RESPONSIBILITY, 1939–51

The official history of the war has much to say about trade unionism. The most pertinent volumes are W. K. Hancock and M. M. Gowing, *British War Economy* (1949); P. Inman, *Labour in the Munitions Industries* (1957); and H. M. D. Parker, *Manpower* (1957). The unions' part in the early stages of the war is described in John Price, *Labour in the War* (1940), and H. Tracy, *Trade Unions Fight – for What?* (1940). Lord Citrine, *Two Careers* (1967) throws light on the T.U.C.'s relations with the government and with foreign Labour movements in wartime. See also A. Bullock, *Life and Times of Ernest Bevin* (vol. ii, 1967). B. C. Roberts, *National Wages Policy in War and Peace* (1958), is valuable for the whole period. There are two useful surveys of trade unionism just after the war: N. Barou, *British Trade Unions*, (1947), and the P.E.P. report, *British Trade Unions, 1948* (1949). G. B. Baldwin, 'Structural Reform in the British Miners' Union', *Quarterly Journal of Economics*, lxvii (1953), describes the creation of the N.U.M. The report of the British trade-union team which visited the United States under the auspices of the Anglo-American Productivity Council was published by the T.U.C. under the title *Trade Unions and Productivity* (1950). See also A. Carew, *Labour under the Marshall Plan* (Manchester, 1987). For the international movement, see L. L. Lorwin, *International Labour Movement* (New York, 1953). V. L. Allen, *Trade Union Leadership* (1957), is a study of Arthur Deakin; G. G. Eastwood, *George Isaacs* (1952), may also be mentioned.

CHAPTER 12: ON THE PLATEAU, 1951–62

B. C. Roberts, *Trade Union Government and Administration* (1956), provided a more complete survey of union institutions than any work since the Webbs' *Industrial Democracy*. This may be supplemented by H. A. Clegg, A. J. Killick, and R. Adams, *Trade Union Officers* (Oxford, 1961). For a general discussion of problems of the 1950s, see G. Cyriax and R. Oakeshott, *The Bargainers* (1960), E. Wigham, *What's Wrong with the Unions?* (Penguin Special, 1961), and B. C. Roberts, *Trade Unions in a Free Society* (2nd ed., 1962). Bryn Roberts, *The Price of T.U.C. Leadership* (1961), expressed the views of a left-wing union leader. On wages policy, there is an interesting symposium in the *Scottish Journal of Political*

Economy, v (1958); see also the O.E.E.C. publication, *The Problem of Rising Prices* (1961). M. Stewart, *Frank Cousins* (1968) is a short biography of the most powerful leader of the second post-war decade. H. A. Clegg and R. Adams, *The Employers' Challenge* (Oxford, 1957), is an account of the engineering and shipbuilding strikes of that year. On strikes, see also W. McCarthy, 'The Reasons Given for Striking', *Bulletin of the Oxford Institute of Statistics*, xxi (1959), and J. Bescoby and H. A. Turner, 'An Analysis of Post-War Labour Disputes in the British Car Manufacturing Firms', *Manchester School*, xxix (1961). The pioneer study of apathy at branch level was J. Goldstein, *Government of British Trade Unions* (1952). The E.T.U. case is summarized in C. H. Rolph, *All Those in Favour?* (1962), and in Olga Cannon and J. R. L. Anderson, *The Road from Wigan Pier* (1973), a life of Les Cannon. A. Flanders, *The Fawley Productivity Agreements* (1964), discusses a novel achievement in industrial relations.

CHAPTER 13: THE STRUGGLE AGAINST STATE INTERVENTION, 1962–70

The Donovan Report and its associated research papers are of especial importance for this period. The story of the Rookes case, from the point of view of the plaintiff, is convincingly told in D. Rookes, *Conspiracy* (1968). For changes in the structure of trade unionism see G. S. Bain, *Growth of White-Collar Unionism* (Oxford, 1970). W. E. J. McCarthy, *Closed Shop in Britain* (Oxford, 1964) is relevant for the period. H. A. Turner, G. Clack and G. Roberts, *Labour Relations in the Motor Industry* (1967) discusses the problems of the most strike-prone of British industries. But Professor Turner is sceptical of the term 'strike-prone' as applied to British industry generally: see his *Is Britain Really Strike-Prone?* (Cambridge, 1969). T. Lane and K. Roberts, *Strike at Pilkingtons* (1971), is a study of a seven-week unofficial strike. The views of the Oxford school of industrial relations experts will be found in a series of essays by A. Flanders, *Management and the Unions* (1970): it might be said to reveal the philosophy behind the Donovan Report. P. Jenkins,

Further Reading

Battle of Downing Street (1970) is an able journalist's account of the Labour Government's attempt to pass an Industrial Relations Act. W. W. Paynter, *British Trade Unions and the Problem of Change* (1970), is a plea for industrial unionism uttered by a very experienced trade unionist. Among biographies and memoirs of leading union officers, A. Moffat, *My Life with the Miners* (1965), and W. W. Craik, *Sydney Hill and the National Union of Public Employees* (1968), deserve mention. For the attitude of the unions to coloured immigration see S. Patterson, *Race Relations in Britain, 1960–1967* (1969); E. J. B. Rose (ed.), *Colour and Citizenship* (1969); and B. Radin, 'Coloured Workers and British Trade Unions', *Race*, viii (1966).

CHAPTER 14: THE INDUSTRIAL RELATIONS
ACT AND THE SOCIAL CONTRACT, 1971–9

J. E. Mortimer, *Trade Unions and Technological Change* (1971), discusses some of the problems of the 1970s. R. W. Rideout, *Principles of Labour Law* (1972), describes the state of the law as it was under the Act. For its introduction, operation and failure, see M. Moran, *The Politics of Industrial Relations* (1977). But the most thorough account of its working is B. Weekes *et al.*, *Industrial Relations and the Limits of the Law* (Oxford, 1975). For a study of the T.U.C. General Secretary of 1969–73, see Eric Silver, *Victor Feather, T.U.C.* (1973). G. S. Bain *et al.*, *Social Stratification and Trade Unionism* (1973), contains some fresh thought on the reasons why people join unions. On Grunwick see J. Rogaly, *Grunwick* (1977). Shopfloor organization in a large motor works is described in E. Batstone, I. Boraston and S. Frankel, *Shop Stewards in Action* (Oxford, 1977). R. Taylor, *The Fifth Estate* (1978) is a good general survey. On the development of the closed shop and the 'check-off', see W. Brown (ed.) *The Changing Contours of British Industrial Relations* (Oxford, 1981).

CHAPTER 15: ON THE DEFENSIVE : THE 1980s

An officially-sponsored survey of trade unionism in 1980

was published as W. W. Daniel and N. Milward, *Workplace Industrial Relations* (1983). A second work from the same data was W. W. Daniel, *Workplace Industrial Relations and Technological Change* (1987). A further survey four years later was by N. Millward and M. Stevens, *British Workplace Industrial Relations 1980–1984* (1987). There is a full account of the steel strike of 1980 in C. Docherty, *Steel and Steelworkers* (1983), and for the miners' strike of 1984–5 see M. Adeney and J. Lloyd, *The Miners' Strike* (1986). For the impact of the depression of the early 1980s, see R. Taylor, *Workers and the New Depression* (1982). The Employment Acts of 1980–90 are briefly described in C. G. Hanson, *Taming the Trade Unions* (1991). For the campaign to retain the political levy, see K. Coates and T. Topham, *Trade Unions and Politics* (Oxford, 1986), chapters 5 and 9.

CONCLUSION

For a historical discussion of the wider legal aspects of trade unionism see O. Kahn-Freund, 'Labour Law', in M. Ginsburg (ed.), *Law and Opinion in England in the Twentieth Century* (1959), and R. M. Martin, 'Legal Personality and the Trade Union', in L. C. Webb (ed.), *Legal Personality and Political Pluralism* (Melbourne, 1958). On the role of unions in determining wages, see Barbara Wootton, *Social Foundations of Wage Policy* (new ed., 1962), and A. G. Hines, 'Trade Unions and Wage Inflation in the United Kingdom, 1893–1961', *Review of Economic Studies*, xxxi (1969). Another general and comparative study is E. H. Phelps Brown, *The Origins of Trade Union Power* (Oxford, 1983).

Bibliographies and details of current work on labour history may be found in the *Labour History Review*, copies of which may be obtained from the Assistant Treasurer, Society for the Study of Labour History, at the Division of Continuing Education. The University, Sheffield S10 2TN. The *British Journal of Industrial Relations* also contains much of interest to the historian of trade unionism.

INDEX

332